THE SECOND BATTALION
ROYAL DUBLIN FUSILIERS IN THE
SOUTH AFRICAN WAR

W. & D. Downey.

H.R.H. THE DUKE OF CONNAUGHT AND STRATHEARN, K.G.,
COMMANDER-IN-CHIEF OF THE MEDITERRANEAN FORCES, AND
COLONEL-IN-CHIEF OF THE ROYAL DUBLIN FUSILIERS.

Frontispiece.

THE SECOND BATTALION ROYAL DUBLIN FUSILIERS
IN THE SOUTH AFRICAN WAR
WITH A DESCRIPTION OF THE OPERATIONS IN THE ADEN HINTERLAND
By Majors C. F. ROMER & A. E. MAINWARING

The Naval & Military Press Ltd

Published by

The Naval & Military Press Ltd
Unit 10 Ridgewood Industrial Park,
Uckfield, East Sussex,
TN22 5QE England

Tel: +44 (0) 1825 749494
Fax: +44 (0) 1825 765701

www.naval-military-press.com
www.military-genealogy.com
www.militarymaproom.com

Printed and bound by CPI Group (UK) Ltd, Croydon, CR0 4YY

In reprinting in facsimile from the original, any imperfections are inevitably reproduced and the quality may fall short of modern type and cartographic standards.

PREFACE

THE 2nd Battalion Royal Dublin Fusiliers is one of the oldest regiments in the service. It was raised in February and March, 1661, to form the garrison of Bombay, which had been ceded to the Crown as part of the dowry of the Infanta of Portugal, on her marriage with King Charles II. It then consisted of four companies, the establishment of each being one captain, one lieutenant, one ensign, two sergeants, three corporals, two drummers, and 100 privates, and arrived at Bombay on September 18th, 1662, under the command of Sir Abraham Shipman. Under various titles it took part in nearly all the continuous fighting of which the history of India of those days is principally composed, being generally known as the Bombay European Regiment, until in March, 1843, it was granted the title of 1st Bombay Fusiliers. In 1862 the regiment was transferred to the Crown, when the word 'Royal' was added to its title, and it became known as the 103rd Regiment, The Royal Bombay Fusiliers. In 1873 the regiment was linked to the Royal Madras Fusiliers, whose history up to that time had been very similar to its own. By General Order 41, of 1881, the titles of the two regiments underwent yet another change, when they became known by their present names, the 1st and 2nd Battalions Royal Dublin Fusiliers.

The 2nd Battalion first left India for home service on January 2nd, 1871, when it embarked on H.M.S. *Malabar*, arriving at Portsmouth Harbour about 8 a.m. on February 4th, and was stationed at Parkhurst. Its home service lasted until 1884, when it embarked for Gibraltar. In 1885 it

PREFACE

moved to Egypt, and in 1886 to India, where it was quartered until 1897, when it was suddenly ordered to South Africa, on account of our strainèd relations with the Transvaal Republic. On arrival at Durban, however, the difficulties had been settled for the time being, and the regiment was quartered at Pietermaritzburg until it moved up to Dundee in 1899, just previous to the outbreak of war.

The late Major-General Penn-Symons assumed command of the Natal force in 1897, and from that date commenced the firm friendship and mutual regard between him and the regiment, which lasted without a break until the day when he met his death at Talana. The interest he took in the battalion and his zeal resulted in a stiff training, but a training for which we must always feel grateful, and remember with kind, if sad, recollections. It was his custom to see a great deal of the regiments under his command, and he very frequently lunched with us, by which means he not only made himself personally acquainted with the characters of the officers of the regiment, but also had an opportunity of seeing for himself the deep *esprit de corps* which existed in it, and without which no regiment can ever hope to successfully overcome the perils and hardships incidental to active service.

As the shadow of the coming war grew dark and ever darker on the Northern horizon, the disposition of the Natal troops underwent some change, and General Penn-Symons' brigade, of which the regiment formed part, was moved up to Dundee, and was there stationed at the time of the outbreak of hostilities. In spite of the long roll of battle honours, of which both battalions are so justly proud, the South African Campaign was the first active service either had seen under their present titles, and the first opportunity afforded them of making those new titles as celebrated as the old ones which had done so much towards the acquisition of our Indian Empire. Imbued with these feelings the regiment lay camped within full view of Talana Hill, waiting the oncoming

PREFACE

of the huge wave of invasion which was so shortly to sweep over the borders, engulf Ladysmith, and threaten to reach Maritzburg itself. But that was not to be. Its force was spent long ere it reached the capital, and a few horsemen near the banks of the Mooi River marked the line of its utmost limit in this direction.

The present work only claims to be a plain soldier's narrative of the part taken by the 2nd Battalion Royal Dublin Fusiliers in stemming this rush, and its subsequent efforts, its grim fights on the hills which fringe the borders of the River Tugela, its long and weary marches across the rolling uplands of the Transvaal, and its subsequent monotonous life of constant vigil in fort and blockhouse, and on escort duty.

All five battalions took part in the war. The 1st sailed from Ireland on November 10th, 1899, and sent three companies under Major Hicks to strengthen the 2nd Battalion. They arrived in time to share in the action at Colenso on December 15th, and all the subsequent fighting which finally resulted in the relief of Ladysmith, after which they returned to the headquarters of the 1st Battalion, which formed part of the Natal army under General Sir Redvers Buller, and later on advanced through Laing's Nek and Allemand's Nek into the Transvaal. The 3rd Battalion sent a very strong draft of its reserve, and the 4th and 5th Battalions volunteered and came out to the front, where they rendered most excellent service. In addition to the battalions there were a good many officers of one or other battalion employed in various ways in the huge theatre of operations. Major Godley and Major Pilson had been selected for special service before the war, and the former served in Mafeking during the siege, while the latter served under General Plumer in his endeavours to raise it. Captain Kinsman also served with the latter force. Major Rutherford, Adjutant of the Ceylon Volunteers, arrived in command of the contingent

PREFACE

from that corps. Lieutenants Cory and Taylor served with the Mounted Infantry most of the time, as did Lieutenants Garvice, Grimshaw, and Frankland, after the capture of Pretoria, while Captain Carington Smith's share in the war is briefly stated later on. Captain MacBean was on the staff until he was killed at Nooitgedacht. The M.I. of the regiment served with great distinction, and it is regretted that it is impossible to include an account of the many actions and marches in which they took part, but the present volume deals almost exclusively with the battalion as a battalion.

The authors are desirous of expressing their most hearty and cordial thanks to all those who have assisted them in the preparation of this volume. They are especially indebted to Colonel H. Tempest Hicks, C.B., without whose co-operation the work could not have been carried out, for the loan of his diary, and for the sketches and many of the photographs. To Colonel F. P. English, D.S.O., for the extracts from his diary containing an account of the operations in the Aden Hinterland and photographs. To Captain L. F. Renny for his Ladysmith notes. Also to Sergeant-Major C. V. Brumby, Quartermaster-Sergeant Purcell, and Mr. French (late Quartermaster-Sergeant), for assistance in collecting data, compiling the appendix, and for photographs, respectively.

C. F. ROMER.

A. E. MAINWARING.

CONTENTS

PART I.—FIGHTING.

CHAP.		PAGE
I.	TALANA	3
II.	THE RETREAT FROM DUNDEE	16
III.	FROM COLENSO TO ESTCOURT	22
IV.	ESTCOURT AND FRERE	28
V.	THE BATTLE OF COLENSO	34
VI.	VENTER'S SPRUIT	42
VII.	VAAL KRANTZ	55
VIII.	HART'S AND PIETER'S HILLS — THE RELIEF OF LADYSMITH	61
IX.	THE SIEGE OF LADYSMITH	76
X.	ALIWAL NORTH AND FOURTEEN STREAMS	83

PART II.—TREKKING.

I.	FROM VRYBURG TO HEIDELBERG	97
II.	HEIDELBERG	111
III.	AFTER DE WET	121
IV.	SEPTEMBER IN THE GATSRAND	141

CONTENTS

CHAP.		PAGE
V.	FREDERICKSTADT—KLIP RIVER—THE LOSBERG	164
VI.	BURIED TREASURE—THE EASTERN TRANSVAAL—THE KRUGERSDORP DEFENCES	182
VII.	THE LAST TWELVE MONTHS	193

PART III.

I.	THE ADEN HINTERLAND	205
II.	THE RETURN HOME AND RECEPTION	217
III.	THE MEMORIAL ARCH	229

APPENDIX 239

ILLUSTRATIONS

FULL-PAGE PLATES.

H.R.H. THE DUKE OF CONNAUGHT AND STRATHEARN, K.G., COMMANDER-IN-CHIEF OF THE MEDITERRANEAN FORCES, AND COLONEL-IN-CHIEF OF THE ROYAL DUBLIN FUSILIERS .	*Frontispiece*
REGIMENTAL BOOK-PLATE	*Title-page*
CASUALTIES AT TALANA	*Facing page* 8
MAJOR-GENERAL C. D. COOPER, C.B., COMMANDING 2ND ROYAL DUBLIN FUSILIERS IN NATAL .	,, ,, 24
CAPTAIN C. F. ROMER AND CAPTAIN E. FETHERSTONHAUGH	,, ,, 32
GENERAL HART'S FLANK ATTACK FROM THE BOERS' POINT OF VIEW (PLAN) . . .	,, ,, 34
CASUALTIES AT COLENSO	,, ,, 36
GROUP OF TWENTY SERGEANTS TAKEN AFTER THE BATTLE OF COLENSO, ALL THAT REMAINED OF FORTY-EIGHT WHO LEFT MARITZBURG .	,, ,, 40
CASUALTIES AT TUGELA HEIGHTS . . .	,, 56, 64
TAKING FOURTEEN STREAMS (PLAN) . . .	,, ,, 88
MISCELLANEOUS CASUALTIES	,, ,, 104

ILLUSTRATIONS

COLONEL H. TEMPEST HICKS, C.B., COMMANDING 2ND ROYAL DUBLIN FUSILIERS, MARCH, 1900–MARCH, 1904	*Facing page* 112
PLAN OF POSITION AT ZUIKERBOSCH	,, ,, 120
PLAN OF BATTLE OF FREDERICKSTADT	,, ,, 168
SKETCH PLAN OF KILMARNOCK HOUSE AND FORTIFICATIONS	,, ,, 184
KRUGERSDORP FROM KILMARNOCK HOUSE	,, ,, 200
OFFICERS OF THE 2ND BATTALION ROYAL DUBLIN FUSILIERS WHO EMBARKED FOR ADEN	,, ,, 216
THE MEMORIAL ARCH, DUBLIN	,, ,, 232
THE SOUTH AFRICAN MEMORIAL, NATAL	,, ,, 238

ILLUSTRATIONS IN TEXT.

	PAGE
THE LAST RITES	10
ARMOURER-SERGEANT WAITE—'DELENDA EST CARTHAGO'.	18
RAILWAY BRIDGE AT COLENSO	23
BOER TRENCHES, COLENSO	36
BRINGING DOWN THE WOUNDED	41
AFTER THE FIGHT	65
THE GRAVE OF COLONEL SITWELL AND CAPTAIN MAITLAND, GORDON HIGHLANDERS (ATTACHED), NEAR RAILWAY AT PIETER'S HILL	67
PIETER'S HILL, FEB. 27TH, 1900	69
PONTOON BRIDGE, RIVER TUGELA, FEB. 28TH, 1900	70

ILLUSTRATIONS

	PAGE
2ND ROYAL DUBLIN FUSILIERS, HEADING RELIEF TROOPS, MARCHING INTO LADYSMITH, MARCH, 1900	72
GENERAL SIR REDVERS BULLER, V.C., ENTERING LADYSMITH	73
THE DUBLINS ARE COMING—LADYSMITH	74
SIR GEORGE WHITE WATCHING RELIEF FORCE ENTERING LADYSMITH	75
SERGEANT DAVIS IN MEDITATION OVER 'LONG CECIL' AT KIMBERLEY. 'SHALL I TAKE IT FOR THE OFFICERS?'	83
ST. PATRICK'S DAY IN CAMP. PRIVATE MONAGHAN, THE REGIMENTAL BUTCHER, IN FOREGROUND	84
A WASH IN HOT WATER—ALIWAL NORTH	87
THE REGIMENTAL MAXIM IN ACTION AT FOURTEEN STREAMS	89
CAPTAIN JERVIS, GENERAL FITZROY HART, C.B., C.M.G., AND CAPTAIN ARTHUR HART	91
ISSUING QUEEN VICTORIA'S CHOCOLATE. COLOUR-SERGEANT CONNELL, 'G' COMPANY, ON LEFT	93
FIRST ENTRY INTO KRUGERSDORP. CAPTAIN AND ADJUTANT FETHERSTONHAUGH IN FOREGROUND	99
'SPEED, DEAD SLOW'	104
HOISTING THE UNION JACK AT KRUGERSDORP	106
JOHAN MEYER'S HOUSE, FIVE MILES OUTSIDE JOHANNESBURG	107
SERGEANT DAVIS, EVIDENTLY WITH ALL WE WANTED	108
PAARDEKRAAL MONUMENT, KRUGERSDORP	110
THE OFFICERS' MESS	120
CORPORAL TIERNEY AND CHEF BURST	123

ILLUSTRATIONS

	PAGE
FOURTH CLASS ON THE Z.A.S.M.	125
FIFTH CLASS ON THE Z.A.S.M.	127
THE VAAL RIVER, LINDEQUE DRIFT	133
THE R.D.F. BATHING IN MOOI RIVER, POCHEFSTROOM	136
FATHER MATHEWS	142
FUNERAL OF COMMANDANT THERON AND A BRITISH SOLDIER, SEPT. 6TH, 1900	149
BUFFELSDOORN CAMP, GATSRAND HILLS	152
A GROUP OF BOER PRISONERS TAKEN AT THE SURPRISE OF POCHEFSTROOM	153
COLOUR-SERGEANT COSSY ISSUING BEER	154
'COME TO THE COOK-HOUSE DOOR, BOYS!'	163
SERGEANT FRENCH AND THE OFFICERS' MESS, NACHTMAAL	170
4·7 CROSSING A DRIFT, ASSISTED BY THE DUBLIN FUSILIERS	172
BOY FITZPATRICK WAITING AT LUNCH	178
'THE LATEST SHAVE.' CAPTAIN G. S. HIGGINSON (MOUNTED) AND MAJOR BIRD	181
THE HAIRDRESSER'S SHOP	192
KILMARNOCK, KRUGERSDORP	193
A BLOCKHOUSE	196
THE 'BLUE CAPS' RELIEVING THE 'OLD TOUGHS'	201
DTHALA CAMP	210
DTHALA VILLAGE, FROM CAMP	211
A FRONTIER TOWER—ABDALI COUNTRY	213
HOMEWARD BOUND AT LAST, AFTER TWENTY YEARS' FOREIGN SERVICE	219

PART I.
FIGHTING.

THE 2ND BATTALION ROYAL DUBLIN FUSILIERS

CHAPTER I.

TALANA.

'The midnight brought the signal sound of strife,
The morn the marshalling in arms, the day—
Battle's magnificently stern array.'
Byron.

THE 2nd Battalion of the Royal Dublin Fusiliers left India for Maritzburg, Natal, in 1897, and therefore, on the outbreak of the war between Great Britain and the South African Republics, had the advantage of possessing some acquaintance with the topography of the colony, and of a two years' training and preparation for the long struggle which was to ensue.

The political situation had become so threatening by July, 1899, that the military authorities began to take precautionary measures, and the battalion was ordered to effect a partial mobilisation and to collect its transport. On September 20th it moved by train to Ladysmith,* and four days later proceeded to Dundee. Here Major-General Sir W. Penn-Symons assumed the command of a small force, consisting of 18th Hussars, 13th, 67th, and 69th Batteries R.F.A., 1st Leicestershire Regiment, 1st King's Royal

---

* It was at Ladysmith that the battalion adopted the green tops on the helmets, a distinguishing badge which was worn throughout the war. The 1st Battalion painted theirs blue on account of the historic nickname, ' Blue-caps,' acquired by them at the time of the Mutiny.

2ND BATT. ROYAL DUBLIN FUSILIERS

Rifles, and 2nd Royal Dublin Fusiliers. Each infantry battalion had a mounted infantry company. The brigade was reinforced on October 16th by the 1st Royal Irish Fusiliers.

The country was still nominally at peace, but the Dundee force held itself ready for emergencies, and sent out mounted patrols by day and infantry piquets by night, while the important railway junction at Glencoe was held by a company. The General utilised this period of waiting in carrying out field-firing and practising various forms of attack. As he was a practical and experienced soldier, he succeeded in bringing his command to a high state of efficiency, and the battalion owed much to his careful preparation. It was due largely to his teaching that the men knew how to advance from cover to cover and displayed such ready 'initiative' in the various battles of the Natal Campaign. The opportunity of putting into practice this teaching soon presented itself, for on October 12th news was received that the South African Republics had declared war on the previous day.

Consideration of the advisability of pushing forward a small force to Dundee, and of the reasons for such a movement, does not fall within the scope of this work; but a glance at the map will show that Sir W. Penn-Symons had a wide front to watch, since he could be attacked from three sides. Although precise information regarding the Boer forces was lacking, it was known that commandoes were assembling at Volksrust, along the left bank of the Buffalo River, and on the far side of Van Reenan's Pass.

Early in the morning of October 13th a telegram was received from Sir G. White, asking General Penn-Symons to send a battalion to Ladysmith at once, as the Boers were reported to be advancing on that town. The General paid the 2nd Royal Dublin Fusiliers the compliment of selecting them for this duty, and they entrained accordingly, about 4.30 a.m., reaching Ladysmith some four hours later.

TALANA

They detrained with the utmost haste and marched at once towards Dewdrop, whither the Ladysmith garrison had been sent; but the report of a Boer advance was discovered to be without foundation, and the battalion was halted five miles outside Ladysmith, and ordered to return. It did not reach the camp at Dundee until 11 p.m.

On the following day Sir W. Penn-Symons moved his detachment closer to the town of Dundee, and placed his camp three or four hundred yards north of the road to Glencoe Junction. It soon became clear that the Boers meant to invade Natal, and Newcastle was occupied by them on the 15th, while the mounted patrols of the Dundee force were already in touch with the commandoes on the left bank of the Buffalo. The detached company at Glencoe was withdrawn on the 18th, and on the 19th three companies of the regiment, under Major English, were sent to the Navigation Colliery in order to bring away large quantities of mealie bags stored there.

Colonel Cooper, commanding the 2nd Battalion Royal Dublin Fusiliers, had been given an extension of his command, and was hurrying back from a short period of leave in England, so the battalion was at this time under the command of Major S. G. Bird.

It was now evident to every one that we were on the eve of hostilities, and a spirit of keen excitement and anticipation ran through all ranks. After a long tour of foreign service, during which the regiment had not had the good fortune to see active service, though on three occasions they had been within measurable distance of it, they were now to have the long-wished-for chance of showing that, in spite of altered denominations and other changes, they were prepared to keep their gallant and historical reputation untarnished. Our advanced patrols had already seen the first signs of the coming torrent of invasion, and one and all were seized with that feeling, common to all mankind, of longing to get the

2ND BATT. ROYAL DUBLIN FUSILIERS

waiting and the preparation over, and to commence the real business for which they had been so carefully and so thoroughly prepared. Full of the most implicit confidence in their brave leader, the regiment knew to a man that they would soon be at hand-grips, and their two years' residence in the country and knowledge of the history of the last Boer War, and the stain to be rubbed out, made every pulse tingle with the desire to show that the past had been but an unfortunate blunder, and that the British soldier of the present day was no whit inferior to his predecessors of Indian, Peninsular, Waterloo, and Crimean fame.

On the night of the 19-20th October, Lieutenant Grimshaw was sent with a patrol of the Mounted Infantry company of the battalion to watch the road to Vant's and Landsman's Drifts, ten miles east of Dundee. About 2 a.m. on October 20th this officer reported that a Boer commando was advancing on the town. At a later hour he forwarded a second message to the effect that he was retiring before superior numbers, one man of his party having been wounded, and that the enemy were in occupation of the hills to the east of the town. On the receipt of this message General Penn-Symons ordered two companies of the Dublin Fusiliers to support Lieutenant Grimshaw. 'B' and 'E' companies, under Captains Dibley and Weldon, accordingly left camp at 4 a.m., and, moving through the town, took up a position in Sand Spruit, which runs along the eastern edge of Dundee. The whole brigade stood to arms, as usual, at 5 a.m., but was dismissed at 5.15 a.m. At about 5.30 a.m. the mist lifted, and everybody's gaze was directed on Talana Hill, where numbers of men in black mackintoshes could be seen. The general impression was that they were members of the town guard, but the arrival of the first shell soon dispelled this illusion.

Soon after 5.30 a.m. the Boer artillery opened fire on the camp. Their fire was accurate enough, considering that the

TALANA

range was near 5400 yards, but the damage done was practically nothing, as very few shells burst, and these only on impact. Our own artillery (13th and 69th Field Batteries, with 'D' company of the battalion as escort) did not immediately respond, as they were at the time engaged in watering their horses; but as soon as possible they were in position to the east of the camp, and began to shell the crest of Talana Hill. They obtained the range almost immediately, and in a short time overpowered the hostile guns, which were thus prevented from playing an important part in the day's battle.

As soon as the Boers started shelling the camp, the battalion fell in on its parade-ground in quarter-column and waited for orders. But when a shell fell just behind the ranks, Major Bird moved it at the double through the camp to a donga which afforded good cover. The men then removed their great-coats, and stayed for some minutes watching the Boer shells passing over their heads. Eventually the King's Royal Rifles, Royal Irish Fusiliers, and the battalion were ordered by the General to move in extended order through the town, and to concentrate in the spruit already occupied by 'B' and 'E' companies. The Leicesters and 67th Battery were left near the camp to watch Impati Mountain, since it was probable that the Boer force which had occupied Newcastle would appear from that direction. The mounted troops (18th Hussars and the Mounted Infantry company of the Dublin Fusiliers, under Captain Lonsdale, less Lieutenant Cory's section, which, fortunately for it, was sent off in another direction), under the command of Colonel Möller, were sent to turn the right flank of the Boers' position on Talana Hill and so threaten their rear.

As the extended lines of the infantry moved through the town they were greeted by pompom fire, which, however, did no damage. It was their first introduction to this hated

2ND BATT. ROYAL DUBLIN FUSILIERS

and under-rated weapon, whose moral effect is so great that, even if the casualties it inflicts are small in number, it is always likely to exercise a marked influence, more especially on young troops and at the commencement of a campaign. Men heard it in wonder, asking each other what it was, and why had we nothing like it, and similar questions. By 6.30 a.m. the three battalions were assembled in the bed of the spruit, and the General rode up with the Staff in order to give his orders for the attack. The 2nd Royal Dublin Fusiliers were to form the firing line, with the 60th Rifles in support and the Royal Irish Fusiliers in reserve. Under Talana Hill is a wood surrounding a small house known as Smith's Farm. Between this wood and Sand Spruit is a long stretch of veld, which on the day of the battle was intersected by several wire fences. The battalion received orders to cross this open ground by successive companies. 'H' company, under Lieutenant Shewan, formed the right of the line, and was the first company to leave the shelter of the spruit. It made for the south-east corner of the wood, where it was afterwards joined by the maxims, and at once opened fire on Talana and Dundee Hills. 'B' company under Captain Dibley, 'A' company under Major English, and 'E' company under Captain Weldon extended to ten paces, and followed in succession. The enemy had by this time developed a vigorous fire, but the range was long and the casualties small. The advancing companies moved on steadily, reached the edge of the wood, and entered it. They now became somewhat separated. 'A,' 'G' (Captain Perreau), and 'F' inclined to the left, 'C' and 'E' remained in the centre with 'B' on their right, while 'H' was held back at the corner of the wood. The latter was bounded on the far side by a stone wall, beyond which stretched an open piece of ground until, further up the hill, there was a second wall. At this point there was a sudden change in the slope of the ground, which rose almost precipitously to the crest.

Lafayette.
CAPT. G. A. WELDON.
Killed.

SECOND LIEUT. GENGE.
Died of Wounds.

Guy & Co.
CAPT. A. DIBLEY.
Wounded.

London Stereoscopic Co.
MAJOR LOWNDES.
Wounded.

Lambert Weston.
LIEUT. C. N. PERREAU.
Wounded.

Marriott.
SER.-MAJ. (NOW QR.-MR.) BURKE.
Wounded.

CASUALTIES AT TALANA.

TALANA

Immediately opposite the point where 'B' company issued from the wood a third wall ran up the hill, connecting the two already mentioned. When the attackers reached the far end of the wood, they came under such a well-directed and heavy fire that their progress was at first checked, in spite of the support afforded by our artillery, which rained shrapnel on the hostile position. The Boers, lying behind the boulders on the crest of Talana Hill, found excellent cover; while from Dundee Hill they could bring an effective enfilade fire on the open space between the two parallel walls. Opposite 'A' company a donga ran up the hill, and at first sight seemed to offer an excellent line of approach for an attacking force. Major English, in command of the company, rushed forward and, in spite of a heavy fire, succeeded in cutting a wire fence which closed the mouth of the donga. He then, at about 8 a.m., led his company into the latter, and was followed by 'G' and 'F' (Captain Hensley) companies; but the donga proved almost a death-trap, since it was swept by the rifles of some picked marksmen on the right of the Boer position.

It was impossible for these three companies to advance any further, and they were therefore forced to limit their efforts to an attempt to keep down the Boer fire. Meanwhile, General Penn-Symons had, about 9.15 a.m., come up to the far edge of the wood, and crying, 'Dublin Fusiliers, we must take the hill!' crossed the wall. Shortly afterwards he received a mortal wound. Captain Weldon was also killed near the same spot in a gallant effort to help a wounded comrade, No. 5078 Private Gorman. Captain Weldon, together with several men of his company, had surmounted the wall in face of a heavy fire, and had taken cover in a small depression on its further side. Private Gorman was hit in the very act of surmounting the obstacle, and was falling backwards, when Captain Weldon, rushing out from his cover, seized him by the arm, and

2ND BATT. ROYAL DUBLIN FUSILIERS

was pulling him into safety when he himself was mortally wounded. Privates Brady and Smith dragged him in under cover, but he only lived a few minutes. His dog, a fox-terrier named Rose, had accompanied him through the fight, and when his body was later on recovered, the faithful little animal was found beside it, and was afterwards taken care

THE LAST RITES.

of by the men of 'E' company. There was no more popular officer in the regiment than George Weldon, and his loss was deeply felt by all ranks. He was the first officer of the Dublin Fusiliers to fall in the war, which thus early asserted its claim to seize the best. He was buried that same afternoon in the small cemetery, facing the hill on which he had met his death.

By this time, 9.30 a.m., the Rifles and Irish Fusiliers had closed up and become merged in the firing line. Slowly, and by the advances of small parties at a time, the attackers gained ground, principally by creeping along the transverse wall which afforded cover from the enemy on Dundee Hill.

TALANA

Helped by the incessant fire of the artillery, which at 11.30 a.m. moved up to the coalfields railway, the infantry gradually collected behind the second wall. They were now within 150 yards of the crest, and the roar of battle grew in intensity. About 11.30 a.m. Colonel Yule came up and ordered the hill to be assaulted, directing the battalion to charge the right flank of the hill, and the Rifles the centre. Captain Lowndes, who was with the companies on the right, led them across the wall and over an open piece of ground. He gave the command ' Right incline,' and so well were the men in hand that the order was promptly obeyed, shortly after which he was badly wounded. Meanwhile, in the centre, men of all three regiments, led by the Staff and regimental officers, dashed over the wall and began to clamber up the steep and rocky slope. The artillery quickened its fire and covered the crest with shrapnel. But the Boers still remained firm. Many of them stood up, their mackintoshes waving in the wind, and poured a deadly fire on the assaulting infantry. Though most of these brave burghers paid for their daring with their lives, they repulsed this first gallant charge. The Dublin Fusiliers suffered many casualties in this first assault. Captain Lowndes, the Adjutant, had his leg practically shattered, as he, with the other officers, ran ahead to lead the charge. Captain Perreau was shot through the chest; Captain Dibley was almost on the top of the hill when hit. He had a dim recollection of the gallant Adjutant of the Royal Irish Fusiliers racing up almost alongside him and within a few paces of the summit, when he suddenly saw an aged and grey-bearded burgher drawing a bead upon him at a distance of a few paces only. He snapped his revolver at him, but only to fall senseless next moment with a bullet through his head. Marvellous though it seems he made a comparatively speedy recovery, and was able to ride into Ladysmith, at the head of his company, in the following February, having been in the hospital in the besieged town

2ND BATT. ROYAL DUBLIN FUSILIERS

in the interval. Evidence of the temporary nature of the discomfort caused by a bullet through the head is afforded by the fact that he is to-day one of the best bridge-players in the regiment. Poor young Genge, who had only recently joined, was mortally wounded, and died shortly after the battle, killed in his first fight and in the springtime of life.

Sergeant-Major Burke's (now Quartermaster) experiences may be best told in his own words: 'It must have been shortly after poor Weldon was killed that I came across "E" company; finding no officer with them I assumed command, and on arrival at the donga handed them over to Major Bird, and accompanied Colonel Yule, who had just arrived, and was ascending the hill. We had only gone a few yards, and were about six paces from the top wall, when I was bowled over, hit in the leg. It was a hot place, for as I lay there another bullet hit me in the shoulder. I crawled as well as I could to a rock, and sitting up underneath it lit a pipe. Scarcely had I got it to draw when a bullet dashed it out of my hand, taking a small piece of the top of my thumb with it. Two men were shot dead so close that they fell across my legs, effectually pinning me to the ground, while two more were wounded and fell alongside of me. At this juncture Colour-Sergeants Guilfoyle (now Sergeant-Major) and James dashed out of cover, and, picking me up, carried me to a more sheltered position, whence I could see what was going on all round, without myself being seen.' He was left at Dundee with the wounded, and subsequently taken to Pretoria with other prisoners of war.

Whilst the men and officers were thus recovering their breath for a renewed attack, a large number were undoubtedly hit by our own shrapnel, as they clung closely to the hillside to avoid coming under fire from the enemy, who still held the top. It was imperative to draw our gunners' attention to their situation, to effect which purpose, an intrepid signaller, Private Flynn, Royal Dublin Fusiliers,

TALANA

jumped up, and at the imminent risk of his own life freely exposed himself in his endeavour to 'call up' the guns. Finding, after repeated attempts, that he could not attract their attention, he boldly walked back down the hillside, torn as it was by mauser fire, and personally delivered his message, a glorious and courageous example of that devotion to duty which proved so strongly marked a characteristic of our N.C.O.'s and privates throughout the war.

Major English now extricated his company from the donga and managed to reach the second wall, where he collected all available men, including 'F' and 'G' companies, and maintained an incessant fire on Dundee and Talana Hills. The artillery behind had never slackened in their efforts to support the infantry, and their shrapnel searched the whole length of the crest line. This combined fire began at last to tell. The rattle of the enemy's musketry, which had lasted since 6.30 a.m., gradually grew feebler, until about 1 p.m. our infantry made a second dash across the wall and this time reached the top of the hill. Below them they saw the stream of flying Boers hurrying across the veld. It was the moment for a vigorous outburst of musketry, but 'some one blundered,' and the fleeting moment sped without being taken advantage of. It is true that those men who first arrived on the summit were firing away, and were joined in doing so by every other man who breathlessly arrived. The company officers had just got their men well in hand, and were directing the fire, when to every one's disgust, and sheer, blank amazement, the 'Cease fire' sounded clear above the din of the fight. There was nothing for it but to stop, but the sight of the enemy streaming away in dense masses just below them, that enemy who had up to now been pouring a relentless hail of bullets on them for hours, was too much. Captain Hensley rushed up to Major English, and after a brief conference, feeling certain the call must have been blown in error, the latter gave the command to re-open fire. Barely

2ND BATT. ROYAL DUBLIN FUSILIERS

was it obeyed when the imperative bugle once more blared forth its interference, and the company officers, the commanders of the recognised battle-units, had nothing left them but compliance.

The guns with 'D' company as escort had come to the neck between Talana and Dundee Hills, but did not fire. The fight was over and Major English formed up the battalion. It then marched back as a rearguard to the brigade, through Dundee to the camp, much as if after a field-day, halting halfway to receive an issue of rations sent out by the A.S.C. It had lost two officers and six men killed, and three officers and fifty-two men wounded. As the troops passed through the town they were warmly cheered by the inhabitants. Late in the afternoon news reached the camp that the Mounted Infantry company, together with a squadron of the 18th Hussars, had been captured, but this was kept from the rank and file of the battalion. As already stated above, Colonel Möller had been sent with the mounted troops round the right flank of the Boers. He succeeded in his task, but proceeded too far, and when the enemy retreated from Talana Hill he found himself with some 200 rifles attempting to stop a force of 4000 Boers. He was roughly handled, but managed to get clear. Then, unluckily misled by the mist, he lost his way, and, instead of returning to camp, moved towards Impati Mountain, where he stumbled into the Boer main commando advancing from Newcastle. He took up a defensive position, placing the cavalry in a kraal and the mounted infantry on some rising ground near. The enemy brought up artillery and soon surrounded him, finally forcing him to surrender.

Talana Hill, in point of numbers, may not rank as a great battle, but its moral effect can scarcely be exaggerated. It was the first conflict of the war. It was Majuba reversed, and the issue had far-reaching consequences. The news of the victory spread quickly through South Africa, and had

TALANA

considerable influence on the Dutch Colonists, who were, to use an expressive colloquialism, 'sitting on the fence,' and kept them sitting there, at a time when had they descended on the wrong side their action could not have failed to be extremely prejudicial to the interests of the Empire; but over and above all else it showed to the world that the British infantry could still attack and carry a position in face of modern rifle-fire, a lesson which was never forgotten by Boer or Briton, in spite of after events. Moreover, Talana must ever be a memorable name in the annals of the Royal Dublin Fusiliers, since it was the first battle in which they had fought under their new title, which was from that day on to become as well known as that of any regiment in the army.

The other regiments engaged had also suffered very severely, the 60th Rifles losing, amongst other officers, their gallant chief, Colonel Gunning. It was curious that on the last occasion the 2nd Royal Dublin Fusiliers had seen active service—the siege and capture of Mooltan—they should then have fought alongside the 60th, as they did in the present instance.

CHAPTER II.

THE RETREAT FROM DUNDEE.

'I am ready to halt.'—*Ps.* xxxviii. 17.

ON the morning of October 21st, Colonel Yule, who, as senior officer, had taken over command of the brigade, received the news that a Boer commando, under General Joubert, was advancing by the Newcastle road. As the camp was within long-range artillery fire from Impati Mountain, the brigade moved off at a moment's notice to the south and took up a defensive position. The tents were left standing, but each man carried a waterproof sheet, a blanket, and great-coat, while the waggons, massed in rear, had three to four days' supplies. Soon after 4.30 p.m. the enemy appeared on Impati, and at once opened fire with a big gun, probably a forty-pounder. The shells at first fell in the vacated camp, but the Boer artillerymen quickly discovered the brigade, and made good practice, although they caused but slight damage. Our batteries attempted to reply, but were outranged, their shells falling far short. Luckily for us a mist came on, and the Boer gun ceased firing.

As soon as night fell the troops began to entrench themselves, for the situation of the brigade was sufficiently unpleasant. In front was an enemy with superior numbers and heavier artillery, and in rear, between Dundee and Ladysmith, another hostile force of unknown strength. To make matters worse, it rained persistently and the night was cold. About 3 a.m. the brigade retreated to Indumana Kopje, some one and a half miles to the south-east of the camp. Here a new position was taken up before dawn, the guns and transport being massed behind the hill in order to be out of sight from Impati.

THE RETREAT FROM DUNDEE

Early in the morning of the 22nd, the spirits of the small force were raised by the news of the victory at Elandslaagte. This caused great delight among the men: they were proud of their own victory at Talana, and this further success roused them to a still higher pitch of enthusiasm. The strategic side of the situation seldom appeals to the rank and file, and the consequence was that when the retreat was commenced they were under the impression that they were being led to yet another victory. When they were undeceived, they were undoubtedly very savage, especially so at, what seemed to them, the callous desertion of their wounded comrades in Dundee.

Since it was possible that some of the defeated Boers might be retreating through the Biggarsberg, a demonstration towards Glencoe Junction was ordered, the troops detailed being the 2nd Royal Dublin Fusiliers, the 60th Rifles, one battery, and some cavalry. No time was given for breakfasts, but the detachment moved off at 8 a.m. with the battalion as advance guard. On arriving within 1500 yards of the Junction, the battery shelled a party of the enemy on a hill to the west of the railway, a proceeding which promptly provoked an answer from the Boer gun on Impati, but another timely mist and rain saved the detachment from this unwelcome attention. No Boers were seen in the pass, so the force, with the battalion as rearguard, returned to Indumana Kopje at 12.30 p.m., when they were able to obtain dinners, the majority of the men having been without food for twenty-four hours.

At 9 p.m. that evening orders were issued for the reoccupation of Talana Hill by the whole force, but the various commanding officers were informed confidentially that Colonel Yule's real intention was a retreat to Ladysmith by the Helpmakaar road. It was an extremely dark night, and the battalion occupied nearly two hours in collecting the companies and reaching the place of assembly at

2ND BATT. ROYAL DUBLIN FUSILIERS

the foot of the kopje. It was not until after 11 p.m. that the brigade actually started on the retreat in the following order: 1st 60th Rifles (advance-guard), 1st Royal Irish Fusiliers, 13th Battery, Mounted Infantry, Transport, 67th and 69th Batteries, 2nd Royal Dublin Fusiliers, 18th Hussars, 1st Leicestershire Regiment (rearguard). The force occupied about four miles of road. The route was through Dundee,

ARMOURER-SERGEANT WAITE.
'DELENDA EST CARTHAGO.'

over Sand Spruit, and down the Helpmakaar road through the Coalfields village. It was impossible to find an opportunity for a return to the camp, which was left standing. All the tents, stores, and baggage, together with the wounded, were left to the enemy. The battalion thus lost its band instruments and camp equipment, while the officers had to sacrifice all their personal kit, and many articles belonging to the mess. The waggons carried nothing but supplies, and no one in the force was able to take away anything beyond what he carried on his person.

The column marched throughout the night, and far into the morning of the 23rd, only halting at 10 a.m., when

THE RETREAT FROM DUNDEE

dinners were eaten on the high ground south of Blesbok Pass, about fifteen miles from Dundee. That the Boers were watching the retreat was proved by one of their heliographs trying to 'pick up' the column. The march was resumed after a two hours' rest, and continued to Beith (twenty-one miles from Dundee), where, at 3 p.m., another halt was made. The men cooked their teas, and had a chance of a brief sleep, but at 11 p m. they had to start again. The road, a very bad one, lay through the pass leading to the Waschbank River. The battalion formed the advance-guard, with two Natal mounted policemen as guides. It was a weary tramp, for, owing to the wretched road, long halts were necessary in order to allow the waggons to close up. At dawn, the 18th Hussars took over the duties of advance-guard, and were supported by 'F' company, under Captain Hensley.

During the night a mysterious heliograph was seen twinkling and blinking away on the left flank. After some difficulty it was ascertained that it was communicating with the farm of a man named Potgieter, professedly a British subject. He was, in fact, caught *in flagrante delicto* in full communication with the unknown Boer signaller, and paid for his crime with his life.

At 10 a.m. on the 24th, the head of the column reached the Waschbank (thirty-six miles), crossed, and halted on the south side of the river. The waggons were not over until 12.30 p.m. A welcome meal and a bathe in the stream refreshed the men, some of whom had had no proper sleep for three nights. Heavy firing was heard from the direction of Ladysmith, and the mounted troops, with the artillery, were sent off to reconnoitre and see if they could render any assistance to Sir George White. They met with nothing, however, and returned before 5 p.m. Meanwhile the infantry had also been disturbed, for at 2 p.m. they recrossed the river in order to occupy a better position to oppose a

2ND BATT. ROYAL DUBLIN FUSILIERS

rumoured pursuit of the Boers. As the latter did not appear, the river was again forded at 4 p.m., and only just in time. A violent thunderstorm burst, and the water rose ten feet in two hours. 'H' company, under Lieutenant Shewan, and a patrol of the 18th Hussars were left on the north bank, and were thus cut off from the main body for several hours.

It rained in torrents until 11 p.m., and the battalion, formed in quarter-column, had to lie down in pools of water, and get what sleep it could. At 5 a.m. on the 25th, in bright sunshine, the retreat was resumed. 'H' company crossed to the south bank a few minutes before the column moved off, although the water was still up to the men's waists. The Dublin Fusiliers formed the rearguard, and marched till midday, when Sunday's River (forty-eight miles) was reached. 'A' company remained on the north bank to cover the crossing of the waggons, and at 2.30 p.m. the column went on, only halting at 4.30 for tea. Everybody hoped to have a long rest here, but at 6.30 p.m. Major Bird was sent for, and informed that, as the Boers were in close pursuit, a night march was necessary.

The brigade accordingly started at 7 p.m., at the same moment that heavy rain began to fall. The road quickly became inches deep in mud, every one was soon wet to the skin, and the night was so dark that a man in each section of fours had to hold on to the canteen strap of the man in front in order to keep the proper direction. As an additional evil, the battalion was still rearguard, which is generally the most tiring position in a column. Halts were frequent, and the men were so exhausted that many of them, when they stopped for a moment, fell down in the mud and slept. Soon after midnight the 18th Hussars, who were keeping connection between the Irish Fusiliers and the rearguard, disappeared. It was so dark that the latter could have no certainty of being on the right road, but was obliged to

THE RETREAT FROM DUNDEE

struggle on blindly. Majors Bird and English established a code of signals by whistle, in order to keep the companies closed up. Dawn still found the battalion marching, dead tired, but luckily in its proper place behind the column, and without a man missing. It was not until 8 a.m. on the 26th that this wearisome march ended. Then Modderspruit, seven miles north of Ladysmith, and sixty-five from Dundee, was reached, and the men sank down, too weary to care about anything. After a brief interval, however, they recovered sufficiently to eat their bully beef and biscuits. It had been a trying march for all, although the column had accomplished only twelve miles in eleven hours. As an instance of the general weariness, it is recorded that a subaltern, during the meal, was asked to pass the mustard, and fell asleep with his arm outstretched and the mustard-pot in his hand.

But the brigade was still not allowed to rest. At 11 a.m. it was on the 'trek' again, and marched till 2 p.m., when the long retreat came to an end, and Ladysmith was entered. Here the Devonshire and Gloucestershire Regiments earned the undying gratitude of the regiment by providing officers and men with a meal, as well as by pitching a camp for them.

On arriving at Ladysmith, tents, equipment, mules, and, in fact, all that had been lost at Dundee, were issued, and the battalion went into camp near the cemetery.

The column was fortunate in having Colonel (now General) Dartnell with it. This officer, after serving with distinction for many years in the regular army, had, on retirement, settled down in Natal, where he was, previous to the war, in command of the Natal Police. A great hunter and fisherman, he knew every inch of the country, knowledge which proved of invaluable assistance in the trying march.

CHAPTER III.

FROM COLENSO TO ESTCOURT.

'If thou hope to please all, thy hopes are vaine;
If thou feare to displease some, thy feares are idle.'
Francis Quarles.

ON October 28th Colonel Cooper arrived at Ladysmith from England and took over the command from Major Bird. The battalion was able to rest from the 27th to the 29th, and recover from the fatigue of the retreat to Ladysmith.

The Headquarter Staff issued orders on the 29th for a general movement, to take place the next day, against the enemy, who were closing in on the town. The Dublin Fusiliers formed part of Colonel Grimwood's brigade, which also included the 1st and 2nd King's Royal Rifles, the Leicesters, and the Liverpools. The task assigned to Colonel Grimwood was the capture of Long Hill.

In order to be in position for the assault by dawn, it was necessary for the brigade to make a night march, and the battalion paraded about 9.30 p.m. on Sunday evening, the 29th October. It formed the rear of the brigade, to which was attached a brigade of artillery. 'F' and 'B' companies were left behind on piquet duty.

Owing to the difficulties inherent in a night march, and, perhaps, also to faulty staff management, the artillery, the Dublin Fusiliers, and Liverpool Regiment diverged from the route followed by the rest of the brigade. As a result of this mistake the battalion took practically no part in the battle of the 30th, but, after a vain endeavour to find Colonel Grimwood's force, spent the morning lying on the crest of a small ridge near Lombard's Kop. It came under shell and

FROM COLENSO TO ESTCOURT

long-range rifle fire, but lost no men. The attempt to drive back the Boers was a failure, and the army fell back on Ladysmith about midday. The battalion reached camp at 2 p.m. and was dismissed. All ranks were somewhat tired, for the sun had been hot, and after dinner sleep reigned supreme. But about 4 p.m. Colonel Cooper received from Headquarters an order to proceed by train to Colenso, with the

RAILWAY BRIDGE AT COLENSO.

object of protecting the important railway bridge which crosses the Tugela at that place. The Natal Field Artillery, in addition to his own unit, was placed under his command. On the receipt of this order, camp was struck, and the tents and baggage sent down to the station. The piquets found by the Dublin Fusiliers were ordered to be relieved by other corps, but although 'F' company, under Captain Hensley, came in, Lieutenant H. W. Higginson's piquet, on the ridge to the east of the cemetery, could not rejoin in time, principally owing to the fact that the greater part of the Gloucestershire Regiment, which had been detailed to find the relief, had been captured at Nicholson's Nek. Lieutenant Higginson

2ND BATT. ROYAL DUBLIN FUSILIERS

and his men were thus left to share in the siege of Ladysmith. The battalion transport, under Lieutenant Renny, also had to remain behind. An account of their experiences during the siege is given by Lieutenant Renny in Chapter IX.

With these exceptions the whole battalion marched down to the station soon after 11 p.m., and was dispatched in two trains. As Boers had been reported on Bulwana Hill during the afternoon, a certain amount of risk seemed to attend the journey. There was nothing to prevent the enemy from cutting the line at any point in the hilly country between Ladysmith and Pieter's Station, while even a small hostile force could have played havoc with the crowded trucks.

However, the enemy had luckily not penetrated to the railway line, and after an uneventful, though unpleasant, journey, Colenso was reached at 4.30 a.m. on the 31st.

The two railway bridges over the Tugela and Onderbrook Spruit were already protected by a small force, consisting of the Durban Light Infantry, a squadron of the Imperial Light Horse, and a detachment of the Natal Naval Volunteers, with a gun. These units had made good defensive works, notably Forts Wylie and Molyneux, guarding the railway bridges over the Tugela and Onderbrook Spruit respectively.

We encamped some 300 yards south-west of Colenso, and the day (October 31st) was spent in making further defences, and dividing the garrison into sections. Colenso was not, however, an easy place to defend. It was commanded by the lofty hills on the left bank of the Tugela, and by Hlangwane Hill on the right bank to the east of the village. The garrison, moreover, was lacking in artillery, having only some muzzle-loading guns with a very limited range. Colonel Cooper telegraphed to Maritzburg asking for a naval twelve-pounder, which, however, could not be obtained.

The necessity for such an addition soon arose. At 8.15 a.m. on November 1st, the staff at Ladysmith sent a wire to

MAJOR-GENERAL C. D. COOPER, C.B.
COMMANDING 2ND ROYAL DUBLIN FUSILIERS
IN NATAL.

FROM COLENSO TO ESTCOURT

say that a Boer force had moved at daybreak towards Colenso. On receipt of this news the garrison was warned to be ready, and patrols of the Imperial Light Horse and the Mounted Infantry section of the battalion were dispatched towards Ladysmith, Springfield, and the country beyond Hlangwane. These patrols returned soon after 1 p.m., and the party which had reconnoitred towards Ladysmith reported that it had come into touch and exchanged shots with the enemy. Later on in the afternoon, Lieutenant Cory, commanding the Mounted Infantry section, went out again and reported that he had seen a hostile force, estimated at 2000 men, which was off-saddled near the main Ladysmith road, some six miles out. He had skirmished with the scouts of this commando and had lost one man. Another wire came from Ladysmith at the same time announcing that the enemy had guns. Our piquets were, in consequence of these events, pushed forward to the horseshoe ridge on the left bank of the Tugela, while the parties guarding the two bridges (road and railway) over this river were reinforced. The night, however, passed quietly.

Mounted patrols were sent out at dawn of the 2nd, and Lieutenant Cory was able to report, at 6.45 a.m., that the Boers were still in the same position. But two hours later he forwarded another message to the effect that the enemy was advancing on Grobelaar's Kloof. Soon afterwards distant rifle-shots were heard, and the Mounted Infantry retired into camp. About 10 a.m. parties of the enemy appeared on the top of Grobelaar's Mountain, and by the aid of a good telescope it could be seen that they were busily engaged in digging. Their intention was not long in doubt, for a thin cloud became visible on the sky-line, and the next moment a shell buried itself in the river-bank.

Colonel Cooper at once ordered the tents to be lowered and the trenches to be manned. But the enemy made no signs of attacking Colenso, and contented themselves by occasionally firing shells which invariably fell short. The interruption of telegraphic communication with Ladysmith soon after 3 p.m. proved, however, that the enemy was not being idle. Groups of Boers could be seen on the hills overhanging the railway, and a train carrying General French was shelled after leaving Pieters. The activity of our foes assumed a more aggressive character when, about 5 p.m., they began to bombard Fort Molyneux. From Colenso the shrapnel could be plainly seen bursting over the work, and the piquets on the left bank of the Tugela reported that heavy rifle-fire was in progress. As the garrison of the fort consisted only of eighty men of the Durban Light Infantry, some anxiety was felt regarding their safety, and this uneasiness was intensified by the arrival of one of the defenders, who announced that the redoubt was hard pressed. Lieutenant Shewan, with one hundred men mostly from 'E' company, was promptly dispatched to reinforce them in the armoured train. He found that the fort had been evacuated, but managed to pick up several of the garrison in spite of the enemy's rifle and shrapnel fire. Captain Hensley, who was holding the horseshoe ridge, also advanced with 'F' company, and, by firing long-range volleys, helped to cover the retirement of the remainder of the garrison, the whole of which reached Colenso in the night. Colonel Cooper telegraphed an account of these events to Brigadier-General Wolfe-Murray at Maritzburg, who replied at nightfall that, since the safety of Colenso bridge was very important, he would send the Border Regiment next day to reinforce the garrison. But no mention was made of any artillery.

    Colonel Cooper had now a difficult decision to arrive at. In front of him lay a superior force of the enemy with guns far outranging his own obsolete muzzle-loaders, and during the afternoon disquieting rumours, which might be true, of another commando at Springfield had reached him. Ladysmith was invested, and the small garrisons of Colenso and

FROM COLENSO TO ESTCOURT

Estcourt alone stood between the Boers and Maritzburg. Having consulted the senior officers of the garrison, Colonel Cooper sent another wire to General Wolfe-Murray explaining the situation, and in reply was authorised to fall back to Estcourt if he could not hold Colenso. About 10 p.m. he reluctantly determined to retire.

The mounted troops and the Natal Field Artillery went by road, starting at midnight. It was decided to send the rest of the garrison by railway, and the stationmaster at Colenso, with great energy, succeeded in obtaining three trains which arrived in the early hours of November 3rd.

The operation of entraining was at once commenced. The night was dark, and the packing of all the tents, supplies, and equipment in the trucks proceeded but slowly. The Natal Naval Volunteers had to bring their nine-pounder gun down the steep slope of Fort Wylie, a task requiring great care and time; the piquets on the left bank of the river had to be withdrawn, and the two bridges guarded up to the very last moment. Although everything was done in the utmost possible silence, it yet seemed that the necessary shunting of the trains must warn the Boers of the evacuation, and bring on an attack. But there was no interruption, and the last train steamed out of Colenso station half an hour before dawn.

Estcourt was reached two hours later. The little town was already occupied by a detachment of the Imperial Light Horse and Natal Mounted Rifles. During the morning there also arrived from Maritzburg the 2nd Border Regiment,* afterwards to be the comrades of the battalion in the 5th Brigade.

Colonel Cooper took over the command of the garrison and immediately set to work on the arrangement of the defences. The next day, however, General Wolfe-Murray and his staff appeared on the scene. Estcourt had thus the honour of having three different commandants in two days.

* A great friendship sprang up between this celebrated regiment and ourselves.

CHAPTER IV.

ESTCOURT AND FRERE.

'Great men are not always wise: neither do the aged
understand judgment.'—*Job*, xxxii. 9.

THE stay at Estcourt (November 3rd to 26th) was a period of great anxiety and hard work. That there was cause for anxiety may be easily understood when the state of affairs is remembered. The Army Corps had not yet arrived from England, nor could any fresh troops be expected before the 10th. The Boers had invaded Natal, had shut up in Ladysmith the only British army in the field, and could still afford to send five or six thousand men against Maritzburg. The Estcourt garrison alone stood in their way.

There were necessarily many outposts, and tours were long and frequent. Thunderstorms, Natal thunderstorms, visited the town with painful regularity, and rendered piquet work even more uncomfortable than usual. It was a period of strained waiting, when every one wondered whether a Boer commando or a British brigade would be the first arrival. Reliable news was scarce, though rumours of every kind were rife.

The battalion was encamped in the market square, while the officers inhabited a small room encumbered with planks. Trenches covered the town to the north and north-east, and were pushed forward some two miles on the Weenen road The citadel, so to speak, was the sugar-loaf hill, on which Lieutenant James, R.N., constructed, towards the middle of the month, emplacements for his two naval twelve-pounders. These guns arrived on November 14th, a welcome addition to the garrison, which had been strengthened on the 13th by the

ESTCOURT AND FRERE

West Yorkshire Regiment. These reinforcements came at an opportune moment, for the Boers had at last moved forward and on November 14th their patrols were close to Estcourt. Their approach caused a certain amount of alarm, and at first the evacuation of the town was proposed. The camp was even struck, and a great part of the baggage was put on to trains which were kept ready in the station. Later on other counsels prevailed, and tents were raised again. It had rained most of the day, and a general wetting was the chief result of this 'scare.' The Boers quickly made their presence felt, and the next day inflicted a severe blow on the garrison.

Our mounted troops had been busily engaged in reconnaissance work, and in an evil hour it occurred to the authorities that the armoured train was also an excellent means of gaining news. Captain Hensley had taken it to Colenso on the 5th and 6th, and on the latter day surprised a party of Boers engaged in looting the village. The dispatch of the train, unsupported by any mounted troops, soon became almost a matter of daily routine. This defiance of common sense could have only one result. On November 15th, Captain Haldane,* of the Gordon Highlanders, went out in the train with 'A' company and some men of the Durban Light Infantry. He reached Frere and, learning from a Natal policeman that the front was clear, pushed on to Chieveley. Here he saw in the distance a small body of the enemy moving southwards, and, having telegraphed the information to Estcourt, turned back. But as the train was running down a steep gradient the Boers suddenly opened fire with two guns from a ridge to the west of the line. Almost immediately afterwards the train was derailed by stones placed on the line, and the leading truck upset, thus stopping the engine.

* He had been wounded at Elandslaagte, and, being unable to rejoin his corps in Ladysmith, was attached to the battalion.

2ND BATT. ROYAL DUBLIN FUSILIERS

It was a predicament trying to the nerves of even the bravest. The Boer shells were well aimed, and came in quick succession. But Captain Haldane and his men did all that could be done. Lieutenant Frankland directed from the rear truck a vigorous fire, which kept the enemy at a respectful distance, and even made them shift their gun. Meanwhile Mr. Winston Churchill, who had accompanied the expedition as a Press correspondent, collected some men and set to work to push the derailed truck off the line. They were exposed to a heavy fire, but eventually succeeded in their task. The train began to move again; luck did not, however, favour them, for the coupling between the engine and rear truck was broken by a shell. Then Captain Haldane ordered the engine to return to Estcourt with as many wounded men as possible, while he attempted with the remainder of the force to reach Frere station. The engine reached Estcourt, but Captain Haldane was not so fortunate. The men left the trucks and started to run along the line. No sooner did our rifle-fire cease than the Boers galloped down the hill and, before Captain Haldane could realise the danger, they were among the men, and he had no course open but to surrender. The casualties of 'A' company were three men killed, four or five wounded, and forty-two prisoners. Private Kavanagh afterwards received the Distinguished Conduct Medal for his gallantry on this occasion. The sound of the Boer guns could be distinctly heard at Estcourt, and great anxiety was felt. A little group of officers assembled in the trenches to the west of the station, and eagerly scanned the country through their glasses. Nothing could be seen, and the firing had ceased. Suddenly through the air rang the shrill whistle of an engine, and at the sound every one gave a sigh of relief. It was the armoured train, and all was well. Another whistle, and round a sharp curve steamed the engine—but, alas! without the trucks. It was evident that a disaster had occurred,

ESTCOURT AND FRERE

although particulars were not received until late in the afternoon; while it was weeks later before the list of casualties could be ascertained. Luckily this mishap occurred when the situation had in other respects improved. The Army Corps was landing, and troops were being pushed forward as quickly as possible. On the 16th, Estcourt was reinforced by the 2nd Queen's and 2nd East Surreys of General Hildyard's brigade, and General Barton's Fusilier brigade was assembling at Mooi River.

The Boers were thus too late, and so lost the opportunity of capturing Maritzburg. Although they doubtless knew of the arrival of fresh troops, they still advanced, and, moving round Estcourt, appeared on the hills to the northwest of Mooi River station. A detachment reconnoitred Estcourt on the 18th, but a couple of shells from Lieutenant James's naval guns induced them to stay at a distance.

The telegraph line south of the town was interrupted on the 22nd, and for a brief period the garrison was cut off from the rest of the world. But the action of Willow Grange, in which the battalion took no part, caused a retirement of the enemy, who retreated through Weenen on the 24th.

Their retreat was in no degree molested by our troops; but on November 26th the long-desired advance took place. It was an exhilarating feeling to leave Estcourt, and lose sight of those hills and trenches, the scene of so many weary vigils. The army did not, however, make a big stride forward. The advance was only to Frere, some ten miles nearer the Tugela.

As the column started at 8 a.m. there seemed every prospect of an easy day. But on active service it is never safe to assume anything. Although no opposition was met with, and the mounted troops hardly saw a Boer, the progress was very slow, and sunset found the rear of the column still three miles distant from Frere. The battalion had the ill-luck to be in the rearguard, behind a seemingly interminable line of transport. Then the inevitable drift intervened, and waggon after waggon broke down. Finally, part of the transport decided to halt till the morning, and the unfortunate rearguard was obliged to form a line of outposts. As the battalion transport was some distance in front, this meant no blankets, no food, nothing save a limited amount of Natal water. The men were not allowed to consume the emergency rations, and therefore had to suffer from cold and hunger. The night passed somehow, however, and with the break of day we marched into Frere, to find our waggons and obtain food.

Another monotonous fortnight was spent at Frere, the only excitement being the arrival of fresh troops and the building of a temporary railway bridge over the Blaukranz. The arrival of Sir Redvers Buller and his staff gave hopes of an early advance, and everybody discussed what our General ought to do, strategical plans becoming as numerous as sandstorms.

Since leaving Ladysmith, the 2nd Dublin Fusiliers had not been attached to a brigade, and now that the Army Corps had come there were not wanting pessimists who foretold that as the battalion was nobody's child it would be sent to guard the lines of communication. Early in December, however, it was assigned to General Hart's 5th, or Irish, Brigade, in place of the 1st Battalion. The latter was ordered to send three companies, with a total strength of 287 men, to make up for the wastage of six weeks' operations. These companies, which were commanded by Major Tempest Hicks, arrived on December 7th, and were allowed at first to maintain a separate organization, so that the 2nd Battalion had eleven companies.

The 5th Brigade was encamped close behind the ridge which lies to the north-west of the railway station. General Hart utilised the fortnight at Frere in making his battalions

CAPT. C. F. ROMER
(standing) and
CAPT. E. FETHERSTONHAUGH.

ESTCOURT AND FRERE

accustomed to his methods. Every day the whole brigade stood to arms an hour before dawn, and advanced up the slope of the ridge, where it stayed until scouts had reported the front all clear. The General was also very particular about the cleanliness of the camp, and made it a rule to go through the lines every morning.

CHAPTER V.

THE BATTLE OF COLENSO.

'Never shame to hear what you have nobly done.'—*Coriolanus.*

ON December 12th, the 6th and Naval Brigades marched from Frere to Chieveley, and the rest of the army followed the next day. The battalion happened to be finding the outposts, and could not march with the 5th Brigade. Some delay in collecting the companies was experienced, so it was not until 1 p.m. that a start was made, and darkness came on before Chieveley was reached. It was, however, a glorious moonlight night, and marching across the veld had a charm which even the dust could not quite destroy. But romance soon gave way to more worldly feelings when, on arriving at Chieveley about 8 p.m., it became necessary to find the brigade camp among the hundreds of tents already pitched.

On the evening of the 14th, it was known that the army was to advance next day, and attempt the passage of the Tugela. Colonel Cooper assembled his officers in order to explain the Divisional and Brigade orders. He stated that the 5th Brigade would cross the river at a drift two miles west of Colenso, then move down the left bank so as to take in rear the Boers defending Colenso bridge, which would be attacked by the 2nd Brigade. The Brigade orders detailed the Dublin Fusiliers to lead the advance to the river, and afterwards to cover the rear of the brigade when it moved down the left bank. General Hart urged in addition the necessity of keeping the men well in hand. They were to cheer in the event of a charge, but were not to be allowed to make a wild rush.

Every one was early astir on December 15th. Breakfasts were at 3 a.m., but before that hour tents had been struck and

2 miles West of Colenso.

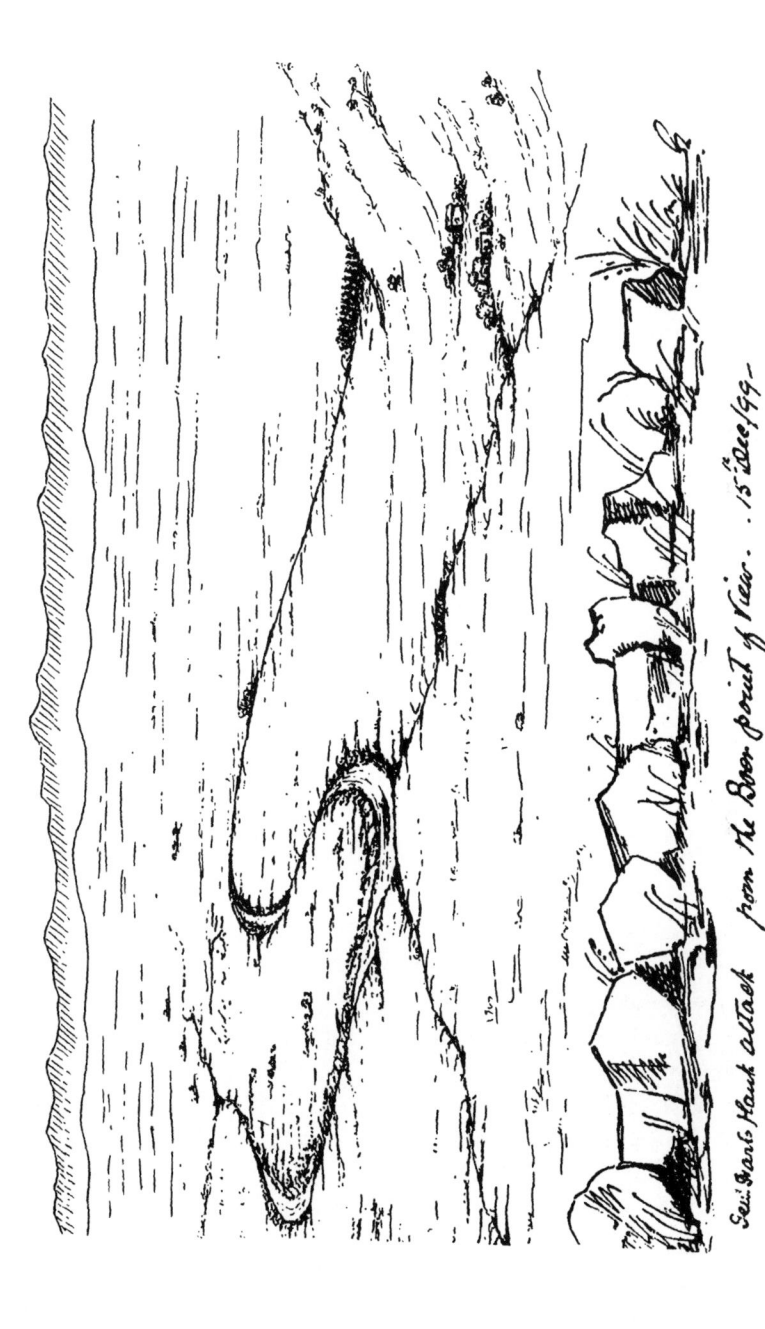

Genl Hart's Attack from the Boer point of view. 15 Dec/99.

From a sketch by Col. H. Tempest Hicks, C.B.

THE BATTLE OF COLENSO

packed in the waggons, on which great-coats, blankets, and mess-tins were also placed, so that the men only carried their haversacks, water-bottles, rifles, and 150 rounds. The brigade fell in at 3.30 a.m. It was still quite dark, and the Brigadier spent the ensuing half-hour in drilling his command. The advance was commenced just as the eastern horizon grew grey with the dawn.

The battalion, which led the brigade, deployed into line to the right, and then advanced by fours from the right of companies. In front rode the General with his staff and a Kaffir guide; behind came the other three battalions of the brigade in mass. The deployment of the battalion had brought ' A ' on the left, and ' H ' and the three companies of the 1st Battalion on the right.

In this order the brigade moved across the broad expanse of veld, leading to the banks of the Tugela. In front, beyond the river, rose tier on tier of ridges and kopjes, backed by the towering mass of Grobelaar's Kloof. In the morning light they looked strangely quiet and deserted. Only on a spur to the left front could be seen a few black specks, the figures of watching Boers.

Soon the naval guns in front of Chieveley opened fire, dropping their shells on the horseshoe ridge to the north of Colenso, and into a kraal further to the west. But no answer came. The brigade moved on, tramping through the long grass, wet with the dew. There was a momentary halt in order to cross a spruit running diagonally across the line of march. The ridges in front grew nearer and plainer. They still seemed deserted, although the eyes of many foes might be watching the advancing khaki-clad troops. Behind came the thunder of the big guns, and the shells screamed in the air overhead. It was past 6 a.m. Suddenly the hiss of a shell sounded marvellously close, there was a metallic clang, and a cloud of dust arose some hundred yards in front. It was a Boer shrapnel, and the battle had begun.

2ND BATT. ROYAL DUBLIN FUSILIERS

Each company of the battalion, without waiting for orders, 'front-formed,' and doubled forward. The mounted officers at once dismounted, Major Hicks' horse being shot under him as he was in the very act of getting off its back. Somehow it did not seem a bit strange to him at the time that his horse should be down, and it never occurred to him then that it had been shot. Another shrapnel burst over the line and then the enemy's musketry blazed forth, finding

BOER TRENCHES, COLENSO.

an excellent target in the massed brigade, which was deploying as best it could.

The battalion was dangerously crowded together, for it had been advancing as if drilling on the barrack square, although Colonel Cooper had tried to open out to double company interval, a proceeding which the General had promptly counter-ordered. But all did their best. The men rushed forward after their officers, and at their signal lay down in the long grass, whence fire was opened at the invisible foe.

It was very difficult to discover the Boer positions. There was one long trench near the kraal which the naval guns

Chancellor.
CAPT. BACON.
Killed.

Watson Robertson.
LIEUT. HENRY.
Killed.

Watson Robertson.
CAPT. H. M. SHEWAN.
Wounded.

Stiles.
MAJOR GORDON
(1st Battalion, attached).
Wounded.

SECOND LIEUT. MACLEOD
(1st Battalion, attached).
Wounded.

CASUALTIES AT COLENSO.

THE BATTLE OF COLENSO

had been shelling, and further to the west could be seen another parapet from which came an occasional puff of smoke betraying a Martini rifle and black powder. But if the Boers could not be seen, they could be both heard and felt. There was one ceaseless rattle of mausers, and a constant hum of bullets only drowned by the scream of the shells.

Short rushes were made as a rule, and the flank companies edged away in order to give room for a more reasonable extension. But no sooner had the battalion opened out than it was reinforced by companies of the Connaught Rangers, and, later, of the Inniskilling Fusiliers and the Border Regiment. In a comparatively short time, after the first Boer shell, the 5th Brigade had been practically crowded into one line. Officers led men of all the four regiments, and encouraged them with the cry, 'Come on, the Irish Brigade!'

There was no control, no cohesion, no arrangement in the attack. No attempt was made to support, by the careful fire of one part of the line, the advance of the remainder; nor did any order from the higher ranks reach the firing line. Small groups of men, led by an officer, jumped up, dashed forward a few scores of yards, and then lay down. Nobody knew where the drift was, nobody had a clear idea of what was happening. All pushed forward blindly, animated by the sole idea of reaching the river-bank.

On the left, part of the battalion was almost on the river when the Boers first opened fire, and quickly reached the bank. After a short halt they turned to their right and moved in single file along the river, being exposed all the time to a heavy fire. They passed through a kraal, and eventually, not being able to find the drift, assembled in a hollow, where they stayed until orders to retire reached them. The centre and right advanced through low scrub into a loop of the river. Some sections of the 1st Battalion, on the extreme right, came upon a spruit, and, under shelter of its banks, pushed ahead of the line.

2ND BATT. ROYAL DUBLIN FUSILIERS

Thus, by short and constant rushes, the assailants worked their way forward. A brigade of field artillery was supporting the attack from behind, but they found it as difficult as the infantry did to locate the Boers, and most of their shells were quite harmless to the enemy, while a few dropped close to the attacking infantry. They aided the latter indirectly, however, since the Boer guns turned their attention to them.

General Sir Redvers Buller had early recognised the difficulties of the 5th Brigade, and sent orders for it to retire. But it is easier to send a force into a battle than to draw it back. The great difficulty at Colenso was to communicate with the company officers, who had to be left entirely to their own 'initiative.' Finally an officer of the Connaught Rangers volunteered to take to the firing line General Hart's written order to retire. He succeeded in reaching the front, but then, thinking he had struck the right of the line, turned to his left. In reality he had gone to the centre of the attack, and, consequently, the retirement was carried out partially and by fractions. The left fell back about 10 a.m. in good order, though the Boers, as usual, redoubled their fire when they saw their foes begin to retreat. The centre and right, having received no order nor warning, clung to their ground, and in some cases even made a further advance. Section after section, however, gradually realised that their left flank was uncovered and a general retreat of the brigade in progress. A score of men, under the command of an officer, would rise up and double back, causing, as they did so, an instant quickening of the enemy's fire. All around the running figures the bullets splashed, raising little jets of dust. Occasionally a man would stumble forward, or sink down as if tired, but it seemed wonderful that the rain of bullets did not claim more victims. They claimed enough, however, of the unfortunate three companies of the 1st Battalion, whom the order to retire never reached. Till

THE BATTLE OF COLENSO

1 p.m., and the arrival of the Boers, they lay where they were, suffering a loss of some 60 per cent. When at last Major Hicks realised the situation, he touched with his stick the man on his right, to tell him to pass the word to retire, but he touched a dead man; he turned to the left, only to touch another corpse. One company was brought out of action by a lance-corporal. Then the Boers arrived, and began making prisoners. One shouted to Major Hicks for his revolver; he replied that he had not got one—it was in his holsters on his dead horse—and stalked indignantly off the battle-field, without another question being put to him.

Major Gordon, who was commanding one of the three companies of the 1st Battalion, had been shot through the knee early in the day by a rifle bullet. He lay for two hours or so momentarily expecting to be hit again. After a time he noticed that as long as he lay still no bullets came in his direction, but that the moment he attempted to move there would be a vicious hiss and spurt of sand and dust close beside him. In spite of this he managed to crawl through a pool of blood to a neighbouring ant-heap, which offered some sort of protection, and into which a bullet plunged just as he reached it. Here he remained till the retirement, when, assisted by two sergeants of the regiment, Keenan and Dillon, he managed to hobble away. Even then he noticed that as long as they kept away from the troops who were still actively engaged few bullets came their way, as though the Boers were purposely not firing at the wounded.

The Boer heavy artillery pursued the retiring troops with shells, which made a prodigious noise, and raised clouds of dust, but seldom did any damage. Gradually a region of comparative peace was reached, where the ground was not being continually struck by bullets, and only an occasional shell fell. The extended lines of the 4th Brigade, ordered to cover the retirement, came into view, and behind them the men of the Irish Brigade collected again in companies and

2ND BATT. ROYAL DUBLIN FUSILIERS

battalions. Then, although the artillery was still roaring fiercely, and the mausers rattled with tireless persistence, the brigade trudged back to its former camping-ground, pitched tents, and began to cook dinners. A prosaic but practical ending to an impossible attack.

But there was still one task to accomplish—the preparation of the casualty list. The regiment had suffered heavily. Two officers, Captain Bacon (1st Battalion) and Lieutenant Henry, had been killed, and three, Major Gordon (1st Battalion), Captain Shewan, and Lieutenant Macleod (1st Battalion), wounded. The total casualties were 219, of whom 52 were killed. Among the latter were Colour-Sergeant Gage (mortally wounded) and Sergeant Hayes.

Captain Bacon (1st Battalion) was killed by a bullet, and must have died immediately. He had previously served for a short time with the 2nd Battalion, in which he had many friends, and his loss was bitterly deplored by Officers, N.C.O.'s, and Privates alike.

Lieutenant Henry had scarcely two years' service, but had in that short space of time endeared himself to every one in the regiment, and was as smart and efficient a young officer as ever joined it. His death must also have been mercifully instantaneous, as he was hit by a shell.

Second Lieutenant Macleod had only joined the 1st Battalion a few days before it left the Curragh on November 10th. He was very severely wounded, his thigh being broken, and although his leg was saved, it was left two inches shorter than it had been, and in the end he had to leave the service on this account.

Major Gordon (1st Battalion), who received a Brevet Lieutenant-Colonelcy for his services, was invalided home, but came out again later on; while Captain Shewan, who had been shot through the leg by a bullet, was back at work again in twelve days, a sterling proof of that devotion

GROUP OF TWENTY SERGEANTS TAKEN AFTER THE BATTLE OF COLENSO.

ALL THAT REMAINED OF FORTY-EIGHT WHO LEFT MARITZBURG.

The names reading from left to right in rows are :—(back row) Sergt. Hanna ; Band-Sergt. Cragg ; Sergt. Davis ; Lance-Sergt. Cullen ; Sergt. Rooney ; Arm.-Sergt. Waite ; Col.-Sergt. Cossey ; Sergt. Smith ; Sergt. Sheridan. (2nd row) Sergt. Keenan ; Sergt. French ; Capt. Fetherstonhaugh ; Col. Cooper ; Col.-Sergt. Guilfoyle ; Sergt. McNay ; Sergt. Hobson ; Pioneer-Sergt. Duncan. (3rd row) Sergt. Moriarty ; Sergt. Purcell ; Col.-Sergt. Connell ; Sergt. Beatty.

THE BATTLE OF COLENSO

to duty which was later on rewarded by the well-merited distinction of the D.S.O.

The three companies of the 1st Battalion had been the greatest sufferers. Being on the right, they were the last to retire; in fact, some of the men did not get in till 5 p.m., while a few were taken prisoners on the banks of the river.

Amongst a host of others who showed their worth under the trying circumstances of this unfortunate day, was Bugler Dunne, a small boy who did his duty well, and had the good fortune to be received by Her Majesty the Queen on his return home. His father was also in South Africa, a Colour-Sergeant in the 5th Battalion. Isolated cases must always receive undue prominence—it is the way of the world—but the spirit of the men was quite remarkable throughout, and made officers and N.C.O.'s proud to command and lead them. Instead of depressing them, the reverse seemed to have a contrary effect, and merely hardened their determination to succeed.

BRINGING DOWN THE WOUNDED.

CHAPTER VI.

VENTER'S SPRUIT.

'Now no chastening for the present seemeth to be joyous, but grievous.'--*Heb.* xii. 11.

THE greater part of December 16th was spent in burying the dead. At nightfall orders were received to strike camp, and the brigade marched back to Frere, which was reached in the early morning of the 17th, when we occupied our former camping-ground.

Another weary wait followed. Frere at the best of times is an uninteresting spot, but it became absolutely repulsive as the grass disappeared and mud and flies reigned supreme. Life in the camp was monotonous, only slightly preferable to the long tours of outpost duty, and a bathe in the river, varied by a walk round the lines, formed the only amusement.

General Hart did not relax any of his precautions, and his command still stood to arms every morning. The rest of the army assembled at Frere seemed, so far as could be seen, to rely on the 5th Brigade, for no other unit followed the latter's example.

Our listlessness was broken on January 6th, when the thunder of the guns around Ladysmith was so distinct that it seemed as if Chieveley must be attacked. Everybody soon learned that the Boers were making a desperate attempt to capture the town, and there was naturally some anxiety as to the result.

A few days afterwards, signs of another forward movement became apparent. One cheerful omen was the arrival of the doctors, whose duty it was to convey the wounded back to the base, and of a large body of civilian stretcher-bearers.

VENTER'S SPRUIT

General Warren's Division, fresh from England, marched in, and the second effort to relieve Ladysmith was begun.

The 5th Brigade left Frere at daybreak on January 11th, and, covered by the 'Royals,' took the Springfield road. It had been raining heavily, and the road, never good, soon became execrable. The column was followed by a long line of waggons carrying baggage, supplies, ammunition, pontoons, &c. On arriving at Pretorius' Farm, the brigade halted and pitched camp. The battalion found the outposts, which were especially ordered to protect themselves by building 'sangars' or digging trenches.

Meanwhile the apparently endless line of waggons had been blocked by a bad drift below the camp, and the brigade was called upon to help. The road was somewhat improved by throwing into the soft mud stones obtained from a wall, and many waggons had to be hauled by ropes through the spruit. For over forty-eight hours did that collection of vehicles continue to cross and require help.

On Thursday, January 12th, the 4th Brigade and General Warren's Division passed through the camp and went straight on to Springfield, since the cavalry had ascertained that there were no Boers south of the Tugela in that direction. The 5th Brigade followed on the afternoon of the 15th, crossing the Little Tugela by a foot trestle-bridge made of spars cut by the Engineers from trees on the bank. As the battalion approached Springfield, the sound of artillery-fire greeted it, and our shrapnel could be seen bursting against a hill which was evidently on the left bank of the Tugela. It was clear that the army was again in touch with the enemy, but nobody knew what Sir Redvers Buller had decided upon, although everybody, of course, dogmatised on what he ought to do.

On the afternoon of the 16th, orders were issued for the brigade to march that night, although nothing was stated regarding its destination. Vigorous operations were

2ND BATT. ROYAL DUBLIN FUSILIERS

plainly intended, since the force was to move as lightly as possible. No tents or blankets were allowed, and the greatcoats were carried by the regimental transport, in which officers were permitted to pack twenty pounds of baggage. Six days' rations were also taken.

The army moved from Springfield at dusk, leaving the camp standing in charge of a few details (cooks, &c.), who had strict orders to light fires and walk about, so that the vigilant burgher might not discover that the army had slipped away. The general direction of the march was north-west. It was a bright moonlight night, but the column moved slowly, for the numerous waggons took up the centre of the road, while the troops moved on the side. About midnight it began to rain, which made everybody cold and uncomfortable, especially as halts were long and frequent. It was not easy to see where the army was going, although the Tugela could not be far off. Nobody knew the plan of operations, which, however, evidently aimed at a surprise crossing of the river, and it seemed as if the enemy must hear the noise of the creaking transport and tramping men.

About 2 a.m. there came a halt on the top of a ridge, where General Hart formed up his brigade. Each regiment deployed into line, and then lay down one behind the other in the following order: Royal Inniskilling Fusiliers, Connaught Rangers, Royal Dublin Fusiliers, and Border Regiment. Fatigued by a long night-march, every one soon fell asleep. Unfortunately, however, the slumbers of the brigade were disturbed by an incident which shows how easily confusion can arise in night operations. A horse from somewhere in front broke loose and galloped over the veld, straight into the ranks of the sleeping regiments. For a moment everything was in confusion, and a general panic nearly took place. Luckily the first glimmer of dawn had come, and the company officers soon regained control of their men,

VENTER'S SPRUIT

but it might have been a different tale had darkness still prevailed.

When daylight came, it showed the army to be on the top of a hill overlooking Trichardt's Drift. On the other side of the river the ground rose to a long ridge flanked on the east by a steep mountain, and on the west by a bastion-like hill. Nobody then knew the country, but that mountain was Spion Kop, and the ridge lying so calmly in the morning light was to be the scene of six days' continuous fighting. At dawn of January 17th, however, the ridge, which the natives called Tabanyama, seemed deserted, and not a Boer was to be seen.

It was now learnt that Sir Redvers Buller had divided his forces, sending two brigades, under General Lyttelton, to Potgieter's Drift, while the remainder of the army, under General Warren, was assembled ready to cross the river at Trichardt's Drift.

The battalion breakfasted quietly, and then 'H' company was sent down to the drift in order to help in the construction of a bridge. As the company descended the steep slope, the artillery from the heights began to shell a farm on the far side of the river, whence a Boer patrol had been sniping. The Engineers had massed the pontoon waggons round a farm by the drift, and were looking for a suitable point for the bridge. The pontoons were launched, and by 11.30 a.m. the first bridge was ready. The infantry immediately began to cross, but the artillery and transport had to wait for a second bridge, which was not completed until after dark.

The 5th Brigade marched down to the river at 2 p.m. and crossed. On reaching the left bank the battalion deployed into line, with four or five paces between the men, and slowly moved up the slope in support of the widely-extended lines of the Lancashire Brigade. Except for an occasional shot from the artillery at Potgieter's Drift, every-

2ND BATT. ROYAL DUBLIN FUSILIERS

thing was still and peaceful; although, as the army moved away from the river, most of the officers expected to be greeted by the familiar 'pick-pock' of the enemy's mausers. The brigade in front eventually halted on the top of a minor ridge, some three thousand yards or more from the crest-line of Tabanyama, and separated from it by open and gently-sloping ground. The Dublin Fusiliers formed quarter-column immediately behind the Lancashire Brigade, and prepared to bivouac. Many of the officers strolled higher up in order to look at the country through their glasses. The main crest-line was evidently occupied, for men could be seen busily digging. It was somewhat trying to think that precious time was being wasted, while the burghers were preparing a defensive position.

Our transport was still on the other side of the Tugela, and consequently we had to do without blankets, great-coats, and kettles. The officers' mess was saved by a subaltern, who succeeded in procuring a Kaffir cooking-pot and some very tough fowls, which Captain Hensley boiled with great skill. The night was unpleasant, for khaki drill is but an inefficient protection against the cold and heavy dew. The experience proved too much for Major Butterworth, R.A.M.C., who had to go on the sick list soon afterwards. He had been with the battalion since Ladysmith, and his coolness and devotion at the battle of Colenso had made him popular with all ranks.

The next day, January 18th, was spent in idleness, and the different corps remained in their bivouacs. There was nothing to do except watch the Boers still digging on the crest-line, and the shells fired by the guns of General Lyttelton, who was apparently making a reconnaissance. The greater part of General Warren's artillery crossed to the left bank and took up a position close to the battalion.

On the 19th the regiment took part in the movement

VENTER'S SPRUIT

which was initiated with the evident purpose of turning the Boer right by the Acton Holmes road. Leaving the artillery and the Lancashire Brigade on the ridge, the remainder of the army descended into the plain, and moved up the left bank of the Tugela. The column marched along the base of the main ridge, and was carefully watched by the Boer patrols from Bastion Hill.

After fording Venter's Spruit the battalion halted about 2 p.m. on some rising ground, whence a good view of the surrounding country was obtained. As there seemed every prospect of a long halt, the men began to take off their boots and putties, in order to dry them, but they had to put them on again hurriedly enough, since the guns suddenly opened fire. At first everybody imagined that the Boers were attacking the artillery and Lancashire Brigade. Soon, however, it was seen that the latter were making a reconnaissance. Not much opportunity for looking at the spectacle was afforded, since we received an order to recross Venter's Spruit and bivouac. The movement by Acton Holmes had been given up for some reason which was unknown, and it was not difficult to see that the alternative was a frontal attack on the position which everybody had watched being fortified.

The battalion halted close to Venter's Spruit, and had a piquet ('H' company) on the Trichardt's Drift road. The transport succeeded in reaching the brigade that night, and the men were thus able to have their great-coats. Not much sleep was, however, allowed. At a very early hour, long before daylight, on the 20th, the brigade was aroused. Great-coats were again packed on the waggons, and then, without breakfast or any opportunity of issuing rations, the battalion fell in and marched off. Owing to darkness and the rough track by which the column marched, progress was at first very slow. When the feeble light of early dawn enabled the country to be seen, the regiment was crossing

2ND BATT. ROYAL DUBLIN FUSILIERS

a spruit near Fairview Farm, lying at the foot of the ridge. It then ascended a small valley leading to Three Tree Hill, where the Field Artillery had concentrated.

The latter soon afterwards opened the battle, and fired on the Boer trenches, which stood out more prominently than usual on the crest of the ridge. The enemy's artillery did not reply, although a vigorous rifle-fire was directed on the skirmishers of the Lancashire Brigade.

The Connaught Rangers had been temporarily detached on escort duty, and General Hart now moved his three remaining battalions to the left in line of quarter-columns. It was a hot day, and the men, who had eaten nothing that morning, suffered some discomfort from such a close formation. The ground, too, was broken and covered with long grass and scrub, so that it was no easy matter to satisfy the General's injunctions in the matter of 'dressing.' The brigade moved in full view of the enemy, and so compact a body of men must have been a great temptation to the Boer gunners, who, however, were either not ready or exercised much self-restraint. After scrambling through a remarkably steep valley, the brigade halted in a gentle depression, where it was safe from the random bullets that were falling near. A long pause ensued, and the men were able to obtain some much-needed water.

It was past noon before the infantry, in this part of the field, advanced in earnest. Then the York and Lancaster Regiment and Lancashire Fusiliers were sent forward as the firing-line against the centre of the Boer position, and were supported by the Borders and 2nd Royal Dublin Fusiliers. The formation adopted by General Hart for the support was two lines. The first line, which was two deep, consisted of the right half-battalions of the two regiments, the Borders being on the right, and was followed at a distance of about two hundred yards by a similar line, composed of the left half-battalions.

VENTER'S SPRUIT

On emerging from the depression where it had been resting, the support came under rifle-fire. The range must, however, have been a long one, and the casualties were few. The attack was moving astride of a spur which ran from the Boer position to the Tugela, a little distance to the west of Three Tree Hill. At first this spur was broad, forming almost a plateau, but further on it narrowed, and consequently the left of the two lines advanced up a narrow valley, which afforded excellent cover.

Led by General Hart, the brigade advanced at a steady pace and, after a time, closed up on the firing-line. It then halted, and from a slight elevation opened fire in order to support the Lancashire Regiments, who, having taken the enemy's advanced position, found that some thousand yards of very open and almost level ground lay between them and the Boer trenches, which lined the northern edge of the summit of the ridge. The attack could now only advance slowly, since it was exposed to a cross-fire from both flanks. Hitherto it had only faced rifle-fire, but about 1.45 p.m. the Boer guns, posted somewhere near Spion Kop, came into action. They were able to rake the whole assaulting line, and, in fact, many officers thought at first that the shells were 'short' ones from our own artillery. The Boers on this occasion managed to burst their shrapnel with some accuracy, and it was fortunate that the attack could find good cover.

This artillery and the increased rifle-fire on the right flank caused the line to swing round in that direction, but any further advance was suspended by superior orders soon after 4.30 p.m. The Borders, who had pushed ahead, were ordered back, and the other regiments took cover among the rocks, and maintained a vigorous fire. The rattle of musketry gradually died away as the light failed, until after nightfall the battalion assembled behind a wall and bivouacked.

2ND BATT. ROYAL DUBLIN FUSILIERS

By great efforts the regimental transport had succeeded in getting touch with the battalion, which was thus able to obtain rations. But it was not until 8 p.m. that the men could get anything to eat.

Thus ended the fight of January 20th. It had cost the regiment one of its most efficient officers, Captain Hensley, who was mortally wounded.* Major English had been hit in the leg—he was back within a fortnight—and of the rank and file four were killed and twenty wounded—among the former being Lance-Sergeant Taylor, a most excellent N.C.O. Athough the opposing forces were so close, the night passed quietly. With daylight (January 21st), however, the rifle-fire at once broke out. The battalion had just managed to have a scratch meal when orders were received to move to the support of the 2nd Brigade, which was away to the left. General Hart ordered Colonel Cooper to move by the straightest line, first down a ravine across a spruit, and then over a hill. While climbing the latter, the battalion was in full view of the enemy, who at once opened fire with guns and rifles. Each company extended in succession, and doubled, so far as possible, over the exposed ground. Once over the hill a region of comparative safety was reached, and General Hart finally formed up his command behind a rocky ridge overlooking the position held by the 2nd Brigade.

* Poor Hensley was not only one of the most popular officers in the regiment, but also one of the best and bravest. All his life he had been devoted to field sports, and his fame as a plucky big-game hunter and skilful shot was well known in many a Central Indian village and Cashmere valley. Educated at the Canadian Military College, he was a master of his profession, while the long months spent in Indian jungles had turned him into a handy man indeed. Wonderful and varied were the uses to which he could put an empty paraffin-tin or biscuit-box, and excellent were the stews he could produce out of a mess-tin. On one occasion in India a wounded panther was mauling one of his beaters. His rifle was empty, but without a moment's hesitation he dashed in, and drove the animal away by beating it over the head. Alas ! poor Hensley, we could spare him ill, but, after all, we know he died the death he would have chosen.

VENTER'S SPRUIT

The latter were having a rifle duel with the Boer trenches but did not advance. The 5th Brigade played a very passive part, and spent the day behind the rocks. Bullets continually whistled overhead, and the hostile artillery near Spion Kop burst an occasional shrapnel along the position. Otherwise there was no excitement.

Towards evening, the regiment received orders to move some few hundred yards to the right, and bivouac. Colonel Cooper directed the companies to close in succession, and march from the rocks to the new position. This movement almost escaped the notice of the Boer artillery, and it was not until the last company ('H') moved that two shells were fired. They fell to the right and in front of the leading fours, and did no damage. The battalion assembled in a narrow amphitheatre just below the southern crest, and at the head of a valley leading to Fairview Farm. Although the bivouac could not be seen by the enemy, except from Spion Kop, it was not altogether sheltered from fire, for every now and then a bullet would clear the crest-line and strike the ground below.

In this amphitheatre we perforce remained for three days, having a far from pleasant time. From sunrise to sunset the rattle of musketry practically never ceased, only at intervals the hum of the passing bullets was drowned by the clang of bursting shrapnel. The Boer guns, posted both directly in front and on the right flank, burst their shells just over the crest, and fired intermittently all day. There were four battalions crowded in the amphitheatre, and each one occupied in turn the crest, whence an uninterrupted fire was directed on the Boer trenches opposite. The enemy's marksmen had the range of this crest-line, and it was a dangerous matter to stand up even for a minute. Stone sangars were built and the companies relieved each other by the men crawling up the slope. The enemy's artillery near Spion Kop could rake the line of sangars, thus necessitating numerous

2ND BATT. ROYAL DUBLIN FUSILIERS

traverses. When not in the firing line, we lay behind the slope in column, each company being protected by a parapet of earth or stone. Immediately below the amphitheatre the ground fell steeply, forming a ravine in which the cooks set up their field kitchens in comparative security. It was characteristic of the British soldier that whereas during the greater part of the day he crouched behind his cover, the sight of a fatigue party with the kettles made him forget the shells and bullets, and he dashed off for his food regardless of danger.

On Tuesday night (January 22nd) the proposed assault on Spion Kop was announced, and every one hoped that a general advance would be the result.

The morning of January 23rd dawned with a thick white mist, which hid everything from view. It was our turn to occupy the ridge, and the companies lay there for nearly an hour before the usual exchange of rifle-fire began. No news of the capture of Spion Kop had reached the amphitheatre, but the fact could be guessed from the absence of the Boer guns in that direction. Only the artillery in front of the battalion's position fired in the morning, and even that ceased during the afternoon. The enemy was evidently concentrating the greater part of his forces against Spion Kop, and parties of mounted burghers could be seen moving from their extreme right. On Spion Kop hung the white clouds of bursting shrapnel, and the stuttering sound of the pompom scarcely ceased for a moment, but the 5th Brigade made no advance. The companies behind the sangars fired hundreds of rounds at the Boer trenches, while their comrades below ate and slept.

At dawn of the 25th, glasses and telescopes were turned on to the summit of the mountain, and it was a bitter blow when the moving figures there were seen to be Boers. It was not until late in the forenoon, however, that the evacuation of Spion Kop was officially communicated. But the renewal

VENTER'S SPRUIT

of the Boer artillery fire against the crest-line had been a sufficiently eloquent announcement of the fact.

As there seemed no reason why the regiment should remain in the amphitheatre when it was not required to man the sangars, Colonel Cooper obtained permission that afternoon to move down the valley below Bastion Hill. The new bivouac was more sheltered, although an occasional Boer shell still fell near.

It was now evident that the second attempt to relieve Ladysmith had failed, and that the army would have to recross the Tugela. On the afternoon of the 25th, fatigue parties were sent by the battalion to improve the track leading to Fairview Farm, and it was rumoured that the retreat would take place that night. At 10.30 p.m. 'H' company was sent to the farm, with orders to hold it during the retirement. But the army did not move until Friday night, January 26th. At 10 p.m. on that date, General Hart's command began to descend the valley in heavy rain, which rendered the track extremely greasy.

Only a short distance had been covered when there was an outburst of rifle-fire from the rearguard, which was still holding the sangars. For a moment it seemed as if the Boers had anticipated the retreat and were attacking. The battalion halted, but the firing soon ceased, and the march was continued, the men stumbling down the track as quickly as the many boulders would permit. At Fairview Farm the column halted for a considerable period, in order to let the rearguard close up. By this time every one was wet to the skin, and the enforced rest was somewhat trying, owing to the cold.

However, after a wait of about an hour, the retirement was resumed. The track was marked by orderlies and tins, but even with this help it was difficult to find the way in the utter darkness. The surface of the road, too, had become so slippery that falls were frequent. Altogether, progress was painfully slow and the march a very fatiguing one. It was past 4 a.m., January 27th, before the pontoon bridge at Trichardt's Drift was reached. The column had another prolonged wait here, and so tired were the men that many of them dropped to the ground and slept in the mud. Early dawn had come when the brigade recrossed the Tugela and toiled up the steep slope on the other side. A Boer gun sent a parting shell just as the column reached the summit.

It was a great relief to look back towards Tabanyama, where the discarded biscuit tins were gleaming in the morning light, and say good-bye to that long line of sangars and trenches. The men's spirits were, moreover, cheered up by the sight of the 'Scotch' cart with the kettles and rations. Breakfasts were cooked, and after a short rest the brigade moved to the camping-ground selected for it. But it arrived only to find that the position was within view and artillery range of Spion Kop. So once more it had to trudge over the veld, General Hart moving it in line of quarter-columns, and being as particular about the 'dressing' as if he were on Laffan's Plain. His command hardly appreciated this smartness at the time. But all were finally rewarded by the arrival of the transport with tents and baggage, and every one spent the night in comparative luxury.

CHAPTER VII.

VAAL KRANTZ.

'The best laid schemes o' mice and men
Gang aft agley,
And lea'e us naught but grief and pain
For promised joy.'
Burns.

ON January 30th we were reinforced by a draft of 400 men, principally militia reservists, who were brought up by Captain Venour. They were a welcome addition, being a physically fine body of men, and, although their training was naturally not so good as that of their 'regular' comrades, they proved equally brave and ready to follow their officers.

The battalion shifted its camp on January 29th to Spearman's Hollow, where it stayed a week. It was here that Sir Redvers Buller visited every brigade in turn, and made his speech stating that the fighting around Spion Kop had enabled him to discover the key to Ladysmith. He had earned the gratitude of the men by putting them on extra rations, and was always a warm favourite with the rank and file, who love a brave man and instinctively know one.

On February 2nd the regiment left Spearman's Hollow for Spearman's Hill, and, on the afternoon of Sunday, February 4th, marched with the rest of the brigade towards Potgieter's Drift. The trek was a short one, and at 6 p.m. we bivouacked behind Swaartz Kop. At nightfall the officers were assembled and informed of the proposed operations for the next day. The idea was to make a feint attack on Brakfontein and then assault Vaal Krantz, the capture of which, it was thought, would break the enemy's line.

We rose at dawn on the 5th, had a comfortable breakfast,

2ND BATT. ROYAL DUBLIN FUSILIERS

and only moved off about 7 a.m., just as the heavy artillery on Mount Alice and Swaartz Kop began the fight by shelling Brakfontein. The hills around rolled with the thunder of the guns, while the faint echoes of the lyddite explosions on the distant ridges formed a piano accompaniment. With this music in its ears, the battalion marched through the gap between Mount Alice and Swaartz Kop by the road leading to Potgieter's Drift. There was a short halt made at the gap, from which a splendid view of the battlefield was obtainable. Immediately below stretched the silver line of the Tugela, with all its many loops and twistings visible. Beyond came a small brown ridge, which had evidently been held by our troops, since a few biscuit-tins glistened on the near slope. Further away was the background formed by the Boer position, extending in a gigantic curve from Spion Kop on the spectator's left to the lofty mass of Doorn Kloof on his right, the centre being formed by Brakfontein and Vaal Krantz, over both of which heavy columns of smoke were hanging. The Lancashire Brigade had commenced the feint attack, and its extended lines could be plainly seen as they advanced slowly in succession, while behind them the batteries of field artillery had unlimbered on the plain, and were already shelling the Boer trenches.

After a short pause the regiment began to descend the hill. The 5th Brigade was following the 4th, both of them marching in 'fours.' Before reaching the drift, the head of the column wheeled to the right and proceeded along the narrow plain between the Tugela and Swaartz Kop. The sight of that long winding line must have been a great temptation to the Boer gunners, but they remained silent. Not even a rifle had spoken. It was only when the Lancashire Brigade began to retire that the enemy disclosed himself. Then Brakfontein spluttered with musketry, and the Boer artillery vented its wrath on the batteries dotted over the plain. But both our infantry and gunners seemed to treat

Spink.
SECOND LIEUT. LANE.
Wounded at Hart's Hill.

LIEUT. J. McD. HASKARD.
Wounded at Pieter's Hill.

SECOND LIEUT. BRADFORD.
Wounded at Pieter's Hill.

Turner & Drinkwater.
CAPT. A. V. HILL.
(1st Battalion, attached).
Wounded at Pieter's Hill.

SECOND LIEUT. BRODHURST HILL
(1st Battalion, attached).
Wounded at Pieter's Hill.

CASUALTIES AT TUGELA HEIGHTS.

VAAL KRANTZ

the fusilade with contempt. The former marched back without apparently quickening their pace, and the latter, limbering up, trotted off to support the attack on Vaal Krantz. This hill was being literally covered with shells, and soon had the appearance of a smoking volcano.

About 1 p.m. the Durham Light Infantry filed over the pontoon under Swaartz Kop, and extended for the attack. At the same time we were moved to a position below the southern end of the Kop in order to cover by long-range rifle-fire the right of the 4th Brigade. 'B' company fired a few volleys at some invisible snipers on the slopes of Doorn Kloof, but with this exception we did not come into action.

Watched by the whole army the Durhams advanced against Vaal Krantz, which they took about 4 p.m. amidst the cheers of the onlookers. But with this success the operations practically ended for the day.

The battalion remained all the afternoon in the same position, and then finally bivouacked there, having luckily succeeded in communicating with the transport, so that the men had blankets. Its outposts were pushed well round the southern slopes of Swaartz Kop, thus overlooking the Tugela. A reconnoitring patrol was fired on from the left bank, but otherwise the night passed without incident.

We did not move on the 6th, and had practically nothing to do. The artillery on both sides fired continually, although the damage done must have been very small in proportion to the noise and expenditure of ammunition.

Every one watched with special interest a duel between our heavy artillery and a large Boer gun which had suddenly been unmasked on Doorn Kloof. This gun fired black powder, and its discharge could be plainly seen, but it was apparently run up for every round behind a parapet. It displayed absolute impartiality in its attentions. One round would be directed against the infantry on Vaal Krantz, another covered with dust a field battery on the plain, a third

2ND BATT. ROYAL DUBLIN FUSILIERS

just missed the battalion, while a fourth shell would crash among the trees on Swaartz Kop. All our heavy guns had a try at silencing it, and their efforts sometimes met with partial success. The Boer gun would cease firing for a time, but it always re-appeared when least expected. Towards the evening it became quite lively and put a shell through the pontoon bridge.

The night of February 6th–7th was spent in comparative peace, although the Boer artillery somewhat spoiled the first part of the night by shelling Vaal Krantz. February 7th was a repetition of the 6th, except that the gun on Doorn Kloof paid slightly more attention to our position. The Colonel found it necessary to post a man on the look-out, whose duty it was, on seeing the white puff of smoke, to blow a whistle, whereupon everybody sought the shelter of the nearest and largest boulder. But although, when the huge shell burst, the air seemed unpleasantly full of whizzing iron fragments, no damage was done, and the gun merely mitigated, to some extent, the monotony of idleness.

By this time it was clear that Sir Redvers Buller did not intend to press the attack home, and no one was surprised to find the army in retreat on the morning of the 8th. The battalion acted as rearguard and marched back between the river and Swaartz Kop in widely extended lines. The Boer guns on Doorn Kloof, the shoulder of Spion Kop, and Brakfontein shelled us on our way, and one man of the rear company ('H') was killed, this being our only casualty between February 5th and 8th. The heavy artillery on Mount Alice covered the retreat and prevented the enemy's guns from being too attentive.

The 5th Brigade halted at Springfield, and two days later went on to Pretorius' Farm. On the 18th it made a march of fourteen miles to the Blaukranz River, starting about 3.30 a.m. The day was hot, and as there was no water on the route the newly-joined militia reservists suffered considerably.

VAAL KRANTZ

After a rest of two days the brigade moved to a camp near Gun Hill at Chieveley, where the naval six-inch gun was in position. The rest of the army was now engaged in the operations against Cingolo and Hlangwane, and the battalion occupied itself in guarding Chieveley, in beginning the construction of a railway to Hussar Hill, and in convoying ammunition to the latter place. This was a somewhat trying task, as during part of the way the convoy became the object of many a Boer shell. The operations against Cingolo and Hlangwane proved successful, and these positions were captured on the 19th. The next day General Hart took the regiment on a reconnaissance towards Colenso. It advanced cautiously on the west of the railway in column of extended companies. The village was found unoccupied, but a party of Boers holding the horseshoe ridge on the left bank of the Tugela opened a vigorous fire. The leading companies at once doubled forward and lined the right bank, whence they answered the Boer marksmen. The left half-battalion remained in support behind the village. A detachment of Thorneycroft's Mounted Infantry appeared on the scene, and having forded the Tugela above the road bridge, turned the Boers out of their position. Later on in the afternoon a train steamed into Colenso station from Chieveley, and took us back just before dusk.

At 6 a.m. on February 21st, the Connaught Rangers and the Dublin Fusiliers went by train to Colenso, where they were joined by a battery. The horseshoe ridge on the left bank was being held by a detachment of Thorneycroft's Mounted Infantry, but General Hart was desirous of crossing the river with at least part of his force. For this purpose he had brought on the train a boat, which was promptly launched. As, however, the boat was small, and hardly capable of holding more than four men, the General gave orders for the construction of a raft. After some trouble

2ND BATT. ROYAL DUBLIN FUSILIERS

this was ready by 4 p.m., and some two hours later about seven companies of the Connaught Rangers had succeeded in reaching the left bank.

General Hart now received an order to cross early next morning, with three battalions of his brigade, the pontoon bridge, which had been constructed under Hlangwane. The regiment bivouacked in Colenso, and at 5 a.m on February 22nd marched down the right bank and crossed the bridge. One company had been sent back to Chieveley for the purpose of striking the camp, and with the transport rejoined the battalion about 7 a.m., after the latter had crossed the bridge and taken up a position on the western side of the horseshoe ridge.

Here it stayed the whole day, all ranks passing the time in examining the Boer trenches, and picking up more or less worthless loot. Heavy fighting was taking place in front, but only an occasional shell fell near the ridge.

CHAPTER VIII.

HART'S AND PIETER'S HILLS—THE RELIEF OF LADYSMITH.

> 'But since I know
> No rock so hard but that a little wave
> May beat admission in a thousand years,
> I re-commenced.'
> *Tennyson.*

LATE on February 22nd, orders were issued for the brigade* to be ready to move at an early hour next morning. Breakfasts were eaten before 4 a.m., and the battalion fell in at about 4.15 on February 23rd. The brigade was to move from the left to the right of the army, and it was probably the intention of the Headquarter Staff for the march to take place during darkness. But there was a hitch in the distribution of biscuits, and it was already broad daylight when we started.

General Hart moved his command in column of route, and the long line soon attracted the notice of the enemy's artillery. It was somewhat trying to the nerves to hear the whistle of a shell coming nearer and nearer, until finally it struck the ground within a few yards of the column. Luckily, the Boers were either using common shell or their shrapnel did not burst, and the battalion had no casualties. Finally the railway was reached, and the brigade turned to the left, each battalion forming column of companies in succession. A halt was made close to the railway line and a short distance to the south of the viaduct over the Onderbrook Spruit. But as a few shells fell dangerously near, and showed that the enemy could still see the brigade, it was moved to the left

---

* The Borders had been left behind at Chieveley. In their place General Hart received half a battalion of the newly-raised Imperial Light Infantry.

2ND BATT. ROYAL DUBLIN FUSILIERS

behind a rocky ridge. The battalion stayed here for the rest of the morning. The Boer gunners fired frequently at the ridge, but the slope of the ground saved us from any losses. Sir Redvers Buller and his staff rode up about midday in order to explain to General Hart what was required of him. This was the capture of the hill known as Inniskilling, or Hart's, Hill. It could be plainly seen from the summit of the ridge behind which we lay, and all officers and section commanders were called up in order to have a look at it. They were told that it formed the extreme left of the Boer position, and that its capture meant the relief of Ladysmith. General Hart desired all officers to inform their men of the necessity for a resolute assault. Our heavy artillery on the right bank of the Tugela now began to shell the hill, which was quickly covered by the smoke and dust of the lyddite explosions.

Meanwhile, the 2nd Brigade was preparing the way by an assault on a ridge some 1000 yards to the front. They had a tough fight, and their wounded were soon being brought down the railway in trucks and stretchers.

The afternoon was well advanced when the 5th Brigade moved to the attack. The hill to be assaulted lay some 3000 yards to the north-east of the ridge which had been sheltering us, and the nature of the intervening ground forbade a direct advance, which would dangerously expose the left flank. It was necessary to hug the river-bank until a position from which a direct attack became possible was reached.

The brigade at first moved along the railway line in file in the following order: Royal Inniskilling Fusiliers, Connaught Rangers, Royal Dublin Fusiliers, and Imperial Light Infantry. The battalion moved with the left in front. A brigade in file takes up a considerable space, and by the time the regiment could start, a heavy outburst of firing showed that the Inniskilling Fusiliers were already engaged.

HART'S HILL

The advance along the railway line, through a cutting and over the Onderbrook Spruit, was very slow, since checks were frequent. The Boer artillery missed this favourable opportunity of shelling their foes, luckily for the latter. After crossing Onderbrook Spruit, the column turned to the right and crept along the river. The enemy were sweeping the bank with pompoms and a heavy rifle-fire, but by crouching under the bank the column obtained good cover for the greater part of the way. But every now and then there came an exposed bit of ground over which it was necessary to double, and so narrow was the track that men had often to jump over the wounded or killed.

The Langverwacht Spruit had to be crossed by the railway bridge. As the latter was in full view of the enemy and was being raked by pompom shells and bullets, it proved a great delay to the progress of the column. It was only possible to cross at more or less long intervals. Each man was forced to run the gauntlet by himself, and had to double over as hard as he could. Beyond the bridge complete cover was obtained except for a small stretch of ground by the Boer bridge. Below the latter, the river ran between high hills, and the column was therefore screened from view.

By the time that the leading company of the battalion had cleared 'Pompom' bridge, the Inniskilling Fusiliers were advancing against the Boer position on Hart's Hill. It was about 5 p.m., and the General could not wait until his brigade had concentrated, but sent his troops forward as they arrived. The left half-battalion of the Royal Dublin Fusiliers formed up near a deserted Boer bivouac overlooking the river, and then, without stopping for the right half, advanced to where General Hart was standing.

Lieutenant-Colonel Sitwell was in command of the left half-battalion, and in a short time he was sent for by the General, who told him to advance and help the Inniskilling Fusiliers to capture the hill.

2ND BATT. ROYAL DUBLIN FUSILIERS

The leading company ('H') was directed to extend to six paces and move forward, the remaining companies ('G,' 'F,' and 'E') following at a distance of 100 yards. No sooner had 'H' company cleared the crest of the hill on which General Hart was standing, than it came under a heavy rifle-fire, principally from the direction of Railway Hill. Lieutenant Lane fell badly wounded—shot clean through the head from one side to another, a wound from which he made a marvellous recovery—and three or four men were hit. The company received the order to double, no easy task down a steep slope strewn with rocks and boulders. The railway line at the bottom of the slope was crossed, and the opposite side of the valley, which was dotted with small trees, ascended. The company had now caught up the lines of the Connaught Rangers, and all climbed up the hill, the crest of which had been gained by the Inniskilling Fusiliers. Although the attacking infantry could not be seen from the Boers on Hart's or Railway Hill, they were still exposed to an enfilade fire from the left.

On arriving with 'H' company at the top of the hill, Lieutenant-Colonel Sitwell found the Inniskilling Fusiliers lying along the crest-line and facing the Boer trenches, which ran at about three hundred yards distance on the far side of the flat plateau. The Inniskillings had already suffered serious casualties, but, on Lieutenant-Colonel Sitwell stating that he had been ordered to charge, claimed the right of leading the assault. To this Colonel Sitwell agreed, but it was decided to wait until the remaining companies of the left half-battalion of the Royal Dublin Fusiliers were up. Meanwhile our guns and the cavalry maxims on the right bank of the Tugela were directing against the enemy's trenches a stream of bullets and shrapnel shells, the latter seeming to burst immediately over the infantry.

The sun had set, and the light was already failing by

Gauvin.
CAPT. A. HENSLEY.
Killed at Venter's Spruit.

Maclardy.
LIEUT.-COLONEL SITWELL.
Killed at Hart's Hill.

Elliott & Fry.
CAPT. MAITLAND
(*Gordon Highlanders, attached*)
Killed at Hart's Hill.

Elliott & Fry.
MAJOR F. P. ENGLISH.
Wounded at Venter's Spruit and Zuikerbosch.

Holloway.
SECOND LIEUT. DENNIS.
Wounded at Hart's Hill. Died of Enteric at Aliwal North.

CASUALTIES AT TUGELA HEIGHTS (*continued*).

HART'S HILL

the time that the four companies of the left half-battalion had come up, principally on the left of the Inniskilling Fusiliers. Then the signal to charge was given, and the whole line rose up, and with a yell dashed forward. But it was met by a murderous fire. In the gathering darkness the Boer trenches quivered with the rifle-flashes, and the bullets struck out sparks as they hit the rocks. At such a short range the enemy's marksmen could hardly miss, and

AFTER THE FIGHT.

the line of charging infantry was almost mowed down. The assault was checked, and the attackers flung themselves on the ground and sought what little cover there was.

Luckily night intervened, and, although the Boers never for a moment ceased their fire, the survivors of that charge managed to creep back to the crest. Here Colonel Brooke, of the Connaught Rangers, and Lieutenant-Colonel Sitwell collected them, and took steps to guard against a counter-attack. A low stone wall was built below the crest, and behind this the night was spent.

It was very dark, and the ground, covered with boulders,

2ND BATT. ROYAL DUBLIN FUSILIERS

most difficult to move over. Wounded men lay all over the hill, but there were no doctors, no stretcher-bearers, and no water. It was impossible to help or to move them. Their groans, combined with the intermittent rifle-fire, made sleep difficult.

We had three officers wounded (Lieutenants Lane, Hill, and Dennis), and some twenty casualties. Lieutenant Hill was again hit as he lay, and subsequently lost his foot in consequence.

The infantry crouching behind the stone wall were unable to communicate with the rest of the army. At dawn, however, Major McGrigor, the Brigade-Major, came up to the line and told Colonel Brooke that General Hart wished him to hold on to his position, to which reinforcements would be sent. Colonel Brooke explained that food and water would have to be sent also, and, above all, that his left must be protected. Having promised to do what he could, Major McGrigor returned to his General. With daylight the battle recommenced. The Boers, from their trenches on Hart's and Railway Hills, kept up a vigorous rifle-fire, and were answered as far as possible by the men of the 5th Brigade behind the wall. Our artillery shelled Hart's Hill, and many of their shrapnel which burst short hit the unlucky wounded who were still lying on the plateau.

But the Boers were not content to remain on the defensive. Gradually their skirmishers worked round the left of the hill, moving by the dongas which ran down to the railway line, and were able to fire up into the rear of the defenders of the wall. Part of the latter were extended at right angles to the wall, and endeavoured to drive off the enemy. But the Boers had excellent cover, whereas the infantry crowded together on the hill presented an easy target. Casualties became numerous. The morning wore on, and there were no signs of the promised reinforcements or of the much-needed water and food. It seemed useless to stay on the hill, and about 8 a.m. Colonel

HART'S HILL

Brooke gave the order to retire. As the men rose to their feet and ran down the hill, the rattle of the Boer musketry increased in volume, and the bullets whistled among the retreating soldiers. Lieut.-Colonel Sitwell was killed as he descended the slope, and Captain Maitland, of the Gordon Highlanders, who had been in command of 'G' company since November, was mortally wounded almost at the same time. Luckily, the distance was not very great, and once over the railway line the stream of bullets ceased.

THE GRAVE OF COLONEL SITWELL AND CAPTAIN MAITLAND, GORDON HIGHLANDERS (ATTACHED), NEAR RAILWAY AT PIETER'S HILL.

Lieut.-Colonel Sitwell's loss was severely felt. Though he had only recently joined us, he had given numerous proofs of his soldierly ability. He had the benefit of considerable previous war service, and had he lived would doubtless have risen to high rank. Captain Maitland, Gordon Highlanders, had been unable to join his regiment in Ladysmith, and had been attached to the battalion since Estcourt. Over and over again he had proved himself to be a most gallant soldier, and had endeared himself to all his temporary comrades

2ND BATT. ROYAL DUBLIN FUSILIERS

(see Appendix). He commanded 'G' company, which was most unfortunate in respect of its commanders, having no less than six during the war. Colour-Sergeant Connell, however, than whom no braver man lives, was with it throughout.

As the retiring infantry climbed up the slope of Hart's Hollow they met the advancing lines of the 4th Brigade, who had been sent to reinforce the 5th. The latter quickly re-formed—there were not many of the Inniskilling Fusiliers left to re-form—and were able to obtain food after a fast of nearly twenty-four hours.

The casualties of the left half-battalion amounted to two officers killed and three wounded, and eleven killed and fifty-six wounded of the rank and file.*

The right half-battalion, under Major English, had, during the assault of Hart's Hill, watched the right flank towards Pieter's Hill. General Hart proposed that they should attack the Boers in that quarter, but Colonel Cooper, who was with the right half-battalion, pointed out that the day was too far advanced. The right half-battalion spent the night of the 23rd–24th February among the rocks on the hill whence General Hart had directed the attack. About 8 a.m. on February 24th, 'B' company was sent to drive off small parties of the enemy who had crept down the dongas and reached the railway on the left. This company came under a severe fire, and Lieutenant Brodhurst Hill was wounded in the leg, but the Boers were driven back. The 24th was spent in a ceaseless rifle-duel with the enemy, who had brought a gun to bear on the hill. During the afternoon, preparations were made for a fresh attack on Hart's Hill, to be undertaken by Colonel Cooper with two battalions, while General Hart,

---

* There were, of course, many narrow escapes, but none narrower than that of Major Romer, whose modesty forbids him to allude to it. His helmet was shot through by a bullet which actually parted his hair in its passage, a feat never before accomplished.—A. E. M.

PIETER'S HILL

with the remainder of the force at hand, assaulted Railway Hill. The attack was, however, postponed.

The enemy evidently feared another assault, for in the course of the night of February 24th-25th, they opened a vigorous fire, which disturbed the slumbers of General Hart's force, and created some excitement. During all this time the unlucky wounded, who had been hit on the 23rd, had been left lying in front of the Boer

PIETER'S HILL. FEBRUARY 27TH, 1900.

trenches. It was impossible to help them, since all attempts in that direction had been frustrated by the enemy. But on the morning of Sunday, February 25th, a partial armistice was agreed upon in order to bring in the wounded and to bury the dead. The armistice ended at 6 p.m., and both sides commenced firing immediately afterwards.

Meanwhile, Sir Redvers Buller had evolved a new plan of operations, and decided to attack with his combined force the three hills—Pieter's, Railway, and Hart's. For this purpose the greater part of the artillery was brought from the left bank and concentrated on the right bank, opposite

2ND BATT. ROYAL DUBLIN FUSILIERS

the points to be assaulted. It was in position by the 26th, and began a slow bombardment of the Boer trenches. During the night, the pontoon bridge under Hlangwane was dismantled, and carried down to a point below the Boer bridge, where it was relaid, an operation which was not concluded until 10 a.m. on the 27th.

On the day before, the Dublin Fusiliers had been ordered to join temporarily General Barton's Brigade. It left its

PONTOON BRIDGE, RIVER TUGELA. FEBRUARY 28TH, 1900.

position among the rocks of Hart's Hollow about 7 a.m. on February 27th, and, moving down the hill through the deserted Boer laager, halted by the pontoon bridge. Here it was joined soon after 9 a.m. by the Irish and Scots Fusiliers, and came under the command of General Barton.

The battalion followed the Scots Fusiliers, and moved along the left bank of the Tugela at the foot of a steep ridge, being covered by infantry and maxim fire from the right bank.

. After a march of two miles, and at the point where the Klip River joins the Tugela, the 6th Brigade turned to its

PIETER'S HILL

left and prepared to attack the Boer position, which, lying some two miles from the river, stretched from the ridges north of Eagle's Nest to the various kopjes constituting Pieter's Hill. General Barton directed the Royal Irish Fusiliers to assault the western end of Pieter's Hill and the Scots Fusiliers the eastern, while the 2nd Royal Dublin Fusiliers formed the reserve.

The assault was successful, and the greater part of Pieter's Hill fell into our hands, but the Boers still held a kopje to the north of the hill, and maintained a heavy fire. General Barton, anxious to complete his victory, directed three companies of the battalion and one company of the Scots Fusiliers to advance against the kopje. 'B,' 'C,' and 'H' were the three companies selected, the first named being on the right and the latter on the left, connecting with the Scots Fusiliers. Guided by Captain MacBean, Royal Dublin Fusiliers, Brigade - Major 6th Brigade, the detachment advanced about 2.30 p.m., and came at once under a heavy rifle and pompom fire. The companies pushed forward, however, by successive rushes until they reached a donga ome three hundred yards from the kopje. Here further progress was checked for a time, and General Barton ordered forward three companies of the Royal Irish Fusiliers. The latter came up about 5.30 p.m., and, supported by the covering fire of 'B,' 'C,' and 'H' companies, rushed the left of the hill, when the above-mentioned companies of the battalion, led by Captain Venour, assaulted the right. The attack was successful, and the kopje was captured.

During the advance Lieutenants Haskard and Bradford, in command of 'C' and 'H' companies, were wounded, and the engagement cost the regiment nine killed and forty-three wounded. 'D' company, under Lieutenant Ely, towards the close of the afternoon came up on the left of 'H' company, in order to fill the gap between the latter and the Scots Fusiliers.

2ND BATT. ROYAL DUBLIN FUSILIERS

The three companies which had made their attack on the kopje spent the night on the captured position. Captain Venour, who was the senior officer present, re-formed the men of the Irish and Dublin Fusiliers, and constructed sangars, with a view of warding off a Boer counter-attack. In the meantime 'A,' 'E,' 'F,' and 'G' companies—with whom was Colonel Cooper—were directed to the right, in order to guard the flank of the brigade against the Eagle's Nest

2ND ROYAL DUBLIN FUSILIERS, HEADING RELIEF TROOPS, MARCHING INTO LADYSMITH, MARCH, 1900.

position. These companies gained about 2 p.m. a ridge opposite the Eagle's Nest, and overlooking the extensive plain which stretches up to Bulwana Mountain. The enemy opened a well-aimed fire on this ridge, and also brought into action a gun which was placed on the shoulder to the north of the Nest. As the right of the four companies was thrown back towards the Tugela, this Boer gun could nearly enfilade part of the line. Sangars were built, however, and there were not more than three or four casualties in this part of the field. The firing ceased at dusk, but otherwise the night was

THE RELIEF OF LADYSMITH

unpleasant, for it rained, and the waggons could not get near the fighting line, so that the men had to do without their great-coats.

Before daybreak on February 28th the battalion collected its scattered companies and was ready for action. There was no reliable news of what had happened on other parts of the field during the 27th, and the full extent of the victory was still unknown. When daylight came it was evident that the

GENERAL SIR REDVERS BULLER, V.C., ENTERING LADYSMITH.

Boers had evacuated the Eagle's Nest, and small parties of them could be seen retiring, while the tents of their laager under Bulwana were gradually diminishing. But even then few could believe that the relief of Ladysmith was practically accomplished.

Before midday an order came, directing the Dublin Fusiliers to move after dinner and join the 11th Brigade, the position of which was not indicated. Major English rode on ahead in order to discover its whereabouts, but by the time he found it, the battalion had gone two miles out of its way. The 11th Brigade was joined about 4 p.m., and the regiment bivouacked between Hart's and Railway Hills. A heavy

2ND BATT. ROYAL DUBLIN FUSILIERS

thunderstorm burst over the country soon after 8 p.m., and made everybody somewhat miserable, although the officers had been cheered by the arrival of the invaluable Corporal Tierney, who, as usual, succeeded in giving them food. The services of this N.C.O. (now Mess-Sergeant) will never be forgotten by the regiment, as long as an officer who was present with it in South Africa remains in it. Over and over again he brought up food to the officers

THE DUBLINS ARE COMING—LADYSMITH.

under heavy fire, and through those desperate thunderstorms. Always cheery, ever ready, there he was in his shirt-sleeves, with a drink and a snack, just as one had resigned oneself to going without anything. A word must also be said in praise of our French *chef*, M. Burst, who cooked for the officers' mess throughout, and proved himself on all occasions a brave man.

After breakfast on March 1st, the 11th Brigade advanced along the railway towards Ladysmith. It was thought that the Boers would be holding Bulwana, and the brigade had orders to attack the hill. But it was soon learnt that the enemy had retired, and we eventually reached Nelthorpe

THE RELIEF OF LADYSMITH

Station about midday and bivouacked. Major English and Captain Venour took the opportunity of riding into Ladysmith.

March 2nd was spent at Nelthorpe. On the 3rd, Sir Redvers Buller's army entered Ladysmith, and the honour of leading the army fell to the 2nd Battalion Royal Dublin Fusiliers—an honour which nobody grudged them, on account of the constant fighting they had taken part in

SIR GEORGE WHITE WATCHING RELIEF FORCE ENTERING LADYSMITH.

since the beginning of the war, and the heavy casualties they had suffered. The route was by the railway bridge, and the streets of the little town were lined by the garrison, who, emaciated but clean, presented a startling contrast to their war-stained relievers.

The entry into Ladysmith, with its enthusiasm and meeting of old friends, formed a fitting ending to the battalion's Natal campaign. Hardly any other unit in the army had suffered such casualties. Only five company officers marched through Ladysmith with it. The others had been killed, wounded, or disabled.

75

CHAPTER IX.

THE SIEGE OF LADYSMITH.

'I am shut up.'—*Ps.* lxxxviii. 8 and *Jer.* xxxvi. 5.

Chronicle of the part taken by the detachment 2nd Battalion Royal Dublin Fusiliers in the Siege of Ladysmith from November 1st, 1899, to February 28th, 1900. By LIEUT. L. F. RENNY, *2nd Batt. Royal Dublin Fusiliers.*

THE detachment which was left behind in Ladysmith when the battalion was ordered to Colenso consisted of two officers, three non-commissioned officers and fifty-one men. The latter were made up by a section of 'G' company which was left on piquet because they could not be relieved in time, and the men of the regimental transport, which had been left behind owing to there being no facility for sending the waggons and animals by train with the battalion.

The morning after the departure of the latter I was ordered by the D.A.A.G. of the divisional troops to proceed to the various camps in Section A, and find a convenient space for the transport waggons. I found the necessary ground in rear of the camp of the 1st Battalion Gloucester Regiment, behind the railway cutting leading to the Orange Free State Junction. Here we were joined in the afternoon by Lieutenant H. W. Higginson, who took command, and the section of 'G' company, when the Gloucesters helped us in every way, and made us as comfortable as they possibly could. All that day we were left in comparative peace, there being no firing on either side; but the next morning about 5 a.m. the Boers opened with 'Long Tom' from Pepworth Hill, and commenced a duel of some hours' duration with our naval 4·7, which was placed on Junction Hill. They also kept up a continual cannonade

THE SIEGE OF LADYSMITH

with their long-range twelve-pounders, but did little or no damage, as they had not yet discovered the exact location of our camps.

For the next three or four days we remained in the Gloucesters' camp and aided in starting the trenches which eventually formed the fort known as 'Tunnel Hill.' This was by no means pleasant work, as it was carried out under fire, the enemy being very quick at spotting our working parties and remarkably so at obtaining our range. We used to watch with great interest the duel every morning between the two big guns. Once the Boers hoisted a large white flag over their epaulement and proceeded to repair some small damage to their gun—they have very weird ideas about the white flag.

On November 7th our detachment was suddenly ordered to proceed to 'Bell's Spruit,' and form the guard there. I was ordered to hand over our transport to the Army Service Corps, so we took away the majority of the men and brought the strength of our piquet up to thirty-one men ; the transport was sent to the railway station yard for the use of the Army Service Corps, where it remained throughout the siege. We were stationed at the mouth of the spruit just where it runs through the ridge opposite the cemetery. Our fortifications consisted of a thick wall with sandbag loopholes running right across the spruit ; about fifty yards in front were strips of high and low wire entanglement, making it practically impossible for the enemy to rush the post at night. By night we had to man two sangars placed on the hills on each side of the spruit. I know nothing more productive of bad language than visiting the sentries on those hills in the dark, scrambling over the hugest boulders up a hill like the side of a house. We were not very comfortable at first, there being absolutely no shelter from sun or rain, but after about a week we managed to obtain a couple of railway tarpaulins, and rigged up shelters on the sides of the spruit. We were all very

2ND BATT. ROYAL DUBLIN FUSILIERS

lucky in not getting hit, as the enemy had a nasty habit of bursting shrapnel over the place and sending common shell on to the crests, which produced a shower of rocks, splinters and stones; but although we were in the spruit for seven weeks with absolutely no cover, not a man in the detachment was hit. During our stay in the spruit our rations were exceptionally good, as we got extras in the way of bacon, jam, chocolate, &c.

The night-work at this time was very hard, as everybody not actually on outpost duty had to work at the trenches from 6.30 in the evening till 3 a.m. the next morning. Sleep being impossible in the day-time owing to the heat and a plague of flies, this continual night-work told on the men severely. On November 9th the enemy made a feeble attempt at capturing the place, and came on in considerable numbers against Observation Hill, but were easily repulsed. On the night of December 7th-8th an attack was made on Gun Hill, where the Boers had a 'Long Tom' and a five-inch howitzer, besides one or two small guns. These guns had been annoying us very greatly for the past three weeks, and we were all delighted in the early morning when we heard the attack had been successful, and the guns blown up. We none of us knew anything about this affair till it was over. I was visiting our posts about 2.30 a.m. when I saw two large flashes on Gun Hill; on listening I could not hear any shells travelling or bursting, so concluded the enemy were amusing themselves by firing blank charges. It was not till we saw our column returning at dawn that we solved the problem. We found the spruit very unpleasant in wet weather, as the water used to come down like a mountain torrent and wash away bits of our wall and shelters; after wet nights we used to spend our time in digging our belongings out of the sand, having spent the night sitting on the rocks.

About December 18th, after the failure of General Buller's first attempt to relieve us, there was a general interchange of posts amongst the troops of our section, and the detachment received orders to proceed to the Newcastle Road examining guard. We were all heartily sick of the spruit, and glad of the change. It was about this time that our rations began to be diminished, and we had completely run out of all extras. The post of the examining guard was on the road just inside the ridge which formed our general line of defence, but by night we moved out as a piquet about half a mile on to the veld into a spruit which ran under the Harrismith line, whence we patrolled out to Brooke's Farm, and the surrounding country. I think this was the worst post we had throughout the siege, as we came in for a long spell of wet weather, and night after night had to lie out on the open veld from 8 p.m. till 4 a.m., wet to the skin and miserably cold. The duties on this post came very hard on our men, as we had to find a double and single sentry by day, so that they never got a night in bed, and only about one day in three off duty.

On Christmas Eve the men came into possession of a fine pig, so that we all had pork for our Christmas dinner, a great change from eternal 'trek ox,' but unfortunately nothing stronger to drink than tea. I'm sure it was the first Christmas any of us had spent in such an uncongenial way.

On January 6th the enemy made their desperate attack on Waggon Hill and Cæsar's Camp. They seem to have completely surprised our outposts, as they succeeded in crawling up the hill in the dark, and the fighting commenced at 3 a.m. The cannonade all day was something tremendous, 'Long Tom' firing 125 rounds. They kept us pretty busy on our side of the defences as well, but never developed any serious attack. Whilst on this post we were subjected to a continuous and daily course of sniping, the enemy getting on the kopjes behind Brooke's Farm, and firing all day at a range of 2800 yards. At this range the

2ND BATT. ROYAL DUBLIN FUSILIERS

bullets used to whiz over the hill and drop amongst us, although we were only a few yards behind the crest. Higginson and I used to spend hours lying on the crest with rifles and glasses trying to spot them, but never succeeded in doing so, as they used to take up their position before dawn and never move all day.

It was about this time that our men began to show the effects of exposure and constant sentry-go, and several of them went down with fever and rheumatism; but we were extremely lucky throughout the siege, having only one casualty: Private Ward, 'G' company, a reservist, who died of enteric at Intombi Camp.

I forgot to mention that on January 6th our section had to be entirely denuded of supports and reserves in order that they might be sent to Waggon Hill, so that if the enemy had attacked us seriously we should have had a hard job to keep them back.

On January 25th the detachment was ordered to garrison Liverpool Castle, a fort overlooking the Newcastle Road, but we had not been there twelve hours before we were ordered to Tunnel Hill. This latter post consisted of a large main fort capable of holding two hundred men, and two small works about a quarter of a mile on each flank, in all of which we had to find a guard. Our fighting strength was at this time reduced to twenty-seven men, so that they did guard and patrol alternate nights. We had to send out five of the latter during the night about half a mile to the front and a mile laterally along the valley. The confinement in this fort was rather trying, and the eternal manning of the trenches at 4 a.m. very monotonous. After about three weeks on this post I was suddenly seized with a 'go' of fever, and was sent down to a room in one of the houses. When I rejoined the detachment, after a fortnight on the sick list, they had moved to the railway station as guard over the bridge across the Klip River. Here we had to endure rather a severe dose of

THE SIEGE OF LADYSMITH

'Long Tom'—this gun never missed a day without dropping shells into and round the station, it was one of its favourite spots, and all the tin buildings about bore evidence of its attentions. One shell, pitching in the parcels office, blew the roof off and the floor in, having first penetrated half-a-dozen walls to get there. We had trenches on our side of the river, which we manned, as usual, at 4 a.m. We also had to man them in the afternoon about 5 o'clock, when the train from Intombi Camp was due. This used to be rather a comic proceeding: a 'key' was made in the line about half a mile outside the station, where the train was brought to a standstill, then either Higginson or myself had to walk out and inspect the train to see there were no Boers inside it. We often used to wonder what would have been our lot if the train had been full of them. On our reporting 'all correct' to the Railway Staff Officer (Captain Young, R.E.), the train was allowed to proceed into the station, and the little play was over till the next day. This was undoubtedly the most comfortable job we had, as the men lived in a shed, whilst Higginson and I had a railway carriage.

On the afternoon of February 28th we heard the joyful tidings of General Buller's victory at Pieter's Hill, and in the evening descried Lord Dundonald and his men crossing the plain; our wild excitement may be left to the imagination. I'm sure we all put on about seven pounds of our lost weight at the mere thought of our being at last relieved. Our troubles were not over yet, however, as the next morning we were ordered back to Tunnel Hill, a spot we had learned to loathe with a truly deep loathing. This move was due to our flying column going out to hurry the enemy's retreat, most of the troops in our section taking part in it. For some unknown reason we were kept four or five days in that smelly fort, and it was not till March 7th that we received orders to rejoin the battalion, which was encamped about two miles out of Ladysmith. We all felt as though we had begun a new life; but it was heartbreaking to see the havoc in our regiment; one had to look about to find faces that one recognised.

Our rations were pretty well reduced towards the end of the siege: one biscuit, one pound of horseflesh, two teaspoonfuls of sugar, and a pinch of tea is not much to keep body and soul together, and we were all pretty feeble and pulled down. I think we must have done the record piquet duty of any men in any service, as we were never relieved throughout the whole siege; I suppose this was on account of being left as a separate unit all through, but we certainly thought it rather hard work. It is a wonder that our little detachment stuck out four months' constant exposure with so little sickness, whilst our luck in sitting under that constant shelling without a man being hit was nothing short of providential.

I have merely chronicled the chief moves and duties of the detachment throughout the siege: it would take a small book to set down all our little experiences, details, and troubles.

CHAPTER X.

ALIWAL NORTH AND FOURTEEN STREAMS.

'But thus much is certain: that he that commands the
sea is at great liberty, and may take as much,
and as little of the war, as he wish.'
Bacon.

AFTER marching through Ladysmith, the battalion proceeded with the 11th Brigade to a camp about three miles to the north of the town and on the left bank of the Klip River. It remained here until March 7th, when it

SERGEANT DAVIS IN MEDITATION OVER 'LONG CECIL' AT
KIMBERLEY. 'SHALL I TAKE IT FOR THE OFFICERS?'

rejoined the 5th Brigade, which was encamped on the south side of the Klip River, and about one mile nearer Ladysmith. On the same date, Colonel Cooper was given the command of the 4th Brigade, and accordingly handed over the battalion to Major Bird.

There was another change of camping-ground on March

2ND BATT. ROYAL DUBLIN FUSILIERS

12th, the brigade moving to the north-east of Ladysmith, under Surprise Hill. It was an uneventful time, although outpost duties were somewhat severe.

In recognition of the gallantry displayed by the Irish regiments in the Natal campaign, the Queen had directed that the shamrock should be worn by all ranks on St. Patrick's Day. Accordingly, on March 17th, every man wore a piece of green, since shamrock was unobtainable,

ST. PATRICK'S DAY IN CAMP.
PRIVATE MONAGHAN, THE REGIMENTAL BUTCHER, IN FOREGROUND.

and the tents were decorated with boughs. A telegram was dispatched to the Queen, who sent the following message in reply:—

'The Queen desires to thank her Dublin Fusiliers for their expression of loyalty.'

The battalion also received many congratulatory telegrams from Irish associations and individuals in various parts of the world.

The detachment of the 1st Battalion was sent back to Colenso on March 21st. It had been just over four months with the 2nd Battalion, and had borne its full share of the

ALIWAL NORTH—FOURTEEN STREAMS

casualties. Originally numbering eight officers and 287 rank and file, it returned with only two officers and 92 rank and file.

The 5th Brigade moved on the 23rd to Modderspruit, and thence on the next day to Elandslaagte, where it encamped a short distance to the west of the battlefield. Here it stayed for ten days, and, as there was little to do beyond outpost work, the battalion resumed ordinary parades and route marching.

On April 4th, General Warren's Division relieved General Hunter's at Elandslaagte, and the brigade marched back to Modderspruit. The 10th Division (General Hunter), which consisted of the 5th and 6th Brigades, was to proceed to Cape Colony for the relief of Mafeking.

On April 7th, Major Tempest Hicks, 1st Battalion Royal Dublin Fusiliers, arrived from Colenso, and assumed command of the battalion. The 5th Brigade began to move by train to Durban on the 9th, and we were ordered to entrain at 1.45 p.m. on the 10th. But during the morning, heavy firing broke out at Elandslaagte, and, as the enemy seemed aggressive, the troops at Modderspruit were directed to be ready to move to Elandslaagte.

We had struck camp and packed all the baggage in the train, and had, therefore, to lie out in the hot sun for several hours, and await with patience the development of events. The Boers apparently contented themselves by a demonstration, and at 6 p.m. the battalion was allowed to depart. The train reached Colenso at 9 p.m., where the 1st Battalion was encamped, and Maritzburg about 4 a.m. Here, in spite of the early hour, a number of friends, together with a band, were on the platform, and the regiment received a warm greeting. The men were given cigarettes and tobacco.

Durban was reached about 10 a.m. on April 11th, and the battalion at once commenced to embark. The head-

2ND BATT. ROYAL DUBLIN FUSILIERS

quarters and about six companies were carried by the *Cephalonia*, while the remaining two companies went in the *Jamaica*. They were both slow ships, but the absolute peace, the good food, the clean baths, and many other luxuries, made everybody regret that they were not even slower.

East London was reached on the 12th, and the battalion was ordered to disembark, since the 5th Brigade was urgently required to relieve Wepener, which was surrounded by the enemy. General Hart, with the Border Regiment and Somersetshire Light Infantry* started for Aliwal North at once, but the battalion remained on board during the whole of the 13th, although 'H' company, under Captain Romer, disembarked in the afternoon, and was at once dispatched by train. The other companies landed on the 14th, and left East London in two trains, starting at 4 and 6 p.m.

Lieutenant Le Mesurier, who had been captured on October 20th, but had, with Captain Haldane (Gordon Highlanders), effected a plucky escape from Pretoria, re-joined us at East London. Unluckily he at once developed typhoid fever, and had to be left behind.

Aliwal North was not reached until 10.30 a.m. on April 16th. 'H' company had arrived the previous afternoon, and was encamped near the station, but the remainder of the battalion crossed the Orange River, and pitched camp about 600 yards from the bridge, with its outpost line pushed forward on the high ground to the north.

Major Hicks became commandant of Aliwal North, and had no easy task. The town was General Hart's base during the operations for the relief of Wepener, and there was consequently much to be done. Moreover, the surrounding country was disturbed, the Dutch population had to be watched, and there were constant rumours of the approach of

* This regiment had joined the 5th Brigade after the relief of Ladysmith in place of the Inniskilling Fusiliers.

ALIWAL NORTH—FOURTEEN STREAMS

commandoes. In the early hours of the 21st, a report reached the commandant that a large body of Boers was marching on the town. He therefore decided to bring the regiment back to the south side of the river, only leaving the piquets on the north bank. We therefore at once struck camp, and, crossing the river, bivouacked near the bridge. But as the report proved to be misleading, camp was re-pitched on a square in the middle of Aliwal North. The outskirts of the

A WASH IN HOT WATER. ALIWAL NORTH.

town were put into a state of defence, and a series of trenches covered the approaches to the bridge. Although this necessitated much labour, everybody enjoyed their stay at Aliwal. It was a pretty place, with trees and gardens full of roses, with plenty of water, including a hot stream running through the camp, with a well-stocked library, and lastly, but by no means leastly, with a hotel possessing excellent lager beer.

The time passed, in fact, too quickly, for on the 26th news was received of the relief of Wepener, and orders were issued for our movement to Kimberley. We started at once in two trains, the first leaving at midnight

2ND BATT. ROYAL DUBLIN FUSILIERS

the second at 1 a.m. on the 27th. It was a long and monotonous journey, the only breaks in which were stops for the purpose of cooking meals. Kimberley was reached at 10 p.m. on the 28th, and the train stopped the night in the station, going on at 6 a.m. on the 29th to Doornfield, about eight miles north of Kimberley, where the Connaught Rangers and the 6th Brigade were already encamped. Since General Hart, with the Borders and Somersetshire Light Infantry were still near Wepener, Colonel Brooke assumed the command of the brigade.

General Hunter's division had been ordered to relieve Mafeking, and the General decided to cross the Vaal near Windsorton with the 6th Brigade, and to advance up the right bank; while General Paget with the Royal Munster Fusiliers, Connaught Rangers, and Royal Dublin Fusiliers, faced the Boer position at Fourteen Streams. Colonel Mahon's mounted column was to move by Barkley West, and reach Mafeking by sweeping round the Boer flank.

The battalion accordingly left Doornfield by train at 9 a.m. on May 2nd, and about midday reached Content, where it detrained and encamped. The next day it marched with the Connaught Rangers to a position about two miles south of Warrenton. The opposite bank of the Vaal was held by the Boers, who were strongly entrenched and had field-guns. On the south bank of the Vaal were the Munster Fusiliers, a battery of field artillery, a six-inch gun mounted on a railway truck, and a balloon, the whole detachment being under Major-General Paget.

As all tents had been left at Content, the regiment bivouacked, and remained more or less idle. The Munsters were holding Warrenton, and there was constant sniping between their posts and the Boer trenches. The balloon ascended daily, and the six-inch gun fired an occasional shot, while the enemy's field-guns came into action at intervals. It was a monotonous and unpleasant time for the Connaught

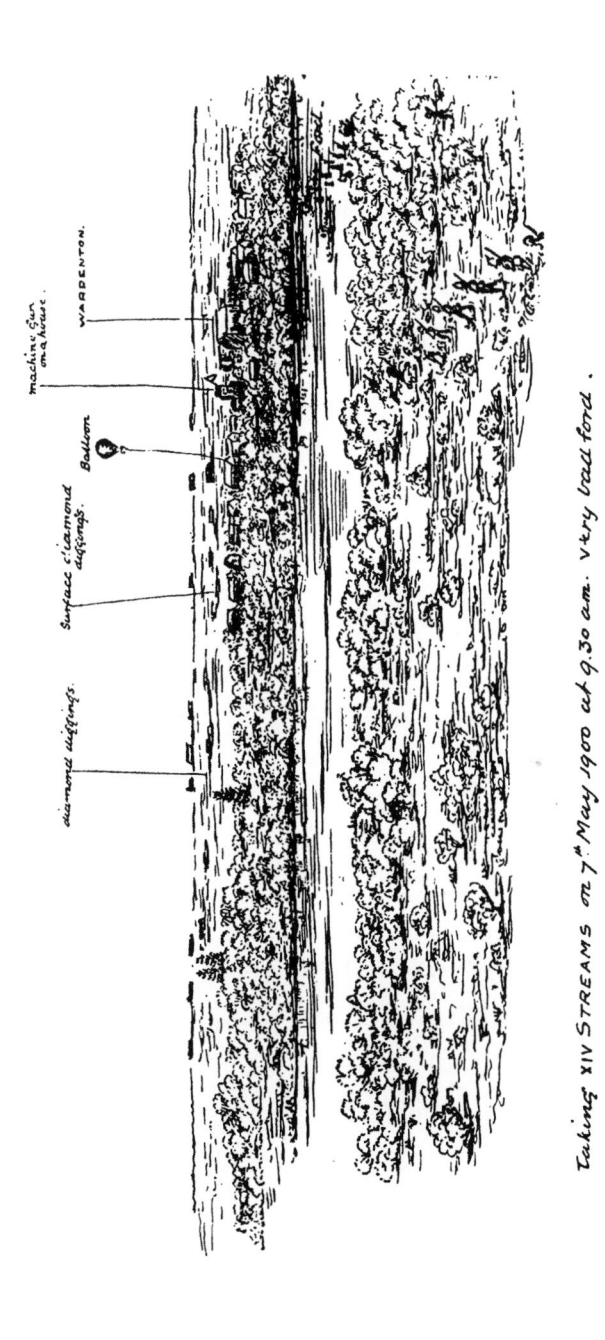

Taking XIV STREAMS on 7th May 1900 at 9.30 a.m. Very bad ford.

From a sketch by Col. H. Tempest Hicks, C.B.

ALIWAL NORTH—FOURTEEN STREAMS

Rangers and ourselves, since there was nothing to do, while it was very hot by day and cold by night.

A little excitement was afforded on May 6th, when the Connaught Rangers and half the battalion made a demonstration against a drift to the east of Fourteen Streams. The object apparently was to draw the Boers' attention from the 6th Brigade, who, after a victory at Rooi Dam, were moving up the right bank. The movement caused a slight

THE REGIMENTAL MAXIM IN ACTION AT FOURTEEN STREAMS.

amount of sniping, and the detachment returned to the bivouac soon after 2 p.m.

The approach of the 6th Brigade, aided, perhaps, by this demonstration, caused the enemy to evacuate hurriedly their trenches during the afternoon of the 6th. Early on the morning of the 7th, the Connaught Rangers and the right half-battalion started to ford the Vaal at Warrenton.

The river at this point was broad and swift. The ford was a difficult one, being beset by rocks and holes, and it took a considerable time for the column to cross, since the water was up to the men's waists. The left half-battalion under Major Bird moved one and a half miles up the river

2ND BATT. ROYAL DUBLIN FUSILIERS

near Fourteen Streams, where there was a ferry-boat. The latter had been rendered useless by the Boers, but as they had left the wire hawser, it was easy for the Royal Engineers to construct a raft, on which the left half-battalion crossed comfortably and quickly.

The right half-battalion joined the left half at the ferry, and breakfasts were cooked. Before leaving the river-bank everybody made an inspection of the Boer trenches, which formed an exceedingly strong position. They were very deep, and so well adapted to the ground, that it was no easy matter to discover them from the opposite bank. Evidences of the hurried Boer retreat were plentiful in the shape of full ammunition-boxes, half-cooked food, blankets, and kettles. One Boer, who was too ill to march, was captured in the trenches.

After breakfasts, the battalion moved through a piece of ground thickly covered with bush, and eventually bivouacked about one mile from the Vaal, near the railway line. The 6th Brigade halted near the same place, and the whole force was occupied for the next fortnight in covering Fourteen Streams. The important railway bridge at this point had been destroyed by the Boers, and the Royal Engineers, aided by large working parties from the infantry, at once commenced to construct a deviation bridge. This necessitated a great amount of labour, and since, in addition, defensive works had to be made, we were all kept very busy.

The stay at Fourteen Streams was interrupted on May 15th by a movement on Christiana, a town in the Transvaal, reported to be held by a strong party of Boers. The whole of the 10th Division took part in the operations, and were thus the first regular troops to enter the Transvaal. The frontier was crossed at 9 a.m. The advance was through an undulating country, at times thickly covered by bush. Towards the afternoon the brigade halted, as news was received that the mounted troops had entered Christiana. A

ALIWAL NORTH—FOURTEEN STREAMS

bivouac was formed in a clearing among the bush, and dinners were cooked. The next day the brigade marched back to Fourteen Streams, and reached that place early on May 17th, having done some twenty-six miles in nineteen hours. Work on the railway bridge was resumed, and, as the 6th Brigade had not returned, the battalion had to watch a more extensive area. Each company was given a section, and constructed a redoubt.

CAPTAIN JERVIS, GENERAL FITZROY HART, C.B., C.M.G.,
AND CAPTAIN ARTHUR HART.

About May 24th, Second Lieutenant Bradford, with twenty-nine men, was sent up the line to garrison Border Siding, where they were picked up three days later.

The deviation bridge over the Vaal having been completed, the battalion was sent forward by train to Vryburg, travelling in two trains. Camp was pitched just outside the station, and for the next two days every one spent their time in buying *karosses* and in shooting partridges.

The 10th Division, when Mafeking had been relieved by Colonel Mahon, was ordered to march to Johannesburg viâ

2ND BATT. ROYAL DUBLIN FUSILIERS

Lichtenburg. As the first part of the route lay through a country very deficient in water, the division marched in several columns, which followed each other at a day's interval. The battalion left Vryburg on May 30th at 7.30 a.m., and proceeded to Devondale, and on the next day made a march of twenty-two miles to Dornbult, where Captain Mainwaring, with Second Lieutenants Newton and Smith, joined.

Their wanderings before they succeeded in doing so are sufficient evidence how little was known, even to our own staff officers of the whereabouts of the several columns. On arrival at Cape Town in the s.s. *Oratava*, they were transhipped to the s.s. *Ranee* and sent to Port Elizabeth. On reporting themselves there they were entrained and sent to Bloemfontein. No one there seemed to know where the regiment was, but at that very time the report arrived of the march on Christiana. Captain Mainwaring then met Captain Carington Smith of the regiment, who was at that time serving in Roberts' Horse (which he later on commanded), and as that officer was shortly going north with some men of his corps, it seemed to both that the speediest way to get to the Dublin Fusiliers was for Captain Mainwaring to be attached to Roberts' Horse. An application to that effect was made to the staff and granted, but shortly afterwards the news of the Christiana column's return to the railway came to hand, so the three officers once more entrained, and proceeded viâ De Aar to Kimberley.

Although Captain Carington Smith did not serve with either battalion during the war, it would not be out of place here to mention the great part he took in it. He commenced by serving in Roberts' Horse, and was with them throughout Lord Roberts' advance to Bloemfontein. In the action at Sanna's Post he was shot through the knee, but resolutely refused to be invalided home. His recovery from this severe wound was little short of marvellous, and he actually managed to rejoin the headquarters of his corps in time to share in the

ALIWAL NORTH—FOURTEEN STREAMS

entry into Pretoria. Shortly after this he was again shot at Heidelberg, this time through the other knee, and again made a second and equally marvellous recovery. Towards the end of the war he commanded Roberts' Horse, and later on the South African Light Horse, and his trekking during the campaign amounted to no less than 9000 miles.

ISSUING QUEEN VICTORIA'S CHOCOLATE.
COLOUR-SERGEANT CONNELL, 'G' COMPANY, ON LEFT.

PART II.
TREKKING.

CHAPTER I.

VRYBURG TO HEIDELBERG.

'None of us put off our clothes.'
Neh. iv. 23.

NOW commenced a different phase of warfare. If, in the constant fighting of the Natal campaign, the regiment had been called upon to prove its fighting capabilities—a call to which their noble response earned them encomiums wherever they went—they were now to be called upon to prove another essential of the true soldier—their mobility. And well they proved it. Day after day, week after week, the tired, footsore, but stout-hearted column-of-route made its slow and wearisome way over the apparently limitless expanse of the swelling veld. And how monotonous that veld can be none can appreciate save those who have experienced its deadly sameness. Ahead, behind, all round, nothing but veld, veld, veld. No trees, no hills, no rivers, no lakes, no houses, no inhabitants! Here and there, perhaps, a miserable shanty of the sealed-pattern South African type: rough stone walls and corrugated-iron roof, a room on each side of the door, a narrow verandah—occasionally occupied by a quiet, peaceful-looking old patriarch, with a grey beard, and an air savouring rather of the pulpit than the sheltered side of a boulder—a scraggy tree or two, and a lick of water in a 'pan'—or pond as we should call it—hard by; a woman, some children, and a couple of goats; a few mealie cobs yellowing on the roof, and a scared, indignant, and attenuated fowl.

Alas! how those quiet-looking, quiet-spoken old gentlemen, open Bible on knee, deceived us. Oh, no! they had

2ND BATT. ROYAL DUBLIN FUSILIERS

never wished for war. Fight? yes; they had fought, and surrendered, and taken the oath, and hoped never to fight again. Peace? yes; they wanted peace, and urged us to hasten on and conclude it. The same story everywhere: in the villages as in the solitary hamlets. A vast, empty, forsaken wilderness, with nothing more bellicose than a lean and hungry boar-hound or two. And yet for two long years to come this very country, over which the battalion trekked so peacefully, fifes and drums playing, officers out on the flanks shooting, mess-president cantering miles away in quest of eggs and their producers, was to be the scene of many a hard-fought fight and many weary nights of outposts. Indeed, it never really succumbed to the very end; the happy hunting-ground of the gallant De la Rey, it was a thorn in the side of our leaders up to the day the Delegates came in.

One day's march varied little from another. Up at dawn, and off after the scantiest of scrappy breakfasts. Good marching while the dew was on the grass, and the sun a welcome ally after the clear, crisp, frosty nights; soon, however, to get hot enough, until the welcome mid-day halt and meal, after which tighten up belts once more and on, and on, one horizon following another with wearisome regularity, and never a sign of the long-looked-for water, till at last, as the sun set behind our backs, its last rays would glint on the miserable 'pan' by whose side we were to halt for the night. And then what bitter feelings of depression and disgust when sometimes the fiat would go forth ' Water for cooking purposes only,' and one had to turn into one's blankets grimy, dusty, clammy, and miserable.

On May 31st, the regiment, having arrived at the railway, was told they would halt there next day. But on the morning of June 1st, the order was given for the column* to march at 2 p.m. to Marigobo Pan, a distance of eight miles only, but

* Border Regiment, Royal Dublin Fusiliers, Bearer Company, and Supply Detachment.

VRYBURG TO HEIDELBERG

quite ten by the route taken. The evenings soon close in at this time of year in South Africa, and it was almost dark when the column arrived. As it was a fine mild night, every one hoped to be allowed to bivouac, but tents were pitched after all, and naturally enough pitched anyhow. In this matter of pitching tents, the battalion particularly prided itself. On arrival at the selected site of the camp the Sergeant-Major blew a whistle, when all those whose duty

FIRST ENTRY INTO KRUGERSDORP. CAPTAIN AND ADJUTANT FETHERSTONHAUGH IN FOREGROUND.

it was to assist ran towards him, the men to mark the tent-poles, bayonets in hand, and two others with the mekometer, to ensure a true right-angle. Every one knew his particular job, so no time was wasted, while the symmetrical lines obtained by the use of the instrument were a joy to the General's eye.*

In the same way, whenever a halt was ordered, it was the regiment's custom to lay out their kits, mess-tins, belts, &c., in lines outside their tents. Each Colour-Sergeant had

* *Vide* General Hart's letter in Appendix.

2ND BATT. ROYAL DUBLIN FUSILIERS

a ball of string, which was stretched between a couple of pegs; the kits were laid along it, the string was rolled up and pitched into a tent, and neatness and regularity prevailed without any extra trouble to any one. This neatness in camp, in addition to its other soldierly qualities, endeared the battalion in the eyes of General Hart, a soldier of the old school, to whom order and regularity particularly appealed.

On the 2nd the column made another short march to Greysdorp, where there were two or three good wells, but where the water in the pan was of a most peculiar green colour.

The Mafeking relief column was met on the way, and very hard and serviceable they looked, while several officers met old friends, amongst others Prince Alexander of Teck, whom we had known at Maritzburg before the war.

A longish march of nineteen or twenty miles on the 3rd, with a halt midway, brought us in the evening to a place called Barber's Pan, somewhat superior to the generality of these places. There was a certain amount of water in the pan, but brackish and unpleasant to drink. Round it were scattered some half-dozen houses, but the most remarkable thing in connection with it was the sunset. As the light faded, a mist rose from the veld, which after a few minutes began to change colour, until at last it settled down to a most beautiful shade of light green. None of us had seen anything similar before, nor did we ever see anything like it again.

A march of about fourteen or fifteen miles on the 4th brought us to a most uncomfortable camp. On the way, Captain Fetherstonhaugh (acting Adjutant since Captain Lowndes was hit at Talana) rode off some distance to a flank to try and get some supplies. He returned with a great story of his reception by crowds of women and one or two men; the latter stated they had been reluctantly compelled to fight against us at Modder River, on pain of

VRYBURG TO HEIDELBERG

being shot, but that their sympathies were entirely with us, &c. They even gave him a pound of butter. And we believed this story at the time.

But, for that matter, who would not have been taken in? Every one coming up the line brought better and better news. Lord Roberts was close to the capital, and, thought we in our simplicity, that of course must end the war. No one guessed there was extra time—two solid years extra time—to be played. So we enjoyed the butter, and said they were sensible people after all, and hoped we'd be in time for the siege of Pretoria.

The next day's march was a pleasanter one than usual, the halts being better arranged, with the result that the troops and transport got into camp quite as early as they would have done under the ordinary circumstances, but very much fresher and fitter. The fact is, staff officers do not understand marching. They go tittuping gaily past long straggling columns, passing the time of day cheerily to friends, and momentarily halting to deliver some ironical knock to acquaintances on the subject of their transport, or their sections of fours, or something of the sort. But the regimental officer, who foots it alongside his company, he understands marching right enough. He will tell you when the going is good, and when it only looks good; he will tell you the effects of five-minute halts, and how much benefit the closing-up rear of the column derives from them; he will tell you when a steady, swinging pace is being set that the men could keep up for ever; and he will also tell you when some long-legged officer in front is going four miles an hour, till some one suggests it is too fast, and he sinks into a slow and tiring two and a half. Colonel Hicks commanded the column on the 5th, and let us march our own way, with the beneficial results already recorded.

And that cheery rumour about Pretoria. French

2ND BATT. ROYAL DUBLIN FUSILIERS

reported to be there, and Mr. Kruger gone off with a couple of millions. What did we care about the latter? We should not have got any of it.

Another short march of a little over ten miles brought us to a camp where there was actually a stream. Here the men got the chance of a much-needed bathe, and how they enjoyed it! Every one, in fact, was in excellent spirits, for the news about Pretoria turned out to be true, and though some of us were disappointed at not being up in time to share in the triumphant entry into the capital, the majority were all for England, home, and beauty.

On the 7th we arrived at Lichtenburg, a small town or village that was to see some heavy fighting later on in the war. On the present occasion all seemed most peaceful. The houses were of the stereotyped South African pattern, with the invariable half-stoep, half-verandah running half-way along their fronts. Clear streams of water ran coolly and pleasingly by the sides of the streets, shaded by the ubiquitous weeping-willow. There was nothing to be bought, and no one to be seen, however, and those of us who went into the town next morning were very soon satisfied, returning to camp minus the various articles we had set forth to buy. It was interesting, however, to see the Boers handing in their rifles and taking the oath of allegiance.

Captain MacBean, who was now on General Hunter's staff, turned up here, and dined with the regiment, and very glad we were to see him. He gave us all sorts of news, too, which we were very deficient of, as the system of daily bulletins had not then started.

After having halted for the 8th and 9th, we resumed our desert march on the 10th, but only made some ten miles. It was most bitterly cold all the way.

The next day proved far pleasanter, and another short, easy march of about ten miles saw us in camp by 1.30 p.m.

VRYBURG TO HEIDELBERG

On the 12th we made a march of sixteen miles. We were then within about thirty-three miles of the railway from Johannesburg to Potchefstroom, and, when a wire came ordering us to do it in two days, we thought a lot of the task, whereas a few months later we were doing that distance in one day, and, curiously enough, almost in the same neighbourhood.

In consequence of this we marched right through Ventersdorp, to our regret, as it looked quite a nice place, and there was a regular trout-stream flowing past it, in which a bathe would have been most welcome. We did eighteen miles before halting.

As indicative of the curious state of the war even in these early days, General Hunter's experience at Vryburg was a good example. He had ridden on with only thirty cavalrymen to Ventersdorp, when suddenly some two hundred and fifty of the enemy appeared on the scene. Fortunately for the General, their only object was to give up their arms and take the oath.

Starting at 7.30 a.m. next day, we made short work of the march to the railway, which we struck at Frederickstadt, a place that many of us were destined to become very well acquainted with before we had done. It is rather prettier than most Boer villages, being situated on the pleasant little Mooi River, whose clear, rapid current reminded us of our home streams. There are a few trees in the vicinity, whilst on the further bank and beyond the railway rise the serrated, well-wooded, and extremely picturesque Gatsrand Hills.

There was only one man to be seen, peacefully hoeing his potato-patch. But if the men were scarce and polite, the same could not be said for the fair sex, who, despite the fact that their knowledge of English was only to be compared with our ignorance of Dutch, did not fail to let us know their opinions of things generally. Indeed, the messpresident, who had gone on ahead on a pony in search of

2ND BATT. ROYAL DUBLIN FUSILIERS

farmyard products, had a battle-royal with an elderly Dutch lady who asked six shillings a dozen for her eggs. We heard more detailed accounts here of the relief of Mafeking, and of the gallant part Major Godley of ours had taken in its defence, while Major Pilson and Captain Kinsman (also Royal Dublin Fusiliers) had assisted in the relief. As Carington Smith had arrived in Kimberley with the cavalry, we were able to claim representation in all three of the great sieges and reliefs of the war.

'SPEED DEAD SLOW.'

But a disappointment was in store for us all the same. The column did not move next day (the 15th), but although engine after engine came puffing up from Potchefstroom they all failed to bring the carriages which our aching legs made us so anxiously look for. We heard of the strike of forty engine-drivers at Potchefstroom, but as they had all been cast into durance vile, and the engines still continued to arrive, that could not have been the reason. However, any doubts we entertained were soon set at rest by an order to continue our march to Johannesburg next day.

LIEUT. ELY.
Died at sea of Enteric.

CAPT. H. CARINGTON SMITH.
Wounded at Sanna's Post
and Heidelberg.

CAPT. WATSON
(Attached to Scottish Horse).
Killed at Moedwil.

CAPT. H. J. KINSMAN.
Wounded in Transvaal.

CAPT. J. A. MACBEAN.
Killed at Nooitgedacht.

LIEUT. ADRIAN TAYLOR.
Severely wounded when serving with
M.I. near Parys.

MISCELLANEOUS CASUALTIES.

VRYBURG TO HEIDELBERG

Starting on the 16th, an uneventful march of twelve miles brought us to Wolverdiend, a place which had not then attained the importance it afterwards assumed.

It was another fifteen on to Blauw Bank Station next day. This march was remarkable in that it was the first occasion since this trek started that the column moved with any military precautions worth mentioning.

Leaving Bank, as it got to be called later on, we struck off from the railway, left shoulders up, in a bee-line for Johannesburg, the city of our dreams, which it was hard to believe was not paved with gold, if one listened to the reports of those who had been there before the war. After a short march of ten miles we halted at a farm called Gemsbokfontein, and looked with longing eyes at the distant ridge, peeping over which could plainly be seen the huge mine-chimneys, like sentinels along the hills, duly noting our arrival.

A fierce grass-fire broke out here, which necessitated the active co-operation of all hands, and all blankets, to oppose it, one too-adventurous officer getting rather scorched for his pains.

As we sat at lunch we could see General Mahon's mounted column ascending the long rise to Randfontein, on our left front, and heard they had gone to Krugersdorp.

'Krugersdorp! Where's that?' 'Let's look at your map,' and so on. Well, we undoubtedly knew where it was a few weeks later. Moreover, there must be Boers there, for had not a party on an engine come out that very day, and after destroying a small bridge, and firing a couple of shots, snorted their way back to the Dorp.

The Royal Dublin Fusiliers supplied the advanced guard on the 19th, and duly started for Johannesburg, but a message very shortly came ordering a left incline, and nominating Krugersdorp as our objective. It was disappointing, but General Mahon had reported the Krugersdorpers 'truculent,' and we had to make a demonstration. This we most certainly did, halting above the railway, just outside the town, and

2ND BATT. ROYAL DUBLIN FUSILIERS

then—producing drums and fifes—forming up and marching through to 'St. Patrick's Day' and the 'British Grenadiers.' But, unlike the peaceful and amiable agriculturist, these townsfolk had no smiles of reciprocation to our advances, and we marched through long lines of scowling male faces, with here and there one or two of the fair sex, but also, alas! sombre to a degree.

After emerging on the far side of the town we passed the famous Paardekraal Monument on our right, and finally

HOISTING THE UNION JACK AT KRUGERSDORP.

camped about half a mile further on. It appears it was a very close thing whether they opposed us or not, and the peaceful solution that eventually took place was largely due to the tactful intervention and determination of an Englishman, Mr. W. Bruce Honman, who had considerable influence amongst the Dutch.

The troops halted at Krugersdorp next day, and the town was formally taken over in the Queen's name, an impressive parade for that purpose being held in the market square. Each regiment furnished a Guard of Honour of 100 men.

VRYBURG TO HEIDELBERG

The Royal Dublin Fusilier Guard was under the command of Major English, with Captain Higginson and Lieutenant Haskard. It was extremely interesting for those of us who were not on duty to watch the faces of the large numbers of Boers, male and female, who watched this ceremony and the hoisting of the Union Jack. On the whole they took it extremely well, and for the most part behaved like brave men, who, having fought and lost, were content to make the best of the situation.

JOHAN MEYER'S HOUSE, FIVE MILES OUTSIDE JOHANNESBURG.

The trek commenced again on the 22nd, and this time we felt convinced our destination must be Johannesburg, as we were marching along the Witwaters Rand straight for it. A halt was made after some ten miles, at Florida, rather a pleasant sort of Saturday-to-Monday resort of Johannesburgers, with a nice lake and pleasant woods.

At last we seemed about to receive our reward, only to have our hopes dashed rudely to the ground. True, we marched to Johannesburg, and even through it, but only through the most miserable of its slums, seeing nothing of its fine buildings, nothing of the wealth and magnificence we

2ND BATT. ROYAL DUBLIN FUSILIERS

had confidently expected. But, indeed, even the finest part of it was only a sorry spectacle in those days, and for many a weary month afterwards. Skirting the racecourse, we marched on to a spot some six miles from the town, near the house of Johan Meyer, a brother of Lucas Meyer. Colonel Hicks and Captain Fetherstonhaugh called on this gentleman, and got a lot of interesting information from him. His house was one of the finest we saw in the whole Transvaal, and from its

SERGEANT DAVIS, EVIDENTLY WITH ALL WE WANTED.

site—at the head of a fine valley—commanded a magnificent view of the country almost as far as Heidelberg.

But, as some set-off to our disappointment and long, tiring march of fifteen miles, Captain Sir Frederick Frankland, who had gone on to Joh'burg, as it is universally called, to buy what stores he could, turned up just before dinner, not only with a large amount of provisions, but also with a case of excellent champagne, which he presented to the mess, God bless him! We were very proud of our noble Baronet that night, and he had to reply to the toast of his health over and over again.

Sergeant Davis, champion forager of the Army, also put

VRYBURG TO HEIDELBERG

in an appearance here, having met with no end of adventures and misadventures since the Colonel had sent him back to the Kimberley-Mafeking Railway. As usual, he had a fine lot of stores, and, also as usual, just what we wanted : baccy, chocolate, biscuits, sjamboks, stamps, etc., etc.

An uneventful march of fifteen miles, with a halt at Reitfontein, was only noticeable for a particularly cold night and the final splitting up of the Irish Brigade, the Connaughts and Borders being ordered to Pretoria.

On the 25th our long march came to an end with a twelve-mile step into Heidelberg. The band of the Derbyshire Regiment played us in, while our old friend, General Bruce-Hamilton, rode out to meet us. We halted on a slope about three-quarters of a mile outside the town, which in its essential features is remarkably like Krugersdorp, the streets being lined with tall blue-gum trees, and the plan of course rectangular, with the usual market square in the centre.

There had been a fight here, and we found Captain Carington Smith again amongst the wounded ; this time, as already mentioned, with a bullet through his other knee, but as cheery as ever, and smiling away at seeing us all again. Lieutenant Adrian Taylor, of the regiment, was also here, and very glad we were to see him once more. Like Captain Carington Smith he was detached from the regiment throughout the campaign, serving with the M.I., and was about a month later very severely wounded near Parys when De Wet crossed the Vaal with Lord Kitchener at his heels. Still another Dublin Fusilier met us at Heidelberg — Major Rutherford, Adjutant of the Ceylon Volunteers, who had come over in command of a detachment of that corps.

In addition to all these, General Cooper (our late C.O.) and his A.D.C., Lieutenant Renny, R.D.F., were also coming up from the south, while the 1st Battalion, who had helped to win Alleman's Nek, were not far off.

On arrival at Heidelberg we had marched just 300 miles

2ND BATT. ROYAL DUBLIN FUSILIERS

in twenty-seven days, and although we had not pressed in any way, we had come along fairly well seeing that we were not bound on any specific object, such as the relief of a town, or the participation in a siege or battle. We averaged just over eleven miles a day, including halts at Lichtenburg (two days), Frederickstadt and Krugersdorp (two days), or just a shade under fourteen miles for each marching day.

PAARDEKRAAL MONUMENT, KRUGERSDORP.

CHAPTER II.

HEIDELBERG.

'Wherever a man's post is, whether he has chosen it of his own will, or whether he has been placed at it by his commander, there it is his duty to remain and face the danger, without thinking of death, or of any other thing except dishonour.'—*Socrates*.

'Such officers do the King best service in the end.'—*Hamlet*.

A CONSIDERABLE force had now assembled at Heidelberg, but it was not to remain there long. General Hunter took over command from General Ian Hamilton, who had had a bad fall from his horse, and shortly moved off to the Free State, where he and his men soon covered themselves with distinction by the rounding-up of Prinsloo's commandoes near Golden Gate, on the Basuto border.

The 2nd Royal Dublin Fusiliers, a half-battalion Somersetshire Light Infantry, and the 28th Field Battery Royal Artillery, with some details, were left to garrison Heidelberg.

The battalion was soon split up into a number of small detachments, and posted at various places along the railway line, which had suffered considerably at the hands of the Boers. Scarcely a bridge remained intact, while the presence of wandering bodies of the enemy in the neighbourhood necessitated the utmost caution and continual vigilance on the part of the companies, half-companies, and even sections, into which some of the companies were at length subdivided.

Headquarters and those companies not on detachment in the meantime had plenty of work cut out for them too. In order to defend the place two hills to the west of the town were occupied, one by the Royal Dublin Fusiliers, known as Dublin Hill, and the other by the Somersetshire Light

2ND BATT. ROYAL DUBLIN FUSILIERS

Infantry. Our hill was put into a most thorough state of defence by many hours of hard labour and efficient work under the direction of Colonel Hicks. Sangars were built on every spur and knoll which afforded a good field of fire; traverses and shelters were numerous; in case of a night attack whitened stones along well-made tracks showed the nearest way to the various posts; while not only every company, but every section, had its well-defined trench or wall to rally on and hold.

To some of us, indeed, all these precautions at the time seemed somewhat excessive, and it is true that no attack was ever made; but just as example is better than precept and practice better than theory, so prevention is better than cure, and there is little doubt that the fortification of that hill, in full view of many a Boer field-glass in the town, whence our movements were of course fully reported as frequently as possible to the enemy in the field, had a deterrent effect on any designs our very active foes might otherwise have contemplated.

On the morning of the 26th the left half-battalion, under Major Bird, was suddenly ordered off to Nigel Road Station, about three miles out on the railway to Johannesburg. The Boers having blown up a bridge between this station and Heidelberg, all stores, &c., arriving from Johannesburg had to be dumped down on the veld here, and it was necessary to have a force on the spot to load them into waggons, as well as to guard them and the trains. These soon began to arrive in large numbers, and as each came up the sides of the railway waggons were opened, and their heterogeneous contents chucked out anyhow into a huge mass. In the mean time R.E. construction trains also arrived, and the quiet little siding was soon a scene of wild bustle and excitement. The R.E. went to work on the broken bridge, and made a most excellent job of it in a surprisingly short time, though a casual inspection of the temporary structure they built for

COLONEL H. TEMPEST HICKS, C.B.
COMMANDING 2ND ROYAL DUBLIN FUSILIERS
MARCH 1900 TO MARCH 1904.

HEIDELBERG

trains to pass over gave the lay mind the impression that an extra strong puff of wind would blow the whole thing over. However, it answered its purpose very thoroughly, and reflected much credit on its constructors.

In the meantime Major Bird soon produced law and order out of chaos. The coolies were made to put mealie-bags in one place and biscuit-boxes in another, while the soldiers built both up into a very serviceable sort of fort for the time being, an example of soldierly adaptability which was not lost on any one who saw it or took part in its erection.

We spent two or three very cheery days at Nigel Siding, the stationmaster's house (two rooms) forming an ideal officers' mess, but on the 28th 'E' and 'F' companies, under Captains Shewan and G. S. Higginson, were recalled to headquarters, 'H' company, under Captain Romer, was sent nine miles nearer Johannesburg to guard Reit Vlei Bridge, while 'G' company remained at Nigel Road to watch over such stores as had not yet been removed. This company was shortly further sub-divided by the left half-company, under Lieutenant E. St. G. Smith, being sent to guard a culvert half-way to Reit Vlei Bridge.

In the meantime Colonel Hicks never for a moment relaxed the soldierly precautions which it was his custom to observe, whether the Boers were reported in the neighbourhood or not; and several times rumours of intended attacks did arrive, though they invariably proved false.

The town of Heidelberg itself was very Dutch and seething with malcontents and treachery. One could easily forgive them for not being exactly content, but what one could not forgive was their slimness, their plausible exterior, and their inner mass of falsehood. No class were more bitter than the clergymen, and one of these gentry was strongly suspected of being in constant communication with the Boers in the field, though his oath of neutrality was taken and he was availing himself of our hospitality. On one occasion Captain G. S.

2ND BATT. ROYAL DUBLIN FUSILIERS

Higginson spent the night in an empty house in the town in an attempt to mark this fox to ground, but unfortunately his vigil was unproductive of result. Lieutenant Haskard was now acting as Railway Staff Officer, and having a very busy time of it, as in addition to hundreds of other duties he had to send rations up and down the line to the various detachments.

On the 9th, Sergeant-Major Burke rejoined the regiment, having been a prisoner since he was wounded at Talana, and left at Dundee. During this time his duties had been ably performed by Colour-Sergeant C. Guilfoyle, now Sergeant-Major, 2nd Battalion Royal Dublin Fusiliers. Lieutenants Marsh and Weldon also joined here, as Lieutenant Supple had done a few days before. The two former had followed the regiment up the line to Mafeking, and thence across the Western Transvaal in a cape-cart, following very nearly in our tracks. They had an adventuresome journey, and were delighted to reach us at last. Captain Clarke, R.M.L.I., who was attached to the regiment, escorted an important Boer commander, named Van Rensburg, to Johannesburg, on his way to St. Helena.

It is necessary to explain briefly here the situation of the three companies, 'A,' 'E,' and 'F,' under Major English, Captain Shewan, and Captain G. S. Higginson, which had been sent out to guard various points on the line from Heidelberg to Standerton.

'A' and 'E' companies had originally gone out, and were posted at Botha's Kraal. Later on it became necessary to hold Zuikerbosch as well. Major English, with Lieutenant Newton as his subaltern, was sent to garrison it. Taking 'E' company with him and leaving Captain Higginson at Botha's Kraal, Major English, with some 110 Royal Engineers, occupied the post, and at once set about to put it into a thorough state of defence. He fully recognised the inherent weaknesses of his situation, and saw that unless well

HEIDELBERG

entrenched he was practically at the mercy of an enemy armed with artillery, as he had none to reply with, while the nearest reinforcements were miles away, and liable themselves to be attacked in force at any moment. He therefore spared no ingenuity in strengthening the position. Having Royal Engineers and a considerable number of Kaffirs at his disposal, he very soon effected his purpose and dug himself comfortably in.

In the meantime signs were not wanting of approaching Boer activity. A large commando, under Hans Botha, was known to be hovering about the neighbourhood, and as it was also known that Botha was occasionally in the habit of spending a night under his own roof—not three miles away—Captain G. S. Higginson made two efforts to catch him napping. But on neither occasion was the chieftain at home, and the unfortunate Higginson, who had selected the darkest and wildest nights as most suitable for his purpose, was foiled each time, and had to withdraw somewhat crestfallen, under a fire of raillery from the ladies of the establishment. He collected some valuable information, nevertheless, and sent in reports of Boers in the vicinity, which, however, were not sufficient to induce General Hart to take any extra precautions.

Such was the situation of affairs when, on the misty morning of July 21st, we at Heidelberg heard the hoarse barking of the accursed pompom, varied by the duller and more menacing note of heavier guns. Anxiously we asked each other what it could be, and reluctantly we came to the conclusion that our comrades were being submitted to shell-fire with no possible chance of reprisal. As the sun rose, the mist did the same, and very soon cheerful messages came twinkling over 'the misty mountain-tops,' announcing that a considerable force of Boers were attacking them, but that they had little fear of not being able to keep them off.

2ND BATT. ROYAL DUBLIN FUSILIERS

General Hart hastily assembled a small column * and marched to Major English's assistance, leaving Colonel Hicks in command of the camp, and as it was quite possible the main attack might be intended for Heidelberg, we took all necessary precautions for the safety of the town.

Before General Hart's force arrived, the Boers had commenced to withdraw, having discovered that on this occasion they had attacked a veritable hornet's nest.

The hill on which Major English had dug his entrenchments is situated in the angle made by the Zuikerbosch River where it turns sharply to the south, and was on the left bank of the stream. On the other side of the river was the hill occupied by the Royal Engineers. Between these two was the new deviation bridge then under construction. The Kaffirs lived in the hollow between the hills, as did also the Yeomanry, of whom there were about ten, under a very young officer. Major English had given this officer orders that, on any attack taking place, he should at once lead his horses down to the river, where there was a kind of hollow place which would have afforded them excellent cover. This order, however, probably from the suddenness of the attack, was not complied with in time, and the horses were in consequence stampeded almost immediately. The natives also were not long in effecting a rapid southerly movement, for which, of course, they cannot be blamed, and the Boers shelled them lustily as they streamed away.

The Royal Dublin Fusiliers' camp was on the southern slope of the hill, the summit being occupied at night by alternate companies, who stood to arms shortly before dawn. Captain Shewan was on the hill, and on the point of letting the men fall out, when the attack commenced. The trenches were at once manned without the slightest noise or confusion, and the Boers' rifle-fire vigorously replied to.

The two Boer guns were in position on the hills to the

* 130 Somersets, 2 guns, 1 pompom, 140 Marshall's Horse.

HEIDELBERG

north, some 3400 yards off, while the pompom came into action near the Fortuna coal-mine. Owing to the excellent disposition and construction of the defences, the enemy's fire made little or no impression, until after a time they began to move round to the flanks of the position. Their rifle-fire then began to have some effect, but at the same time the fire of the defence had a better target, and after a short time the burghers commenced to withdraw from the rear face of the work. In the meantime they had swung round to the west of the Engineers' hill, and under cover of a grass fire, which was lighted by them and spread right up to the trenches, endeavoured to attack this part of the position, in which, however, they also failed. The enemy continued his endeavours until midday, when he commenced to withdraw, his movement being somewhat expedited by the arrival of the reinforcements under the General.

Considering the numbers of the attacking force, and the resolute manner in which they had persevered, the casualties were extraordinarily small, two officers and three men wounded, one of the former being Major English himself; he was struck by a shell splinter in the eye, but most fortunately did not lose the sight of it.

This gallant defence called forth a most eulogistic order from the Commander-in-Chief. The success had come at a time when it was badly needed. The guarding of the railways necessitated the splitting-up of forces, and in more than one recent instance a commander of less foresight than Major English had failed to realise the responsibility of his position, with the result that more additions were made to the already-far-too-long list of 'regrettable incidents.'

The following telegrams passed between General Hart and Major English :—

Helio message received at Zuikerbosch Fort on July 22nd, 1900, from General Hart: 'Received following wire from Lord Roberts. Begins—" Please convey my congratulations

2ND BATT. ROYAL DUBLIN FUSILIERS

to Major English, and all concerned on the gallant manner in which they defended their post on the Zuikerbosch."'

Major English made the following reply:—'All in the Zuikerbosch command thank our General for forwarding Lord Roberts' telegram, which they consider a great honour.'

The following is an extract from Army Orders in South Africa, dated Pretoria, July 26th, 1900 :—

'*Engagement.*—The Field-Marshal Commanding-in-Chief desires that the following account from Major-General A. Fitzroy Hart, C.B., Commanding 5th Brigade, of the successful defence of a post by a small force of infantry against a determined attack of the enemy with guns, be published as an example of what can be accomplished by a small body of resolute men, well commanded and skilfully and judiciously entrenched :—

'From General Hart, Zuikerbosch, to Lord Roberts, Pretoria, July 21st : "Enemy made a determined attempt to destroy my advanced post at Railhead, Zuikerbosch, to-day. Major English, Royal Dublin Fusiliers, commands the post, with two companies of Dublins, ten Yeomanry, and 110 Royal Engineer reparation party, defending the new railway bridge which replaces destroyed one. Boers began attack at daybreak with two or three guns and a pompom, shelling the position hard. They then advanced, and completely surrounded him with mauser fire, keeping it up from 6.20 a.m. to 11.45 a.m., and it was hotly returned. English signalled early to me at Heidelberg, thirteen miles off, that he was surrounded, and holding his own confidently. I started from Heidelberg with two guns, a pompom, 130 Somersets, and 140 Marshall's Horse and Yeomanry, and, on approaching English's position, found he had already beaten off the enemy, and saw them assembled on the heights N.E. of his position, and beginning to ride off N.E. My guns opened fire, and Boers broke into a gallop. The complete repulse of the Boer attack is entirely due to the skill with

HEIDELBERG

which Major English had fortified his position, his vigilant arrangements, and the good fighting of the garrison. Casualties : wounded—Lieutenant Greig, severely ; Privates Mallon, Stanton, and O'Brien, slightly. The bridge and train not injured. Line only injured to the extent of three rails taken up. Numbers of enemy's casualties not known. Boers sent out an ambulance for wounded, and were seen burying dead."'

The following extracts from a letter from Sapper F. Adcock, published in a home newspaper, are also of interest. After a brief description of the situation, he continues :—' It was at this time that the heliographers of the Dublin's showed their pluck, for, fixing up their stand amidst shot and shell, they got their message through to Heidelberg. .... We could watch every move of the Dublins, as the ditch ran in the line of their kopje. ... Another bit of pluck well worth seeing happened just as there was a lull in the firing. Two of the Dublins ran from their entrenchments to their tents, quite a quarter of a mile, and carried all their bread in a blanket between them to the entrenchments. The Boers fired three shells at them when they were going back, but two fell short, and the other was right between them.'

The sapper was right, and it is pleasant to read letters like the above when emanating from an entirely independent source. Major English reported most favourably of the signalling, which was necessarily conducted practically in the open, the enemy's projectiles falling all round the operator and Major English, who stood close beside him. For this service Private Farrelly, who sent the message, was awarded the distinguished conduct medal. The two brave men who went out for the bread were Privates Hayes ('A' company) and Townsell ('E' company).

The remainder of our stay at Heidelberg was uneventful except for what might very easily have been a most un-

2ND BATT. ROYAL DUBLIN FUSILIERS

pleasant accident. We were all seated at lunch one day when there was a sudden and loud report close at hand. Investigation proved that it came from Captain Pomeroy's revolver (an officer belonging to a West Indian Regiment who was attached to us). He had carelessly left it in his tent loaded, while his servant had still more carelessly fired it off. The only sufferer was an unfortunate animal, Major Bird's charger, which was shot in the hoof.

On our departure on the 27th, Major-General Cooper's Brigade took over the defence of the town.

THE OFFICERS' MESS.

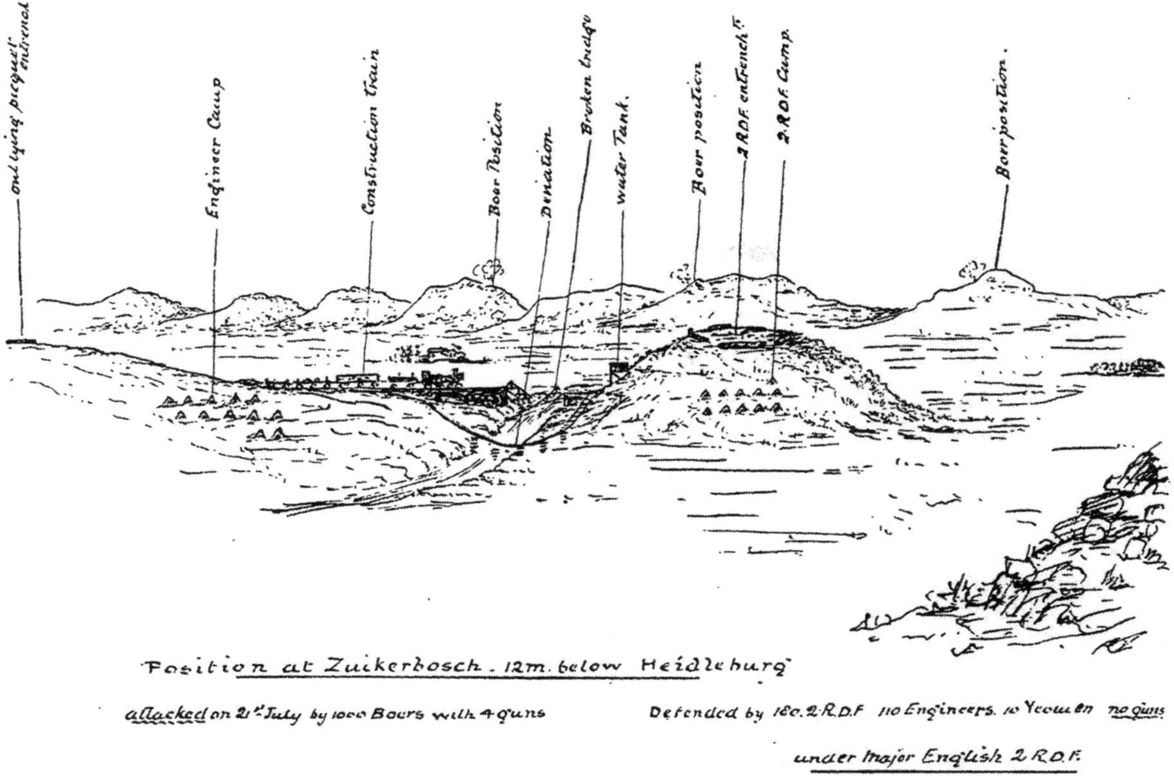
out lying picquet entrench
Engineer Camp
Construction train
Boer Position
Deviation
Broken bridge
water Tank.
Boer position
2 R.D.F. entrench[t]
2 R.D.F. Camp.
Boer position.
Position at Zuikerbosch - 12m. below Heidleburg
attacked on 21st July by 1000 Boers with 4 guns
Defended by 1 Co. 2 R.D.F 110 Engineers. 10 Yeomen no guns
under Major English 2 R.D.F.

From a sketch by Col. H. Tempest Hicks, C.B.

CHAPTER III.

AFTER DE WET.

'It is vain for you to rise up early.'—Ps. cxxvii. 2.

HAVING been for a month at Heidelberg, we had begun to quite make it our own, and felt as if we should finish the war where we were. And although there were still any amount of commandoes in the field, we could scarcely be blamed for thinking that the back of the business was broken, and that a few weeks, or at the outside months, must see us returning to England. Well, we reckoned without our host, or rather the hosts of Messrs. Botha, De Wet, De la Rey, & Co., and if we made a mistake we made it in good company.

The Colonel had never ceased fortifying and improving Dublin Hill, and there is no doubt that at the end of July his efforts had resulted in a very sound and efficient post.

Everything pointed to peace and quiet when, late on the afternoon of July 27th, the ominous 'order' call broke the stillness of the crisp wintry evening.

'Come for orders! Come for orders! Hurry up, hurry up; come for orders!'

Who, that soldiered through those long weary months, but must remember that infernal call? For it was characteristic of the war, and owing, doubtless, to the immense tract of country over which it was waged, that not only the rank and file, but even the officers, with one or two exceptions, knew little or nothing of what was going on. Consequently one never knew what the next minute would bring forth, and waited accordingly with ears at tension for the strains of the bugle, whose notes might portend nothing or everything.

2ND BATT. ROYAL DUBLIN FUSILIERS

On this occasion they were the prelude to one of the most stirring periods in the history of the war—the first great De Wet hunt. It is beside the purport of this volume to discuss the advantages of British infantry pursuing mounted Boers. It has often been maintained that the result of such an apparently hopeless hare-and-tortoise sort of procedure would have been successful on this occasion but for the fact of the unblocking of Oliphant's Nek. On the other hand, there are not wanting many who are equally prepared to argue that, although this bolt-hole being open may have facilitated the guerilla's escape, that astute leader would easily have found some other nook or cranny quite sufficient for his purpose had it been shut; while, if the worst had come to the worst, from his point of view, he could, at the sacrifice of his waggons and guns, have dissolved his commando in the night, only to unite again at some more suitable and less column-infected time and place.

At the time we knew nothing of all this; all we knew was that some big move was in progress, for, as we neared the railway next day, train after train steamed through, reminiscent of the vicinity of Epsom on a Derby Day, but that was all. Where we were going, when we were going, why we were going, were all questions quite beyond our ken—not to be answered, indeed, until some days later, when an officer on General Hunter's Staff told us what it was all about.

Our march to the railway on the 28th was a long and trying one, variously computed at from twenty-one to twenty-three miles. Whatever its exact length may have been is immaterial; it was the method in which it was conducted that was so desperately trying. After the usual sketchy apology for a breakfast, the column moved off with the Somersets as advance-guard, and 'F' and 'G' company of the Dublins as rearguard. From a variety of causes the progress was uncommonly slow, and, no halt being made of greater length than a few minutes, the men of the rear-

AFTER DE WET

guard had a trying time, for any one who has marched behind a column of waggons, &c., miles in length, knows that one practically gets no halt at all from these five-minute snatches, owing to the necessity of continually closing up. It was quite dark when the rearguard hove in sight of the passing trains, and then, to make matters thoroughly uncomfortable, some half-dozen waggons stuck firmly in a snipe-bog, scarcely a mile from their destination.

CORPORAL TIERNEY AND CHEF BURST.

It looked uncommonly as if the unfortunate rearguard would have to bivouac in that miserable marsh. As everybody was pouring with perspiration from their endeavours with the waggons, and as it was beginning to freeze, while there was no chance of getting at great-coats, blankets, or food unless the waggons came out, out they jolly well had to come—and came. It was ten o'clock before the men got anything to eat, and 11.30 p.m. before our arrangements for the night were completed. Our invaluable French 'chef' had kept some hot soup for the rearguard, and seldom was soup more appreciated than by those famished and frozen warriors.

2ɴɴ BATT. ROYAL DUBLIN FUSILIERS

We now heard that we were going south, and going south by train, and that at all events was something to look forward to. At least it was a change—something to look forward to with anticipation ; and certainly it is something to look back upon with a certain amount of amusement, but at the time that railway journey was certainly the reverse of comfortable.

We could not get off as early as we expected to on the 29th. The first train started all right, but owing to the amount of work to be done in getting kit over a small drift that lay between our bivouac of the night before and the station, the second train did not follow it till 3.30 p.m.

After this the difficulty of dispatch increased with each succeeding train, until when it came to entraining reluctant horses and still more reluctant mules practically in the dark, for there was no other light but the dim glimmer of two candle-lamps, the task became herculean, and required an infinity of patience and tact. The General and his staff having gone by the first excursion, the task of bringing along the remainder of the column devolved on Colonel Hicks, with Captain Fetherstonhaugh as his staff officer. They did not complete the entraining until the early hours of the 30th, and then only to find the line blown up in front of them. The fact that no disaster occurred here was owing to Colonel Hicks' determination not to try to get through that night, as he clearly foresaw what actually took place, and that there was nothing to prevent the enemy blowing up the line.

It is necessary now to turn our attention to the second train, which conveyed most of the regiment, under command of Major Bird. Some forty men with their arms and accoutrements were told off to each open truck, necessitating the tightest packing, which, however, had a beneficial effect in so far as it took off the worst part of the constant succession of jerks and jolts which the journey consisted of. But everybody was full of fun, and the men as merry as crickets at the

AFTER DE WET

change from the long days of uninteresting 'foot-slogging' and the prospect of a brush with the elusive De Wet. The officers—about twenty in number—travelled in the guard's van, on the floor of which they made themselves as comfortable as possible under the circumstances. After passing Vereeniging and duly admiring the excellent work of the sappers, the mess-president proposed that they should sample the hampers he had provided for them. This

FOURTH CLASS ON THE Z.A.S.M.

was carried unanimously, but at that moment the train began to slow up, and, anxious to see every new place, we determined to wait until the train started again, and then enjoy our dinner in peace and comfort.

The sudden explosion of a shell from 'Long Tom' in our midst could not have had a more demoralising effect than the news which greeted us when we came to a standstill. It arrived in the shape of a telegram from the General, ordering the officers to ride in the trucks with the men, and to keep a sharp look-out for attacks from both sides. So there was no chance of any dinners after all, and all our visions of chicken and tongue, whisky and sparklets, and a hot cup of tea or

2ND BATT. ROYAL DUBLIN FUSILIERS

chocolate resolved themselves into a lump of chocolate out of one's haversack and a pull at one's water-bottle. The mess-president proved himself a man of resource on this trying occasion. With hunger gnawing at his vitals he saw a beautiful dinner laid out in a waiting-room for some staff officers. Unable to satisfy his comrades he saw no reason why he himself should go unsatisfied, and in the three or four minutes occupied by the engine in watering he hastily bolted a fine plate of roast beef and potatoes, not omitting a bottle of beer standing hard by, and jumped into the train at the last moment, thanking his astonished host and friend, Major Hickie of the 7th Fusiliers, as the train moved off into the darkness.

Anything more cheerless than the remainder of that night journey it would be hard to conceive. In the first place, when there are forty men in an open truck, it is very difficult to find room for two more. In the second place, it was bitterly cold, and a pitch-dark night. In the third place, the even-money chance of a slab or two of gun-cotton on the line ahead was not a pleasing one to contemplate. In the fourth place, the men were ordered to 'charge magazines,' and to spend several hours jolting along with the cold barrel of a loaded rifle poking one in the ribs, or insinuatingly tucking itself into the nape of one's neck, could by no stretch of imagination or fire-eating ambition be called comforting. However, there was one fine piece of news at any rate to act as a compensation, the surrender of Commandant Prinsloo and three or four thousand men to General Hunter.

Once or twice ghostly forms on horseback loomed suddenly out of the blackness of the veld, momentarily lit up by the glare from the engine. On each occasion they shouted some warning, but what it was nobody could make out. Our engine-driver fully expected to be blown up, and had taken the bit between his teeth, cracking on at a pace that stirred up the living contents of the trucks

AFTER DE WET

behind him, until if any one of them had had a spare morsel of fat on him, he must inevitably have been churned into butter. Carrying on at this rate, we soon arrived at our destination, a small station called Kopjes. And when very shortly after our arrival two or three dull explosions in the direction whence we had come signified that the line had been blown up right enough, our gratitude to the engine-driver was considerably increased. Nor did his

FIFTH CLASS ON THE Z.A.S.M.

solicitude for our welfare end even then, for having effected his object, he said we could have as much boiling water out of the engine as we liked, and in less than sixty seconds we were drinking steaming hot chocolate, and returning grateful thanks to our host. If any one class more than another deserved special recognition during this war, it was the railway staff—the drivers, stokers, and guards. It is no exaggeration to say that during the whole war no train was ever run at night but that these men did not run the risk of being blown sky-high, in addition to all the other incidental dangers of their hazardous calling.

2ND BATT. ROYAL DUBLIN FUSILIERS

The break in the line necessitated our waiting some two or three days at the station, until the remainder of the column got through. When it was at last assembled, we marched off due west, towards the sound of heavy firing in the distance. A march of fourteen miles brought us within sight and almost within range of a long, low line of kopjes, and here, we were informed on our arrival, was the famous guerilla chief, surrounded—so we were informed—at last, and only awaiting the arrival of our column to be finished off altogether. Without going so far as some of the subalterns, who on hearing he was surrounded seemed to anticipate the sight of De Wet in the middle of a sort of cock-pit, with the British forces sitting round, there still seemed a considerable number of sufficiently large gaps in the chain of columns and brigades slowly and ponderously extending round either flank of the Boer position. The firing we had heard had been from the Boer guns, they having shelled the Derbyshire Regiment out of their camp, which had been pitched imprudently close to the harmless-looking kopjes. Needless to say, there was not a move of any sort to be seen, and how on earth three or four thousand men managed to conceal themselves so absolutely must ever remain a marvel. True, their camp was beyond the crest-line, but it is certain they had outposts and sentries on the look-out, and these must of necessity have been posted where they could see us; but certain it was we could not see them, carefully as telescopes and Zeiss glasses swept every inch of the hills.

Unfortunately we had to leave eighty-nine men behind at the railway, as they had no boots, a serious matter with every probability of a stiff fight on our hands: for General Hart's orders were to prevent De Wet going south; to attack, if necessary, to make him go north, but not to allow him to go in any other direction. This being so, our object was effected, as will appear later on.

Another and equally sudden interruption to a meal took

AFTER DE WET

place on August 1st. Marshall's Horse, a Colonial corps of whom we saw a good deal, had gone out on a reconnaissance in the morning, and had some scrapping with the enemy's patrols, &c. But now word suddenly came that they were surrounded, and in a tight corner. Hastily dropping knives and forks, we fell in almost at the double, and, though somewhat struck by the incongruity and apparent anomaly in the fact of our cavalry being surrounded by the Boers when we had been distinctly informed that it was we who were surrounding them, set off as hard as we could lay legs to the ground. After marching between four and five miles, well within the hour, we met the doctor of our mounted corps, who said he had been taken prisoner and released, and that there was no necessity for going any further, as our friends had beaten off our enemies and were on their way back. So back we trudged too, meeting on the way what most of us thought was a squadron of cavalry, but which turned out to be Brigadier-General Little's cavalry brigade. The sight of the attenuation of this force afforded us food for reflection, and made some of us begin to understand a little how it was that, in spite of our magnificent paper forces, we still found such difficulty in rounding-up our foes.

The next three or four days were uneventful. Lord Kitchener arrived and took over the chief command of all the forces, which now really seemed to be closing in on De Wet. The noose was being drawn tighter and tighter daily, and the Boers' position became more and more precarious. What would have happened but for Lord Kitchener's arrival it is hard to say, as General Hart, ever impatient of passivity, a very Ney for pertinacity of attack, personal bravery, and confidence in his troops, was undoubtedly on the eve of launching an attack. But in the light of the succeeding events, it is clear now that such an attack would have been premature and ill-timed. In the event of its non-success—and we had a very small force to carry it out with—the

2ND BATT. ROYAL DUBLIN FUSILIERS

general operations would have been completely ruined, for we being the Southern force, there would have been nothing to prevent De Wet going south. In the event of success it would merely have meant that the Boers would have slipped away north two or three days sooner than they did, when, seeing that our arrangements to intercept them were not even then complete, an earlier start would have enabled them to carry out their retreat with even greater ease.

Major King, of General Hunter's staff, now arrived in camp with a Boer prisoner, one of Prinsloo's staff. The latter was being sent through with a message to De Wet, informing him of the full magnitude of the Boer surrender at Golden Gate, and advocating his own relinquishment of further operations. They went through to the Boers' position, and were courteously received, but General De Wet declared it was impossible for him to think of giving up now, as he had President Steyn with him. Nobody believed in the excuse, and its purport is somewhat difficult to understand, but it ended the conference, and Major King and his prisoner returned to camp.

Major English, whose eye had proved troublesome and kept him behind, now rejoined the battalion, to everybody's gratification, for the publication of Lord Roberts's army order, which took place at this time, had made us all very proud of him and his men.

On the 5th an order was given to send out a small force, consisting of two companies of the regiment, a pompom, and a troop of Marshall's Horse, to a point five miles N.N.E. of the camp, in order to fill up a somewhat big gap between General Hart and the 3rd Cavalry Brigade. 'B' and 'G' companies, under an officer of the regiment, with Captain Nelson, R.M.L.I., and Lieutenants Smith and Molony as subalterns, and Lieutenant Nek of Marshall's Horse, were selected, and started as soon as the men's dinners were finished. General Hart rode out later on, and, catching this force up,

AFTER DE WET

selected a site, and gave orders to the officer commanding it to dig himself in, promising that the pompom, which had not turned up, should be sent on.

In the meantime the remainder of General Hart's force also started digging, a very different state of affairs to his premeditated attack a couple of days earlier.

The detachment sent out patrols on the morning of the 6th to see if they could draw the enemy's fire, with strict injunctions to content themselves with doing so and then withdraw. This they soon succeeded in doing. On their return they passed a farmhouse, and received information that an important Boer General was in the habit of sleeping there sometimes. Visions of a capture of De Wet inflamed the minds of some of the younger officers, and on the night of the 6th–7th Captain Nelson and Lieutenant Smith, with a few picked men, made a raid on the house. However, they found nobody but womenfolk, and returned empty-handed.

Next day commenced our memorable pursuit. De Wet and his merry men had slipped away over the ford bearing his own name as neatly as a cherry-stone from between finger and thumb, and, with their heads turned north, were to give us, and many another converging column like us, the hunt of our lives. The regiment started at 11.30 and only halted at dusk, some three miles from a range of hills on which rumour said the Boers were going to stand and fight it out to the bitter end, even if the whole British Army came against them. 'B' and 'G' companies did not get in until 9 p.m., as, in addition to having an extra five miles to march, they had some trouble with their waggons.

We marched all day on the 8th in an easterly direction along the left or southern bank of the Vaal River—a long, tiring, uneventful trek. Expecting momentarily to see our prey delivered over to us, our spirits sank lower and lower as the day dragged on with no sign of any Boers. There was the usual aggravating little drift to be negotiated at 6 p.m.

2ND BATT. ROYAL DUBLIN FUSILIERS

only half a mile short of our camping-ground for the night, but eventually we got all the waggons over, and men and officers obtained something to eat. This proved one of the coldest nights of the winter, and there was ice instead of water in most of the water-bottles next morning when reveille went at 3.30 a.m.

Starting at 5 a.m. we again went steadily on till 6 p.m., making well over thirteen hours without food. We skirted round the south of Parys, a name which appealed strongly to a good many of us, and suddenly heard the welcome sound of heavy firing not very far ahead. The column halted, and word soon came that this time our pains were really to be rewarded; the Boers were only six miles ahead, and Lord Methuen was engaged with their rearguard. All signs of hunger and fatigue at once disappeared, the regiment started trekking off once more, instinctively 'stepping out' as they went. The guns still thundered invitingly just ahead, and as we topped each fresh horizon or rounded the slope of the next kopje we all expected to see our prey close in front. But it was not to be. As the afternoon wore on the sound of the guns died away, until at last we came to a halt at dusk in a sort of amphitheatre among the low hills. Too tired to want much food, the men sank down with the delightful nightcap that reveille might again be expected at 3.30 a.m.

The 10th proved more or less a repetition of the preceding days. Starting at 5 a.m., we did not halt till well after dark, the waggons, kits, food, &c., not getting up to us till 10 p.m. Seeing that there was no chance of any other food, some bullocks were commandeered, and the men cooked them in little chunks in their mess-tins over the grass fires. Tired out as they were it was too cold to get any sleep without blankets, and long lines of melancholy soldiers could be seen standing along the edges of the grass fires, against which their figures were outlined in bold silhouette, and from whose scanty flames they endeavoured to get what little warmth they could. Everybody was wet through to the knee, a good many to the

AFTER DE WET

waist, while some were soused all over, for in the course of our march we had turned due north, and crossed the Vaal at Lindeque Drift. The river is very broad here, and split up into numerous small streams, in the wading of which many humorous incidents took place, owing to the slippery nature of the rolling stones in the bottom of the river. A rolling stone may not gather much moss, but it is undoubtedly capable of gathering a considerable quantity of slimy weeds, and when

THE VAAL RIVER, LINDEQUE DRIFT.

concealed by two or three feet of running water it offers about as precarious a footing as it is possible to imagine.

Winding our way through the low hills on the Transvaal side of the river, we at length emerged on to an enormous plain. The far horizon was bounded by the Gatsrand hills, with which, as with another detached clump of rounded kopjes on our left, known as the Losberg, we were destined ere long to become closely acquainted. As we finally turned in about 11 p.m. we heard reveille was not to sound till 4.30 a.m., but when some subaltern attempted a feeble joke about a 'Europe morning,' his effort met with nothing but silent contempt.

2ND BATT. ROYAL DUBLIN FUSILIERS

There is little doubt that any one who shared in that next day's march will never forget it. As we proceeded across the illimitable plain a strong head-wind began to blow, increasing in strength as the day wore on. De Wet had fired all the grass ahead of us, with the result that the air was laden with millions and millions of particles of minute ashes and sharp cinders. These soon filled eyes, ears, nostrils, throats, and lungs, until breathing became well-nigh impossible, and the agony caused by their penetration into our eyes almost intolerable. But woe to him who endeavoured to alleviate his distress by wiping his eyes with grimy hands. Such action merely had the effect of 'rubbing it in,' and so accentuating the misery and discomfort. The men very soon began to fall out in ever-increasing numbers. On one occasion Captain Nelson, R.M.L.I., was seen straggling off right away from the column. Lieutenant Bradford went after him and found that he was temporarily quite blind. At last, after hours of torment, we reached a pass in the Gatsrand, on the far side of which we halted, as night fell. A big grass fire almost immediately broke out, and as the grass was long and thick, and a strong wind still blew to fan it, things looked very ugly. The flames swept right through the camp, but luckily the tents were not up. But what would happen when they reached the guns and ammunition? What, indeed, might have happened, but for the gallantry of the gunners and naval detachment, it is hard to say. As it was the ammunition-waggons caught fire and were sufficiently charred to demonstrate the closeness of the danger. But, as ever, 'the handy-man' was to the fore, and with promptitude and courage, that could not have been excelled, managed to extinguish the flames.

And now for a wash—what, no water! No water, which, hungry and exhausted as they were, every one wanted even more than food. But, alas! it was too true, and after contenting ourselves with some liquid mud, flavoured with

AFTER DE WET

charcoal, called coffee, and some few mouthfuls of tough old trek-ox, liberally peppered with burnt grass, we only waited to hear that reveille was to be at 1.30 a.m. before sinking down to snatch what rest was possible. This delightful spot rejoiced in the refreshing name of Orange Grove.

The 12th of August. Shade of St. Grouse! At 3 a.m. we were on the move in bright moonlight and sharp frost, with a wind blowing which cut like a knife. After doing some sixteen or seventeen miles we arrived about 10 a.m. at Wolverdiend station—a large force of cavalry and infantry assembled there, moving out as we moved in. Camp was pitched, and a good meal cooked—our first respectable one for three days—and then—then came the order to start off again in the afternoon. Wearily we resumed that march, but even as we started the prospect was brightened by the sound of heavy guns ahead, on our right front. We finally bivouacked for the night on the most stony kopje in all South Africa. It was impossible to find a spot anywhere that did not consist of sharp, jagged rocks, rendering sleep, to any troops less tired than we were, an utter impossibility. A rumour credited Lord Methuen with again having brought De Wet to bay, and we were almost positively assured that next day would end our laborious march.

No less than ten mules were lost during the day, from utter exhaustion. Many a heart, weary in itself, ached yet more deeply for the sufferings entailed on the dumb animals.

Reveille at 2, off at 3, was our time-table for the next day. After proceeding some five or six miles, the force came to the pretty little Mooi River. The Colonel found an excellent place for us to cross it, compared to the spot where the Somersets were obliged to plunge in. A halt was called on the far side, and a scratch meal taken. While thus employed, some of our troops who had been De Wet's prisoners, amongst them a couple of our own men, came in.

2ND BATT. ROYAL DUBLIN FUSILIERS

They had been with De Wet's rearguard, and told us that when Lord Methuen had shelled it the day before, they had managed to escape; also that the fire of Lord Methuen's guns had knocked over a Boer gun and exploded one of their ammunition waggons. They added that De Wet was in command of a very considerable force, and some distance ahead.

We presently resumed the pursuit, finally camping in

THE R.D.F. BATHING IN MOOI RIVER, POTCHEFSTROOM.

some very desolate country, where the water was scarce and bad. Signs of over-fatigue and want of sleep were now becoming very apparent, a large number of men falling out and riding on the waggons. Poor fellows! they stuck it out as long as ever they could, but their socks gave out from the constant wettings, and they pitched them away, marching on in their boots until the pain of the raw chafes became too much to bear. There was never a grumble or complaint: a man simply asked to see his Captain, and respectfully said his feet had given way, and he must regretfully fall out. The officers knew it was true, and felt for their comrades whose emaciated kits precluded the possibility of a change. To

AFTER DE WET

such a state was the column now reduced that the General, who had ordered reveille for 2 a.m. the following morning, actually put it back till 6 o'clock.

The regiment acted as rearguard on the 14th, and did not start till 9 a.m., halting for a short time at mid-day near a blown-up Boer ammunition waggon. Every conceivable sort and kind of small-arm ammunition lay scattered around on the veld, and those who were keen on curios of this description made quite a collection of full and empty cases.

The battalion lost eleven more mules, the poor brutes simply falling to the ground from utter exhaustion, being perforce left where they lay. We arrived in camp at 5.30 p.m., and then for the first time, in at all events some of our lives, heard two reveilles in one day, the hated call blaring in our ears at 10.30 p.m. Starting at 12, we pushed on, belts tightened, teeth clenched, and simply determined *not* to give in. We were told that the cavalry brigades had De Wet at last at the foot of the Magaliesberg, only sixteen miles ahead. So on we went into the sheer and bitter night, more like ghostly shadows than anything else, as the spectral column wound its way through sleeping villages and over mile after mile of dark and silent veld. At last our eyes were gladdened by the sight of twinkling watch-fires on the slopes of some hills just ahead, and as the first signs of dawn began to become manifest, we sank wearily down to enjoy a few minutes' repose. But it was broad daylight when we woke, and alas! for all the hopes of the past eight days, the hills ahead were only occupied by our cavalry. Theirs had been the watch-fires of the dark hours of the night. The game was up, and we were told the first great De Wet hunt was over. Some one had failed to stop the earth; the fox had foiled his pursuers, and the various Generals reluctantly whipped off their hounds.

It was a bitter disappointment. We had been so buoyed up by the promises held out to us. Every one had so

2ND BATT. ROYAL DUBLIN FUSILIERS

thoroughly entered into the job, and plodded stolidly along; and all for nothing. Work which, if successful, would have lived in history, but which, being unsuccessful, was fated to be forgotten and ignored; and unsuccessful through no fault of any of the troops engaged in it. There was no General or Staff to blame: no regiment or department which could be hauled over the coals. No; some one had blundered, that was all. The point has never been exactly cleared up, and probably never will be, and there the matter ended.

> 'Lay not your blame on me: if you have lost him,
> Why, I have lost him too.'—*Othello*.

So we turned over and fell asleep again, and woke up at 9 a.m. and had some breakfast, and were about to fall asleep again when the word came to fall in and march on to some other bivouac. The one we were in was good enough for us, but of course there was nothing for it but to obey, and we marched to a small village called Rietfontein. Here we heard that Colonel Hore's column was surrounded, and in a bad way, some eighty miles off, and that we were to form part of a small force, and make a forced march to his relief.

Accordingly the column marched at 8 a.m. next morning. After going about two miles, an order arrived saying we were to go back; and back we went—a somewhat profitless proceeding, but doubtless unavoidable. The remainder of the day was spent resting, but it was known that reveille was to sound at midnight, and that we were to make a big effort next day.

Starting at 1 a.m., and steadily tramping on till 9.30 a.m., we put twenty miles behind us. A halt was then made for a meal in rather a pretty spot, which actually boasted of some trees sufficiently large to afford shade, and under the foot of some well-wooded kloofs on our right. Resuming our march, we did some two or three miles more

AFTER THE DE WET HUNT

when word came that Colonel Hore was all right, having made a most gallant resistance and suffered many casualties, and that we were to go back the way we had come and march to Pretoria.

By the time we got back to our bivouac it was still early in the day, and we had already marched twenty-five miles. Five more mules had fallen dead, making a total of thirty-eight since we started on the 7th.

On the 18th we resumed our return journey, if return journey it could be called, since wherever we were going it was a hundred to one against its being the place we had come from. After a short trek we out-spanned for breakfasts, and an order was then given that we were to stay where we were and bivouac there for the night.

We moved to Vlakfontein next day, a distance of about sixteen miles, and the march quite uneventful. Rumour, however, pointed to Krugersdorp as our destination, and this must have been the exception that proves the rule, for on this occasion rumour proved right.

Another long and equally uninteresting march of eighteen or nineteen miles, only relieved by the arrival in hot haste of an indignant Marquis. It appeared he had been at a farm some two miles off on our left front, and had been offered some tea, which he had refused, and on leaving the house had been shot at by about a dozen Boers. What it was all about, or what he had been doing alone at this farm, and why the Boers should not shoot at him when he withdrew, none of us could quite make out. However, there were some Boers there, so the Colonel fired a few long-range volleys in the direction indicated, but declined to make a deviation with a view to reprisals.

Another eighteen miles on the 31st brought us to within about eight of Krugersdorp. About time too, for the men's boots were giving way badly, and scarcely one in ten had any socks.

2ND BATT. ROYAL DUBLIN FUSILIERS

The eight miles proved to be very long ones, however—longer than even Irish miles—and although we had made an early start, it was noon before we at last reached Krugersdorp for the second time. On this occasion we halted on a hillside just outside the north of the town, and beside a sort of small suburb on the further side of the creek.

Since leaving Heidelberg we had marched 289 miles. But of this distance 123 had been covered in the week during which we pursued De Wet, and 228 in the fortnight commencing August 7th. The longest distance covered in any one day had been the 25 miles on the day we turned. This marching was not done on roads it must be remembered, but across country, over hills, and through rivers, with frequent troubles with the unfortunate transport to overcome, and with very little food, and that of an inferior quality.

So ended our attempt on foot to catch De Wet on a thoroughbred. It was hopeless from the first, and yet went within measurable distance of succeeding, though even if we had rounded up some of his force at Olifant's Nek, it is very doubtful if De Wet himself would have been caught.

CHAPTER IV.

SEPTEMBER IN THE GATSRAND.

'Why gaddest thou about so much?'
Jer. ii. 36.

FROM August 23rd to 28th we obtained a very welcome week's rest, which would have been more enjoyable had the weather not broken badly, resulting in a succession of cold, high winds and heavy thunderstorms. These latter were of the most abominable description and a severe trial to those of us whose nervous systems were so constituted as to be affected by them. Some declared that they liked them; others frankly admitted that they detested them. They seemed to have a way of coming along about 4 p.m., and as soon as they got into position, immediately above our heads, opened fire. Needless to say, in the course of the long campaign there were a good many very narrow shaves, and one of our men was actually killed by lightning. The storms were almost invariably accompanied by torrential rain, which, though adding greatly to our discomfort, mitigated the danger, the local cognoscenti assuring us that even they looked upon a dry thunderstorm as no joke.

The regiment was a good deal split up at this time owing to the men we had dropped behind us on our late trek; they had fallen out from a variety of causes, but ninety per cent. of them on account of sore feet or lack of boots. There were no less than 160 at Wolverdiend, 50 at Rhenoster, 40 at Wolverhoek, and so on. The Colonel made many attempts to gather up his chickens once more, but when we started on our next trek we were still deficient of a good many. Major Bird left us at this time to go to Natal, where he was to arrange about our property, and organize orderly-room

2ND BATT. ROYAL DUBLIN FUSILIERS

papers, etc. Major English was unfortunately down with a severe attack of dysentery, and had it not been for Major Rutherford's arrival on the morning of the 29th the battalion would have been Majorless. Our padre, Father Mathews, presented us with a very fine pair of koodoo horns which he picked up at a store while we were here. He had originally been attached to the Royal Irish Fusiliers, but had come to us after Nicholson's Nek. He remained with us till

FATHER MATHEWS.

the end of the war, and proved himself a brave soldier and a welcome member of the mess.

Orders were eventually issued for a start at 6 a.m. on the morning of the 29th, but a night of heavy rain and succession of thunderstorms put an early start out of the question, and we did not get off till 3 p.m. The force was known as the Pochefstroom Column,* and our mission, as far as we knew, was to lay waste the country between Krugersdorp and

* South Wales Borderers, Royal Dublin Fusiliers, half-battalion Somersetshire Light Infantry, 4·7 Naval Gun, 28th Battery Royal Field Artillery, Marshall's Horse, and Yeomanry.

SEPTEMBER IN THE GATSRAND

that place, to fight the enemy whenever we met him, to bring in women and children, to destroy anything in the way of forage, &c., which might be useful to our enemies, if we could not bring it along for our own use ; to collect waggons, cape-carts, animals, harness, &c. ; and generally to carry fire and sword throughout the land.

Moving off in a southerly direction through the town, we came to what should have been a harmless little drift, about two or three miles out. The recent rains had, however, transformed it into a formidable obstacle, and waggon after waggon stuck hopelessly in its miry embrace. The General, therefore, determined to halt on a rising slope on the far side, and as many waggons as possible were man-handled over the bog. Tents were pitched, but scarcely were they up when a furious storm burst overhead. In a minute everything and everybody was soused through and through, the scene being vividly lit up by the almost continuous flashes of vivid lightning, while the crashing, bellowing boom of the thunder in our ears made voices inaudible and orders perfectly useless. What sort of teas the regimental cooks prepared we did not know, but the invaluable and ubiquitous Corporal Tierney managed to bring each of us a cup of hot tea and a rasher or a steak in our tents. The storm lasted till dawn, when the heavy clouds, as if despoiled of their victims by the rising sun, reluctantly drew off northwards. A glorious morning was the consequence, but, of course, there was no chance of trekking for some hours to come.

At 2 p.m. a start was again made, but as the tents and everything else were soaked through, and weighed fifty per cent. more than they would under ordinary circumstances, there was little hope that our transport animals would be able to drag them through any bad drifts. We only managed to do some seven miles before darkness came on, when we camped for the night at the Madeline Gold-mine. It was jumpy work here, as the whole place was honeycombed with

2ND BATT. ROYAL DUBLIN FUSILIERS

prospecting-holes and ditches, varying in depth from three feet to about three hundred. How on earth no one fell in must ever remain a mystery, as, to add to the delightful freshness of the situation, a large herd of bullocks took command, and meandered through the camp, one of which moved the mess president on some considerable distance, fortunately for him with a horn on each side of him, instead of one through him, as was doubtless intended.

We marched from the Madeline at 7 a.m. on August 31st, and after trekking some miles arrived at a large coalmine, which seemed to be in very good order. This country had been the scene of a goodish bit of fighting. Not far off the ill-fated Jameson raid had come to its inglorious conclusion; a little further on the Gordons had suffered severely during the advance on Johannesburg; and here the Pochefstroom column was to be 'blooded.'

We did not know that anything interesting was on the tapis until we saw the white cotton-wool puffs of our shrapnel bursting against a range of kopjes in our front. Then the Colonel told us that there were supposed to be a good many Boers on ahead, and that the General had gone off with a portion of the column to attack them, while we were to advance and seize and hold a nek, with a view to cutting off the retreating Boers, or threatening their left flank, or reinforcing our right, or some obscure purpose. It was the same in so many of our days of scrapping and trekking. Talk about the fog of war: we who were actually in the battle knew nothing about it. Doubtless the Commanding Officer was in the know, but the Company Officer, the commander of what is now recognised as the real fighting unit, he knew nothing. It was a funny fight. We trekked along, unconcernedly watching the pretty effect of our friends the gunners' practice; able with glasses to see the stones and dust driven ahead when the shells burst low; but unable to see any Boers. On reaching our destined spot we lay down

SEPTEMBER IN THE GATSRAND

and had a smoke, and thought of all sorts of things other than fighting, until at last news came from the General, and we heard we had fifteen casualties. So it had been quite a battle after all, as fights were going in those days, when any scrap that resulted in a casualty was known as a hardly-contested engagement.

On the 1st we moved to a rather pretty camp, close under the far side of the hills, called Jakfontein. The General and the troops he had with him on the 31st arrived at about 5.15 p.m., and camped alongside. The General told the Colonel they had had quite a victory yesterday, driving the Boers from their position, and occupying it at nightfall. They also thought they had done a good deal of damage to them with our guns, as they withdrew.

The column did not march on the 2nd, but two companies ('E' and 'F') under Captain Shewan proceeded to Bank Station as escort to the wounded, while two more ('A' and 'B'), under Major Rutherford, were sent off to commence the burning and looting, which, as far as we could understand, was the *raison-d'être* of the column. However that might be, there was a tremendous fuss on their return, and all sorts of accusations made *re* looting. There is no disguising the fact that we were altogether too squeamish, and that the orders on these and subsequent occasions were capable of more than one interpretation. Here were we in an enemy's country, badly off for a cart, let us say, for the officers' mess; the very thing is found in an unoccupied farm; to bring it along and use it was to loot: to burn it was to obey orders. At this length of time it is easy to write dispassionately, and there can be no harm in saying that it was vexing to be found fault with when under the impression that one was doing one's best for the general good, and not in any way profiting oneself. A few days later an officer searching a farm for concealed weapons, &c., came across a heavy ebony stick—just the thing he wanted. The

2ND BATT. ROYAL DUBLIN FUSILIERS

old Boer lady made a great fuss about his taking it, saying it was all she had to beat the Kaffirs with. That finally determined him, more especially as he was not exactly standing on ceremony at the time, seeing the next company was being sniped at, and his turn liable to come at any moment.

Captain G. S. Higginson was appointed Remount officer, and from this moment we began to lose sight of him, to everybody's great regret.

After spending another day in bringing in forage and supplies, the column started at 9 p.m. on the 3rd on a night march. For the first four or five miles all went well, and the advance-guard, under the careful leading of Captain Romer, maintained the right direction. Then, however, the road made a sharp turn, and although Captain Romer's party followed the turn right enough, part of his advance-guard, under a subaltern, went wandering off into the black night. It took some time to retrieve them, and as the column immediately afterwards came to a deep drift, it was considerably delayed. 'G' company was sent up a high hill on the left to guard that flank until the whole of the transport and rearguard was past, and the cold on the top was a thing to remember. The main column got into bivouac shortly after 1 a.m., but this unfortunate company was out till 5, which, seeing the march was resumed at 6, was rather hard luck. However, there was plenty of that going for everybody in those days, and after the usual short 'grouse,' the sleepless night was forgotten.

After moving into the hills about eight miles further, and passing through some beautiful farms, with every peach-tree a mass of glorious bloom, the column halted. The Imperial Yeomanry, who had been scouting far ahead, now found themselves perilously involved with a small body of the enemy. General Hart, with a portion of the column, including the artillery and naval gun, moved out to extricate them, and very soon we heard heavy fighting going on. He

SEPTEMBER IN THE GATSRAND

succeeded in his object, however, at the expense of four of the Yeomanry wounded and one man killed. In the meantime, Colonel Hicks had thrown out outposts on the hills, 'G' company coming in for another sleepless night, probably through some mistake in the roster. Captain Nelson, R.M.L.I. (attached), had a somewhat peculiar experience. Having been detained for some purpose when his company was going out, he gave Lieutenant Marsh, his subaltern, orders where to go, and later on followed himself. But then he couldn't find them. Nor could the other companies on other hills see anything of them, though signals were flashed in the direction they had taken. It was not until next morning that they were discovered, quite close to the place they had been ordered to go to. It was characteristic of the nature of the country in which we were operating, and the excellent manner in which they hid themselves, that Captain Nelson should have missed them, for at one time he must have passed quite close to the piquet.

Next morning Boers were reported in the vicinity. It is impossible to say they were in our front, as our front coincided with the report of the first visible Boer, and we simply went for anything we saw. Rumour put this force at 700 strong, but most people considered that an exaggerated estimate. We moved off in three columns: the South Wales Borderers took the right, moving along the difficult, serrated tops of the hills; the cavalry and yeomanry took the lower, more undulating, easier hills to the left, while the rest of us with the guns moved along in the centre; the General, conspicuous by a large red flag which a trooper carried behind him, moving wherever any opposition presented itself. It must be the unanimous opinion of all troops who knew our General, that a braver man never fought in action, but at the same time the man who carried that red flag deserved some honourable distinction. Perhaps he got it; probably he did not.

2ND BATT. ROYAL DUBLIN FUSILIERS

After moving some two or three miles, our further way was blocked by mauser-fire from a very ominous, black-looking kopje which stretched down into the valley from the high ground on our left. The guns came into action against this hill at a range of about two thousand yards, and it seemed as if a golden-crested wren could not have escaped if it had been unlucky enough to be there. The shrapnel kept up an almost incessant hail, covering the wooded sides of the kopje with jets of round white balls of smoke, while every now and then the deeper note of the 4·7 was followed by a huge cloud of dust and yellowish vapour thrown up, and off, by the explosion of the lyddite in the huge projectile. How many Boers held that hill will probably never be known; only four were found. But a strange spectacle ensued. Emerging from the cover on the far side, rode, *ventre-à-terre*, a solitary horseman. Immediately two companies extended in our front opened fire on him. How he escaped was a marvel, for in front, behind, on every side of him could be seen 'the bullets kicking dust-spots on the green.' But escape he did, and many a 'Good luck to you' went after him, for he was a bold man to have stayed as long as he had, and fully deserved to escape. Our bombardment had effected one useful purpose. Amongst the killed was a Commandant called Theron, a brave, enterprising young fellow of about twenty-five years of age, whose exploits had already stamped him as a born leader of men. Our own casualties amounted to four yeomen wounded.

We camped a little further on, and buried our enemy, and one of our own men who had died from his wounds, side by side, with all due honour, ceremony, and respect.

September 6th was an unpleasant day. In the first place we made a very early start, which, after the two previous nights' work, was rather hard on the troops. Several had been without sleep for two nights, and engaged with the

SEPTEMBER IN THE GATSRAND

enemy all day. As far as fighting went this long-range scrapping was not of course worthy of the name, but as far as discomfort and fatigue were concerned, the operations were entitled to the most dignified and resonant title in the vocabulary. The 6th was an example. In the first place there was no fighting; in the second place, there was very little marching; in the third place, there was no rest; in the fourth place, there was no food. In the absence

FUNERAL OF COMMANDANT THERON AND A BRITISH SOLDIER.
SEPTEMBER 6TH, 1900.

of definite orders the commanding officers delayed for a long time ere venturing to outspan and cook: when they did do so orders immediately arrived, scattering companies right, left, and centre, on the burning and capturing expeditions. Finally, when orders were published, they were for another night march, the object and destination of which were concealed even from officers commanding regiments. However, there was nothing for it but to make the best of an unpleasant state of affairs, to snatch a few mouthfuls of food whenever possible and a few minutes' sleep at any opportunity and once more the long column wound its way through the

2ND BATT. ROYAL DUBLIN FUSILIERS

night. It arrived on the morning of the 7th at Wolverdiend station, where there was now a considerable garrison, among them 140 of our own men, who had been there since the De Wet trek. The day was passed in shifting camp and fatigue work in the station, where there was much to do in the way of loading and unloading trains.

Captain Romer got three days' leave here to meet his father, the famous judge, who had come out as President of the Royal Commission.

At 9 p.m. the column started on another night march, the battalion supplying the rearguard. It was weary work waiting on those occasions. Tents were struck, and coats, blankets, &c., packed on the waggons an hour before the advance-guard was due to march off, after which there was nothing to do but lie down on the ground in the bitter cold, and wait till all the transport had got away. Nor did the advance-guard have very much the best of it, as they of course arrived hours before the waggons, and had their shivering turn in the early morning, at the other end of the march.

By 10 a.m. the column arrived at Klerkskraal, a small and very widely scattered village on the banks of the beautiful Mooi River, a stream of the clearest and most delicious water. Companies were sent to clear out the neighbouring farms as usual, and a good deal of information was gathered about a considerable quantity of the enemy, who had been trekking through for some time past in small groups.

A dozen fine Indian tents, the gift of Rai Bahadur Boota Singh, of Rawal Pindi, were handed over to us here for the use of the officers. Very welcome they proved, as our old ones were nearly worn out.

Sunday, September 9th, 1900, was a day that will live long in the annals of the battalion. It was given out that in view of the hard work done by the troops, the day would be treated as a day of rest, almost immediately following which order came another, detailing two companies of each

SEPTEMBER IN THE GATSRAND

corps to go out on the unpleasant foraging duties. The roster declared that 'G' and 'H' companies were next in succession, and these two companies started immediately, officers and men snatching a hasty and very scratch breakfast before starting. They were out all day, from 8 a.m. to 6 p.m., during which time they were gathering in supplies of straw, fodder, &c., together with all carts, waggons, and harness in a serviceable condition, burning such as they could not carry away with them. At about 5 p.m. a heliograph message recalled them to camp, in reaching which they had to cross a small stream with a snipe-marsh on either side: the waggons of course stuck, but the men set to with a will, impelled doubtless by a keen desire to get back to their dinners in camp, and dragged them out one by one with ropes. A dismal surprise was in store for them. For even as they came in sight of the camp, it was struck, and in place of the dinners they had so fondly anticipated, some tea alone awaited them. The officers were even worse off, for as the mess president had been employed with the two companies out foraging, no one else had thought of keeping even a cup of tea for them, and, exhausted as they were by ten hours' work without food, under a burning sun, they received the pleasing intelligence that the column was starting at once to march to Pochefstroom, a distance variously estimated at from thirty-five to thirty-eight miles.

The force marched in three parts. First, mounted men, guns, and 'A' and 'E' companies Royal Dublin Fusiliers in waggons. Then the main body of infantry, and lastly the transport with 'G' and 'H' companies Royal Dublin Fusiliers as rearguard. There was a moon for most of the way, but it only served to make the surroundings more weird. Parallel to our right ran a low range of hills, whilst on the left was the Mooi River, with a farm looming up out of the night every mile or so along the way. There was one halt of half an hour towards midnight, but the remainder of the

2ND BATT. ROYAL DUBLIN FUSILIERS

halts were merely of the usual five minutes' duration. And hard it was to resume the weary way at the end of even those brief spells of rest. Every one was so fit that the actual marching was nothing like so trying as the difficulty of keeping awake through the long, dreary hours, and one would time after time drop asleep as one walked mechanically along, only to wake in the very act of falling. Frederickstadt was reached in the small hours of the morning, and the stream

BUFFELSDOORN CAMP, GATSRAND HILLS.

crossed to its left bank. There was then a halt of about an hour to close up the transport, and very welcome it was, for we were still an ordinary day's march from our destination. Turning to our right, we brought the Gatsrands on our left, and the word went forth that the Boers were in them, a report which seemed to be confirmed a moment later as a blaze of light suddenly appeared above their summits. 'There they are!' 'That's their signal lamp!' were the comments that greeted the glory of the morning star, whether Jupiter or Venus, on that as on many a previous and subsequent occasion. On straggled the column, many of the men completely worn out,

SEPTEMBER IN THE GATSRAND

having been reluctantly compelled to avail themselves of the permission to ride on the waggons; the remainder, with grim determination to march till they dropped, trudging patiently and silently on. At last came the welcome flush of dawn; no 'envious streaks' these, but the first message from the longed-for day which ended that abominable night. When Pochefstroom finally came in sight it was still a good five miles off, and those last five miles were as bad as any part of the march. For though in some mysterious way the coming of day had dispelled to a great extent the deadly sleepiness from which most of us suffered, our aching limbs now began to make themselves manifest, and those far-off trees never seemed to get any nearer. However, by ten o'clock the last man was in, but very nearly done. It had been a remarkable march—very remarkable seeing the conditions under which some of the troops performed it.* For to do from thirty-five to thirty-eight miles, most of it by night, on an empty stomach, after a hard ten hours' work under a hot sun, in sixteen hours, is a performance of which any troops may be justly proud.

Nor was it altogether without result, for our mounted and waggon-carried troops had arrived much earlier, and, fairly taking the place by surprise, had surrounded it, killed seven, and captured some seventy or eighty prisoners, and put a good many more to ignominious and hasty flight.

We also obtained some draught beer. Beer! None of us had tasted it for months. How it went down! Yet our memory of it is sad, for the unfortunate manager of the brewery was afterwards shot by the Boers for selling it to us. The column remained at Pochefstroom till the 12th, our stay being darkened by the melancholy death of the signalling officer,

* That minor operations such as these should receive but scant recognition at the hands of historians is not to be wondered at, but neither the official nor the *Times* histories in their accounts of this surprise of Pochefstroom found space to mention the length of this march, an omission which is very greatly to be wondered at.

153

2ND BATT. ROYAL DUBLIN FUSILIERS

Lieutenant Maddox, of the Somersetshire Light Infantry, who was shot through the heart while going round his stations. On the 12th Colonel Hicks took command of a small force* which moved out to occupy some kopjes overlooking two drifts over the Mooi River. Starting at about 3 p.m., we did not reach our destination (some five miles south of Frederickstadt) till dark. Somewhat to our surprise, the hills were unoccupied, as Boers were known to be in the vicinity,

A GROUP OF BOER PRISONERS TAKEN AT THE SURPRISE OF POCHEFSTROOM.

while there had been a certain amount of distant sniping throughout the march. Putting piquets at the drifts, the infantry and guns occupied one hill, and the mounted troops another hard by. We had just turned in for the night when a sharp rifle-fire broke out all along the front, to which our sentries were not slow to respond. We immediately occupied the posts to which we had been assigned, but the firing soon died away. No one was hit by the enemy, but an unfortunate trooper in Marshall's Horse was shot by a comrade, and later on succumbed to the wound.

* Royal Dublin Fusiliers, 100 cavalry, two guns.

SEPTEMBER IN THE GATSRAND

At daybreak on the 13th, we located a Boer laager some five miles out on the plain. One of our officers had a deer-stalking telescope, with which it was possible to follow the movements of the Boers as they woke up, a most interesting spectacle. They were of course far out of range of our fifteen-pounders, but just as we were regretting our inability to get at them, General Hart's force from Pochefstroom could be seen trekking slowly in their direction from our left front.

COLOUR-SERGEANT COSSY ISSUING BEER.

We, from our elevated position, could see what the Boers could not, and to watch our comrades creeping slowly nearer, while the Boers were loitering about and stretching themselves, was a sight the opportunity to view which was seldom afforded in the course of the war. But long before the General got close enough to do any harm, the alarm went. Any one who has ever seen a pebble cast into an ants' nest can realise the proceedings of the next two minutes. Darting about in every direction, the Boers caught their horses and inspanned their transport with a celerity which fairly took our breath away, and in what seemed an incredibly short

2ND BATT. ROYAL DUBLIN FUSILIERS

space of time they were trekking away across our right front, their movements still more hastened by a few rounds from the naval guns. Moreover, they came within very long range of our fifteen-pounders, so we were enabled to return them a 'quid' for their 'quo' of the previous night, with probably about the same result to their skins, though one riderless horse could be seen careering about.

A helio message from the General instructed us to march off and join him at Frederickstadt, where we arrived that afternoon, spending the morning in the usual domiciliary visits, getting a really handsome waggon for the mess, and carefully searching a farmhouse belonging to the Bezuidenhouts.

On the 14th there was a considerable amount of firing in the neighbourhood, but nobody seemed to take much interest in it. As, however, it resulted in the loss of twelve mules and some waggons, and one gunner wounded, it is hoped that we did some damage in return.

On the 15th Colonel Hicks again took out a small force of all arms,[*] for the purpose of getting in more stores, of burning Bezuidenhout's farm (it being now clear he had murdered two telegraphists), and to hold the kopjes we were on the 13th, while the Somersetshire Light Infantry marched to join us from Pochefstroom. The country was now thoroughly infested with Boers, who made some slight effort to oppose Colonel Hicks. He very soon brushed them aside, however, and, marching his force along two parallel ranges of low hills, arrived at the place where we had bivouacked on the night of the 12th–13th. Dinners were cooked on arrival before the companies went out marauding. Whilst they were being prepared a cartridge went off in one of the fires, and severely wounded one of the cooks, the bullet penetrating his chest. This poor fellow was later on sent into hospital at Krugersdorp, and, as the wound

[*] Royal Dublin Fusiliers, two guns, twenty-five Yeomanry.

SEPTEMBER IN THE GATSRAND

never improved, was eventually invalided home. But the line was blown up just in front of his train, and he was brought back to hospital. He soon began to recover, and one day went wandering about without his hat, got sunstroke, and died, one piece of bad luck on the top of another, and a melancholy example of how 'when sorrows come, they come not single spies, but in battalions.'

A convoy under Captain H. W. Higginson, arrived at Frederickstadt at this time, after having been considerably pestered by some Boers who had shelled him with a ninepounder Krupp, and severely wounded one of our men. Luckily, the General had sent out a small force with two guns to meet this convoy, or it might have had a very much worse time.

Next day Bezuidenhout's farm was duly burnt, and at 3 p.m. the force started to march back to Frederickstadt, the Somersetshire Light Infantry (wing) under Major Williams, with eighty prisoners, a large number of refugees and waggons, starting an hour earlier, having of course further to go. The march was not interfered with, and the force reached its old quarters once more before dark.

The dreary monotony of these days and nights of trekking and foraging suffered a variation on the 17th. In the morning 'A' company, under Major Rutherford, took over the eighty odd prisoners from Pochefstroom, and marched off with them to Wolverdiend. In the afternoon a shell suddenly burst in the middle of the camp. The cheek of these foes of ours. The first arrival was shortly followed by several more in quick succession, some of which landed in camp, and some of which went over our heads. We turned out, lowered the tents, and then lay down in extended order, trying to locate the position of the hostile gun. At last some one saw the flash, after which our naval gun and fifteen-pounders picked up the range with admirable celerity, immediately silencing the opposition. At a range of 3600 yards, the second shot from the naval gun had burst within

2ND BATT. ROYAL DUBLIN FUSILIERS

four feet of the marks of the Krupp nine-pounder which had been shelling us. At the time the enemy opened fire a regimental court-martial for the trial of twenty-one prisoners had just assembled, under the presidency of Captain Shewan. On the arrival of the shells, the court, escort, witnesses and prisoners dissolved themselves with one accord, and were not afterwards reassembled.

> 'In such a time as this it is not meet
> That every nice offence should bear his comment.'
> *Julius Cæsar.*

The sun was in the enemy's eyes, and the village of Frederickstadt almost immediately behind our camp, which may account in some measure for the indifference of their fire, as we must have offered a magnificent target to them. As it was, our only losses were four horses, not a man being hit. But we were fairly caught napping.

The General ordered the regiment to take possession of the hill, which was done without any further fighting, two companies being left on outpost duty on its summit.

On the 18th some of the usual desultory sniping commenced on the other side of the camp, but a demonstration by the inlying piquet ('G' company, 2nd Royal Dublin Fusiliers) was sufficient to put a stop to it.

Major Bird arrived back from Maritzburg. Next day the trek commenced once more. A small force* was left behind under command of Major Bird to hold the hills from which we had been shelled, and to take care of most of the transport. The remainder of the column marched at 11 p.m. on Ventersdorp, where some Boers were reported. After marching all night and covering some twelve miles, the enemy opened fire in front and on both flanks. Our guns came into action, and a sort of running fight was maintained. Eventually the

* Half-battalion Royal Dublin Fusiliers, one company Somerset Light Infantry, two guns 28th Battery Royal Field Artillery, and twenty Marshall's Horse.

SEPTEMBER IN THE GATSRAND

enemy took up a more definite position, when General Hart ordered Colonel Hicks, with two companies of the regiment, two guns and a pompom, to advance to a small ridge on one flank, while he with the remainder of the force marched round the enemy's rear. This resulted in the evacuation of their position, when Colonel Hicks's small party got an opportunity to deliver an effective fire on them.

Next day sniping at the bivouac began at dawn, but the troops were allowed a meal before resuming their march. Colonel Hicks was again detailed to take a kopje from which a considerable but ineffectual fire was coming. Moving steadily on, with his 200 men in widely-extended order, he brought a maxim into action, which had the effect of clearing the hill, but the long-range fighting went on without a break till the evening.

Having more or less broken up the Boers in this direction, orders were issued for the return march to Frederickstadt. An early start was made, and at 10 a.m. a halt and outspan ordered. At mid-day the officers commanding units were sent for, when the General informed them that a large force of Boers, under Steyn and De Wet, with women and children, 3000 strong, was reported in the neighbourhood of Klerksdorp. Rumour further said that they were so bewildered by our apparently aimless midnight movements that they neither knew where to go nor what to do. The General added that it was his intention to march again in the afternoon in their direction, to have another outspan at dusk, and then to march all night and surprise them next morning. The commanding officers looked at one another in blank amazement, for they knew better than the General could the effect these constant nights without sleep and days of fighting without food were having on their men, but there was nothing for it, and the General called upon his troops for one more supreme effort. At the same time he heliographed to Major Bird to march from Frederickstadt and join him *en route*, which was done.

2ND BATT. ROYAL DUBLIN FUSILIERS

Major Bird's force had not been left altogether unmolested during this time. The company of Somersetshire Light Infantry were holding a small knoll in prolongation of his left, and some 2000 yards off. Against them the Boers brought up their Krupp gun which they had used against us two or three days before. The range was considerable, but they managed to reach their target; yet, though they fired twenty-three shells into the camp of this company, the only damage they did was to knock the top off a box of eggs *without breaking a single egg*. They also managed to pitch a shell or two amongst the transport. Our fifteen-pounders endeavoured to reply, but, in spite of digging deep holes for the trails, were unable to reach the ridge from which the Boers were firing.

Major Bird's force having joined hands with the main column shortly after dark, the long march was resumed at 10 p.m. It was a pitch-dark night, and the difficulty of keeping in touch, and the still greater difficulty of keeping the transport in touch, wore out tempers as well as sinews. On one occasion the regiment as nearly as possible got left. We were following the first-line transport of the corps immediately in front of us, and keeping close up to it, but the Colonel got anxious, and, after several times asking the adjutant if he was certain we were in touch, told him to ride on and see. He came back in a few minutes to say that there was nothing to be seen ahead. The carts in front had lost touch, and they were all we had to guide us. The adjutant at once cantered on, and had the good fortune to shortly pick up the tail of the column, when everything was soon all right again. The march continued the whole night, dawn being heralded by the corncrake-like note of the pom-pom, which led us to hope we had effected our object. But once again it was not to be, for the Boer laager had moved off, and from the top of a small hill could be seen trekking away about 7000 yards distant. Men and horses had been at it since 6 a.m. the day before, and any further pursuit was out

SEPTEMBER IN THE GATSRAND

of the question. Indeed, an extra two or three miles that had to be done to reach a better camping-ground almost proved the last straw. The right half-battalion had marched thirty-three miles in the twenty-four hours, and only slept on one night out of the last three, while the left half-battalion had done twenty-six miles in eighteen hours.

Our enemy had slipped away once more at the critical moment, but our spirits were raised all the same by the arrival of a dispatch, which we understood called us back to Krugersdorp and hinted that the war was over.

After a day's rest at this rather pleasant camp, the force moved into Pochefstroom (eighteen miles), and marched past the General in the Market Square on the 25th, remaining there until the 27th. It had been on the move for nearly a month with very little rest, during which time men and horses had undoubtedly got very wiry and fit. But beyond collecting a certain amount of stores, cattle, and forage, it is doubtful whether all the forced marches and strenuous exertions had been of much benefit, or whether they served to bring hostilities much nearer to a conclusion. Although the enemy, in more or less force, had been viewed practically every day, it had always been impossible to bring him to close quarters, and the policy of wearing out infantrymen's hearts, tempers, constitutions, and boots in abortive pursuits of mounted enemies was, and in the light of all that we now know still is, open to question, for a reference to the *Times* history of the war shows that all our wanderings and meanderings are summed up in very few sentences, the most pregnant of which is to the effect that word had gone out to the Boer Commandoes not to interfere with us.

On the 27th the column started on its march back to Krugersdorp, and did the distance (sixty-two miles) in four easy stages. It marched by the road south of the Gatsrand Hills, with the Losberg on its right, and with the exception of one day (29th) without molestation from the enemy. On that

2ND BATT. ROYAL DUBLIN FUSILIERS

occasion they made a somewhat determined attack on the rearguard, attempting to cut off some waggons, and the last few miles of the march took the shape of a running fight. The General had ridden on ahead with the cavalry to our next camp, so Colonel Hicks sent back a couple of guns to the rearguard, who shook off the terrier-like attentions of the enemy without very much trouble; but they had delayed the march a good deal, and it was not till late in the evening that every one got in, and heard that the war really was over at last. An officer in the regiment who was considerably exhausted sank on to his valise, too tired to care for anything. His servant said to him, 'We'll be in Krugersdorp to-morrow, sorr, and I'll be able to get yiz some claning matherials,' to which his weary master replied, 'I don't care a damn whether I'm clean or whether I'm dirty.' In answer his man made the following cryptic remark: ' 'Tis no use talking like that, sorr. Lord Roberts says the war is over, and we'll begin soldiering now.'

The following summary of the work done was published for information:—

'SUMMARY OF WORK OF POCHEFSTROOM COLUMN.

' The Pochefstroom column started from Krugersdorp on the 29th August, and returned on 30th September. The task of the column is to assist in stamping out the resistance of the remaining scattered forces of the enemy by hunting them, and depriving them of their supplies of food and transport, with a view to bringing the war to an end. In the first cruise of 33 days the column has marched 310 miles—the length of England from Portsmouth to Scotland—and was in action with the enemy on 29 days, putting them to flight on each occasion. The column's casualties were only 3 killed, 24 wounded, and 3 missing. The Boers lost considerably according to accounts of Kaffirs present; we found some of their dead, including General Theron. In prisoners

SEPTEMBER IN THE GATSRAND

of war and important arrests, the column took 96 of the enemy. Loyal inhabitants, numbering 316 men, women, and children, were rescued from Pochefstroom, and safely conveyed to Wolverdiend. General Liebenburg ordered General Douthwaite to attack this convoy, but Douthwaite thought it dangerous, and was arrested by Liebenburg for suggesting that he, Liebenburg, " had better do it himself." The convoy was not attacked. The column took from the enemy the

'COME TO THE COOK-HOUSE DOOR, BOYS!'

following cattle: 2720 sheep and 3281 goats; 1066 sacks of mealies, 104 sacks of meal, 2 waggon-loads of mealie cobs, 12 sacks of wheat, 847 loaves of bread, 162 sacks of potatoes, 68 sacks of oats, 33 sacks of bran, 36,000 bundles of oat-hay, 299 bales of chaff, 400 bundles of manna-hay, 90 horses, 28 ponies, 11 mules, 36 waggons, 31 carts, and destroyed 45 waggons and carts that could not be taken away.

'(Signed)   A. HART (Captain),
'*C.S.O. Pochefstroom Column.*

'*Krugersdorp, 2nd October,* 1900.'

'We looked for peace, but no good came.'—*Jer.* viii. 15.

CHAPTER V.

FREDERICKSTADT—KLIP RIVER—THE LOSBERG.

'Have I not heard great ordnance in the field,
And Heaven's artillery thunder in the skies?'
Taming of the Shrew.

OUR camp, on this our third visit to Krugersdorp, was on the south-west side of the town. The 6th Brigade (General Barton's) was also in Krugersdorp, and had been for some time, so it was with somewhat mixed feelings that we heard we were to set out on the trek once more almost immediately. However, in the end the other brigade went out, with what result will presently appear. Krugersdorp was now surrounded by a large circle of forts and fortified houses. The perimeter of these defences was very large, not far short of twelve miles, but the positions themselves were well selected from a tactical point of view. As they were continually being strengthened, improved, and added to, in a few months' time it would have been very difficult for the Boers to have taken the place, provided a sufficient garrison remained in it.' But this strength, or sometimes weakness, was a constantly varying one—about the middle of December sinking as low as 300—which of course was risking a good deal. Moreover, it was not until some time later, when the Officer Commanding Town Guards devised an inner series of defences, that the town could be said to be in any way safe from a midnight raid; and it was this, more than even the capture of the place, which seemed so likely to occur, when the banks and stores could have been cleared out in a few minutes, and the raiding party gone before any force could have been assembled to interfere with it. The town

FREDERICKSTADT

was, of course, full of spies and friendly enemies, ever on the look-out for any chance of getting a bit of their own back—and who could blame them?—but on the whole remained very quiet and well-behaved throughout the occupation.

The regiment's headquarters were destined to remain here for the rest of the campaign, with the exception of the three treks which form the subject of this chapter, and Krugersdorp will ever be identified with our name in South Africa in consequence. As we got to know its inhabitants better, and as they got to appreciate our men better, a kindlier feeling was generated on both sides, with which improved state of affairs the cricket and football we played with them had not a little to do.

General Barton moved off on October 5th, with much the same commission that General Hart had carried, and immediately came into contact with the enemy, the noise of the fight sounding loud in our ears, while from Captain Nelson's piquet the bursting shells and even some of the Boers could be plainly seen. The day before a flag of truce had come in with a letter, saying that one of our men was lying wounded in a farmhouse a little way outside the outposts; a waggon was sent out and brought him in, when he proved to be one of our mounted infantry, who had been wounded in Colonel Rochfort's dashing attack on a Boer laager near Pretoria.* The Boers had looked after him as well as they could, and dressed his wounds according to their homely lights, and altogether played the game so far as he was concerned.

Next day still brought the sound of General Barton's artillery, and the right half-battalion under Major Bird went out as escort to two waggon-loads of ammunition for

* The writer was recently dining with Colonel—now Major-General—Rochfort, when that officer particularly asked him to mention how splendidly the party of Dublin Fusiliers under his command had behaved on this occasion, and his admiration of their soldierly conduct at all times while serving under him.

2ND BATT. ROYAL DUBLIN FUSILIERS

him. The General sent half-way to meet him, and our men got back all right about 6 p.m.

With the advent of summer the thunderstorms increased in frequency and severity, and it was no joke to have to suddenly jump up and hang on to the pole of one's tent to prevent it being blown away, with the uncomfortable knowledge that lightning has a partiality for running down tent-poles. We had one really bad experience in this way, to be narrated later, but nothing to touch the blizzard that struck the camp of the 5th Battalion Royal Dublin Fusiliers near Mafeking, when sheets of corrugated iron flew about like packs of gigantic cards, and Colonel Gernon and Captain Baker, the Quartermaster, together with many others, sustained very serious injuries. Still, our share was bad enough, and quite spoiled the summer for a good many of us. The mornings would break clear, cloudless, and invigorating; but about 3 p.m. on about three days of the week, a bunch of cotton-wool clouds would appear from the south. As these rose higher and higher, they swelled into enormous piles of grand, rolling cloud-masses, like stupendous snow-clad mountains, whose bases grew black and ever blacker, until they would suddenly be riven by blinding flashes of flickering ribbons of lightning, and the air torn and rent by reverberating booms of awe-inspiring thunder.

Second Lieutenant Tredennick joined at this time. Second Lieutenant R. F. B. Knox should have arrived with him, but had to remain behind in Johannesburg, as he was seedy. The train they were in had been attacked by Boers near Heidelberg.

Rumour now began to be busy with General Barton's force, and on the 22nd an order came for General Hart to join him. We had just packed up, when an order came countermanding the move.

Next day, however, another order came to the same

FREDERICKSTADT

effect, but detailing Colonel Hicks to command the column. Though small in point of numbers,* it would have been hard to have picked a better one in point of quality. A finer body of horsemen, or one more adapted to the work in hand, than Strathcona's Horse it would be impossible to conceive. Without making any invidious comparisons, it is only just to say that these Canadian troops appeared to us to have no superiors, while the truly magnificent way in which they literally brushed away the opposition, on the morning we joined hands with General Barton, was a sight to be remembered.

The regiment was entrained, but did not get off till about 5 p.m., our departure being marked by a peal of thunder which made even those who declared themselves fond of such phenomena nearly jump through the roof of the guard's van. We only got as far as Bank Station, as the line was reported infested with the enemy, and it was important that we should not be blown up. Indeed, we had scarcely arrived there, when a loud explosion—fortunately behind us—proved the activity of our watchful foes. After making teas we bivouacked in the train.

The regiment reached Wolverdiend next day, in the course of which the remainder of the force assembled, preparations being made for an early start next morning.

Fearing that information would get through, the Colonel gave orders that the column would start at 6 a.m., but at the same time issued confidential orders to officers commanding units that he really intended to start at 3.30 a.m. Unfortunately, however, it rained so hard all night that it was impossible to start until 5 a.m. Colonel Hicks sent Strathcona's Horse out to the front and left flank, while Brabant's Horse took the right flank and front. The Essex Regiment supplied the advance-guard, while one company

* 600 Strathcona's Horse, 160 Brabant's Horse, 2 Elswick guns, 1 pompom, Essex Regiment, ½-battalion Royal Dublin Fusiliers.

2ND BATT. ROYAL DUBLIN FUSILIERS

of the Dublin Fusiliers acted as rearguard and escort to the waggons. In this order the force approached a low line of bush-covered hills, which separated them from General Barton. These hills were occupied by two or three hundred Boers, who had been detailed to check our advance. On arrival within rifle-range of the hills, Strathcona's Horse made a dash right at them, the effect of which was so imposing that the enemy immediately resigned all idea of resistance, and bolted as hard as they could go. With this range of kopjes in our possession, the rest was plain sailing, and we marched on to the hill on which the larger part of General Barton's force was posted. The column had barely arrived when a fierce rifle-fire broke out in front. It was impossible to see what was going on, as the hillside was covered with thick mimosa bush, but that a fierce fight was raging in our close proximity was very evident from the prolonged and heavy fire, in which the pompoms soon began to take part, while the naval gun and smaller field-pieces joined in. Colonel Hicks, accompanied by an officer of the Dublin Fusiliers, then climbed some little way up the hill in the direction of the 4·7, and there a sight met their eyes which was seldom seen in this war. The plain at their feet, stretching from the railway west to the village of Frederickstadt, was covered with flying Boers—Boers flying on their feet, a most unusual occurrence with them. As they fled across the open veld in full view, they were pursued by every variety of missile. In one spot, seven Boers were running side by side. The officer with Colonel Hicks had just drawn his attention to them, when a shell from the naval gun burst in the air behind them, and a second later tore up the ground all round. Five fell at once; the other two staggered on a few paces and then fell also, all seven being afterwards found stone-dead. It was all over in a very short time, and then the stretcher-bearers began to come in with their patient, gruesome burdens, and

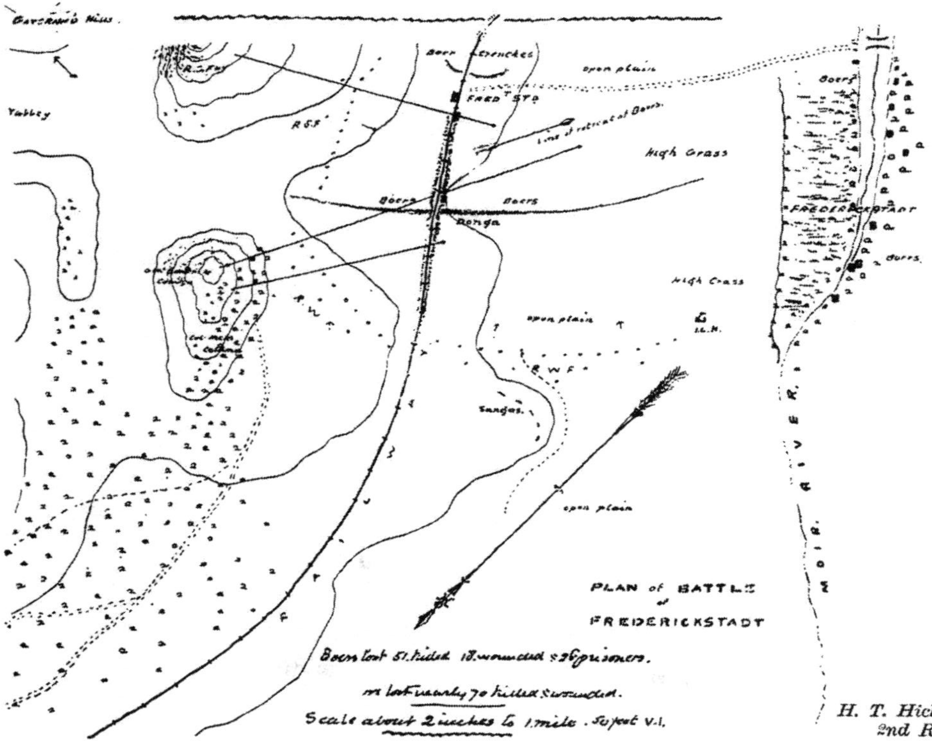

H. T. Hicks, Lt.-Col.
2nd Roy. Dub. Fus.

FREDERICKSTADT

the prisoners arrived under escort, to be handed over to the Royal Dublin Fusiliers for safe custody.

Then we heard the story of the fight. General Barton's position, which he had occupied for some days, extended along a line of low hills, the two main features of which were divided by a valley running back at right angles to the railway into the Gatsrand, the general line of the position being parallel with the railway. The station was held and used as a hospital, while the hill on which General Barton's camp was situated extended down to the railway, and was the nearest point to the river. For some days the Boers, under De Wet, had been gathering round this position, and the force had been subjected to a constant shell-fire and the intermittent attentions of a particularly aggressive and unlocatable pompom. Under the railway, about midway between General Barton's two main positions, ran a small, dry donga. Into this underfeature De Wet had ordered about 200 men on the night of the 24th-25th. The first indication of their presence was a somewhat foolish attempt made by them to capture some mules. Unaware of their numbers—and truly the situation was such that any one could be pardoned for not grasping it at once—a company or part of a company was sent forward to dislodge them and clear up matters. The Boers allowed them to approach quite close, and then annihilated them. It was now very evident that the donga was held in force, and, as the General was aware by this time of the arrival of Colonel Hicks' column, he launched a vigorous attack. This was the heavy firing we heard on our arrival. After offering a slight resistance, some of the enemy surrendered, the remainder flying on foot as already stated to their horses, which they had left amongst the trees near the river. It is not often the Boer leaves his horse thus, and it offered strong presumptive evidence of their confidence in their ability to rush the position, in accordance with De Wet's intention.

The battalion bivouacked on the hill, and threw out out-

2ND BATT. ROYAL DUBLIN FUSILIERS

posts. To them was also assigned next morning the intensely unpleasant duty of shooting three prisoners who had been tried and found guilty of showing the white flag and afterwards resuming their fire. 'G' company, being the nearest piquet to the place selected for the execution, was detailed to carry it out. The casualties on our side had been about forty-one killed and wounded, while twenty-four Boers were killed, sixteen wounded, and twenty-six taken prisoner.

SERGEANT FRENCH AND THE OFFICERS' MESS, NACHTMAAL.

After remaining at Frederickstadt on the 26th, orders came for our return to Krugersdorp on the 27th. We had an uneventful march to Wolverdiend, and there entrained, reaching our destination late in the evening. The officers, as usual, rode in the guard's van, and, as these trains used to bump and jolt in the most unpleasant manner, we made ourselves as comfortable as we could in a sort of 'zariba' composed of our valises and a number of large packages sewn up in sackcloth. Our feelings when we later on discovered that these packages were corpses may be left to the imagination.

We returned to our last camp, and set to work to make it

KLIP RIVER

more comfortable, running up wood and corrugated-iron shelters for stores, officers' mess, &c. We were also kept perpetually busy in building more forts and improving those already in existence. Captain Romer gave his name to a work which he erected and on which he expended much time, pains, and ingenuity. Posts and piquets also had to be held on all the principal roads into the town. Captain Nelson, R.M.L.I., in command of one of these, one afternoon shouted to two men who were driving through his posts to stop. Unfortunately for them, they paid no attention and drove on, so he seized a rifle and fired, killing one of the occupants stone-dead, an exemplary lesson to the inhabitants to make them understand that outposts were not posted for amusement.

General Clements' column was now stationed at Krugersdorp, and we saw something of Captain MacBean, Royal Dublin Fusiliers, his Brigade-Major. Alas! poor MacBean; he was killed a few days later, standing close beside his General, at the battle of Nooitgedacht. A universal favourite, and one of the most popular officers in the regiment, he was also probably the ablest. Passing brilliantly into and through the Staff College, he went on to the Egyptian Army, taking part in all the principal actions up to and including the battle of Omdurman, receiving a D.S.O. in recognition of his services. In the present campaign he had commenced the war as a Brigade-Major, later on serving on General Hunter's staff, and now transferred to General Clements', who had the highest opinion of his capabilities. Amongst many other accomplishments he was one of the best bridge-players in the service. There is little doubt that if he had been spared he would have risen to the highest rank. He was gazetted to a Brevet-Majority after his death.

On November 15th Lord Roberts inspected the regiment, and congratulated them on the work they had done, afterwards speaking to Major English and telling him how highly he had thought of the Zuikerbosch affair. It is these little

2ND BATT. ROYAL DUBLIN FUSILIERS

acts of kindness and remembrance that make all the difference, and their effect is much more far-reaching than those who confer them often imagine. One only does one's duty, of course, but yet one is only human, and it is very pleasant to feel that that duty has been appreciated.

Captain Lowndes, the adjutant, who had been home after his severe wound at Talana, now rejoined the regiment, and took over the adjutancy from Captain Fetherstonhaugh. That officer had filled the post with marked zeal and ability for over twelve months, and was the only officer who was present with the Headquarters of the battalion from the start of the war without being wounded.

On November 16th the regiment formed part of a column,[*] ordered to march off and scour the veld, though our destination was, as usual, shrouded in mystery. The night of the 15th–16th however, precluded any possibility of carrying out the intended early start, as the rain descended in torrents, deluging kits and country. At about 2 p.m., however, a start was effected, and all went well till a small drift was reached, when the 'cow-gun,' which had taken the place of our old and tried friend, the Naval gun, stuck hopelessly. Colonel Hicks fell out 120 men and put them on to the dragropes. Their first pull was too much for the rope, which broke, with the inevitable result that the whole 120 were deposited on the veld, on the broad of their backs. Another and a stouter rope was produced, which proved itself equal to the strain, and with a long pull, a strong pull, and a pull all together, the heavy weapon was dragged on to *terra-firma*, and the march resumed, a halt being made for the night about eight or nine miles out, and almost on the historic site of Doornkop.

The trek was resumed next morning under more favourable auspices, but these soon proved a delusion and a snare. The column was making for a pass in the Gatsrand, not far from

[*] South Wales Borderers, Royal Dublin Fusiliers, 28th Battery, R.F.A., 4.7 inch gun, mounted details.

KLIP RIVER

the waterworks, known to be in the enemy's occupation, when at about 11 o'clock a violent thunderstorm broke directly overhead. Marching along, soaked to the skin, with a lightning-conductor in the shape of a rifle over one's shoulder, was not conducive to steady nerves, but so dense was the rain that it had, at all events, one beneficial effect, for the Boers holding the pass left their positions and took shelter in some farmhouses, with the result that they were very nearly

4·7 CROSSING A DRIFT, ASSISTED BY THE DUBLIN FUSILIERS.

captured by our cavalry, who, indeed, succeeded in taking possession of the pass without opposition, the enemy, taken completely by surprise, having only just time to jump on their horses and gallop off. Getting the 'cow-gun' over the pass, however, was no easy matter, but it was eventually accomplished, and after a march of about sixteen miles, the force halted for the night in rather a pretty camp, on a farm known as Hartebeestfontein.

The column marched to Klip River, about seventeen miles, next day, arriving there about 5 p.m. The rearguard was sniped at the whole way by our friends of the day before, but without effecting much damage. A cavalry brigade under Brigadier-General Gordon was here on our arrival, and an exchange of troops took place, we receiving some Greys and Carabineers in exchange for half a battalion of South Wales Borderers.

A halt was now made for a day, most of us taking the opportunity to get a bathe in the river.

Leaving Klip River on the morning of the 20th, we marched back in the direction whence we had come two days before, and were soon engaged with the enemy's snipers, of whom we captured one; but they had the best of the argument, as they killed two of our column. One of these poor fellows had very bad luck: he had received a letter at Klip River only the day before, telling him he had come into a sum of money, sufficient to enable him to retire and spend the remainder of his days in peace and quiet.

Nor was the day to prove uneventful for the rest of us. About 1 p.m. it began to cloud over, and presently to rain; this soon turned into hail, of the variety which one is accustomed to at home. This was at first refreshing, and one would pick up the cool hailstones—they were about as big as peas—and eat them, and the rattle they made on the helmets was quite musical. When they grew to the size of gooseberries, and began to sting, they provided less amusement, shoulders being shrugged up and necks arched to obtain as much protection as possible. The unfortunate dogs, of which a variety invariably turned up with every column, howled with pain, and the cattle and horses grew very restive. But soon the stones, driven by a gale of wind, increased to the size of cherries and strawberries, with occasional jagged lumps of ice an inch in diameter. As there seemed no particular reason why they should not run through the whole gamut of the orchard, and rival plums, peaches, and melons, and as there was no earthly chance of obtaining a vestige of shelter of any kind, men began to wonder what was going to happen

KLIP RIVER

next, with an occasional sharper-than-usual belt between the shoulders or on the boot to quicken their fancy. It was only with the greatest difficulty that the horses were controlled, but the stones providentially grew no larger, though the storm continued. The entire country-side was a rolling mass of ice nearly over the tops of boots. Runnels and rivulets became roaring torrents, roads became rivers. When the storm eventually subsided the transport of course could not go another yard, and camp was pitched where we were. The carpet of hailstones in the tents slowly melted into mud, and we made ourselves as comfortable as possible under the circumstances. Several kids and lambs we had with us were killed by the stones. Not one of us had ever been out in such a storm before, but, as those who had not been on 'the Natal side' confidently predicted, those who had been declared that this was mere child's play to the hailstones they had seen there.

What became of the Boers we never knew: up to the commencement of the storm we had been merrily sniping away at each other at extreme ranges, but during and after it they entirely disappeared, so entirely that even next day we never got a sign of them, and concluded they had all been drowned.

There was, however, nothing to complain of on this score the day after, as sniping was carried on all the time. Though this form of fighting resulted in few casualties, it was destructive to peace and comfort and enjoyment of the scenery. It was interesting to notice what officers recognised when we arrived at places we had visited on previous treks, and instructive to note that it was almost always those who were addicted to sport and field-pursuits who were the first to pick up their bearings and the lie of the land. The force eventually encamped at the foot of the hill on which 'G' company had spent such a cold and miserable night when waiting for the transport to pass, two months before.

2ND BATT. ROYAL DUBLIN FUSILIERS

On the 23rd, the march took us up again through Orange Grove and on past Leeuwport Nek, moving along the south side of the main ridge of the Gatsrand, with three companies making the best of their way along their jagged peaks. Two of Roberts' Horse were hit on this march, one being killed.

The column reached Buffelsdoorn Pass on the 24th, after a spirited rearguard action, the brunt of which fell on the South Wales Borderers, who had several men and one officer hit. We remained in this pass for some days, sending out small expeditions among the adjacent hills, and erecting fortifications to cover the defile. It was in its way an important place, being within a few miles of Wolverdiend Station, and providing an excellent door through the rocky, serrated peaks of the Gatsrand into the broad plain which lay between them and the Vaal. Our camp was situated just on the north side of the pass, in a picturesque place, with easy access to the railway, and from a tactical point of view an excellent position.

Next day a convoy with nearly ten thousand cattle, sheep, &c., was dispatched to Wolverdiend, without seeing any signs of the enemy.

The night of the 25th–26th could scarcely have been worse; heavy rain, howling wind, and vivid and frequent lightning with its sonorous accompaniment, put sleep out of the question; indeed, at one period it became necessary to get up and hold on to the tents to prevent them being blown away. With the advent of dawn the forces of nature gave us a rest, our friends the enemy immediately filling their place. They opened fire from some kopjes to the east of the camp, and endeavoured to round up some of our cattle. The South Wales Borderers undertook to dislodge them, and speedily did so, the 'Cow-gun' joining in at long range as soon as the Boers evacuated their positions. Having disposed of man for the time being, Nature again rolled up in dense masses of magnificent clouds to the attack. The storm which followed was also one to be remembered; the lightning could be seen striking the ground in the close vicinity of the camp, and though no one was hit, we heard that two men of the regiment at Kaalfontein were not so fortunate, one poor fellow being killed and the other severely wounded. 'C' company, 2nd Royal Dublin Fusiliers, was on piquet through both these night and day storms, and had, as may be imagined, an unenviable experience.

On the 27th, General Hart rode down to Wolverdiend to see Sir John French. While he was away, word arrived that a party of Roberts' Horse who were out scouting had been held up. Colonel Wilson—the senior officer in camp—detailed 100 Carabineers to go to their assistance, but they found the opposition still too great, so two companies of the regiment were sent out to reinforce them, while the guns opened fire from the summits of the hills. In the middle of the operations a thunderstorm joined in to swell the general din, under cover of which the Boers crept in round three sides of the force. There was never any question of their succeeding in cutting it off, but the boldness of their tactics was characteristic of the phase the war had now begun to assume. There was a good deal of rifle-fire on both sides, and the 28th Battery R.F.A., under its new commander, who had replaced our esteemed friend, Major Stokes, D.S.O., promoted to R.H.A., fired nearly one hundred rounds. What casualties the enemy suffered was not ascertained, but on our side there was only one, a man in Roberts' Horse being badly hit. Those of us who were not engaged sat among the rocks on the tops of the hills, whence a fine panoramic view of the skirmish was obtainable by the aid of telescopes and binoculars.

The 28th and 29th passed uneventfully, Captain Romer occupying the time in again demonstrating his architectural capabilities in the erection of a fort near the pass.

2ND BATT. ROYAL DUBLIN FUSILIERS

On the 30th a reconnaissance in force was made along the Gatsrand in a westerly direction, the left half-battalion of the Royal Dublin Fusiliers acting as the infantry of the force. Moving along the summits of the hills in four lines of widely extended companies, they marched to within sight of Frederickstadt before they returned. Imagine exaggerated Pyramids of Cheops; imagine each block of stone carved by stress of weather into a thousand needle-

BOY FITZPATRICK WAITING AT LUNCH.

points and ankle-twisting crevices; plant a dense growth of mimosa and other thorny scrub in every cranny and interstice. Take a dozen such pyramids, and do your morning constitutional over them, after the scrappiest of breakfasts at 5 a.m., and you will find twelve or fourteen miles quite as much as you care about. But the march was not devoid of interest, though we met with no Boers. Small buck, hares, and partridges were there in sufficient number to afford a good day's sport under other circumstances, while a profusion of various kinds of flowers afforded satisfaction to the eye, in strong contrast to the bare and barkless trunks

THE LOSBERG

of trees riven by the frequent storms that devastate these hills. In one place a most gruesome sight was met with. Under a small tree beside a tiny stream stood a three-legged cooking-pot, and round it lay three skeletons, with a scattering of shrapnel bullets to silently tell the story of the tragedy. Beside one body lay a Rifleman's haversack, an eloquent if speechless travesty on the fortunes of war, for undoubtedly they were the remains of Boers, over whose head a chance shrapnel must have burst months before.

A similar reconnaissance, but in the opposite direction, was made next day, resulting in one man being wounded. Convoys were also passing to and fro, and on the 2nd, Captain Fetherstonhaugh took over the duties of provost-marshal, temporarily, from Captain Thompson, of the Somersetshire Light Infantry, who had hurt his knee. Rumours of an early move also began to circulate, with the Losberg, the grim and solitary hill rising out of the plain to the south of the Gatsrand, as our probable destination. For some time past the Boers had used it as a sort of headquarters and rallying-place for their frequent raiding parties. Columns were now converging on it from all points of the compass, but as they could be plainly seen from its summit, the high hopes entertained in some quarters of rounding up a large number of the enemy were not shared by everybody.

Yet the start at 9 p.m. on the 3rd was sufficiently impressive. The officers were assembled, and had their several duties clearly pointed out to them, one peak of the hill being assigned to the South Wales Borderers and the other to the Dublin Fusiliers. To 'A' company of the latter regiment, under Major English, was given the honour of leading the attack, which was to be made at dawn next morning. Silently and with all due precautions the column slowly wound its way down the pass, like some gigantic boa-constrictor, and out on to the plain below. Whenever a farm

2ND BATT. ROYAL DUBLIN FUSILIERS

was reached it was entered, and steps taken to prevent lights being shown or signals flashed: three Boers, booted and spurred, being taken in one. It was a perfect night for marching, all Nature hushed in deep repose save the loud-mouthed bull-frog; the moon set an hour before dawn, reminding one of Whyte-Melville's line:

> 'The darkest hour of all the night is that which brings the day.'

But dark as it was our objective could be seen ominously looming up—a lamp-black mass against the velvet softness of starlit sky. The movement had been admirably timed, and as day broke the two regiments advanced to the attack, the South Wales Borderers on the right, the Dublins on the left, while the artillery opened fire against the hillside between the two summits. But that was all. Not a shot was fired in return. Not a Boer was even seen. Nothing. Except, indeed, large quantities of most delicious and most acceptable oranges, after eating which the tired troops lay in the rain, which commenced to pour down, and slept peacefully till the transport came up.

Before we started next morning, a huge herd of blesbok suddenly appeared on the scene, wildly galloping about in every direction, being continually brought up by the barbed wire fences of the farms. A good many were shot, but it was cruel to kill them, or try to, with hard bullets, and many and many a beast must have got away badly wounded, whilst the indiscriminate manner in which the sportsmen fired in all directions was a source of danger, not only to themselves and the buck, but to the camp as well. One fine old fellow, with a good head, charged right through the camp, altogether eluding one regiment, in spite of every variety of missile, from cooking-pots to helmets, to finally fall a victim in another regiment's lines to a tent-pole. After which interlude the force marched to Modderfontein.

THE LOSBERG

Next day a helio from Bank directed the column to make its way to that station, a party of the South Wales Borderers being left behind to watch the pass at Modderfontein, where they were to have a rough experience later on. The remainder of the force moved to Bank on the 7th, and marched again the same night for Krugersdorp, making a total distance of thirty-three miles in the twenty-four hours, a good wind-up to the three weeks' trek. An enormous number of cattle and sheep were brought in, but it was the end of the Pochefstroom column, which was now finally broken up into a number of small posts.

The regiment camped once more on the same site it had last occupied.

'THE LATEST SHAVE.'
CAPTAIN G. S. HIGGINSON (MOUNTED) AND MAJOR BIRD.

CHAPTER VI.

BURIED TREASURE—THE EASTERN TRANSVAAL—THE KRUGERSDORP DEFENCES.

'They are wet with the showers of the mountains, and embrace the rock for want of a shelter.'—*Job*, xxiv. 8.

BY this time we had begun to regard Krugersdorp as our base, and to look upon our returns to it as more or less getting home. But on this occasion there was to be no rest of any length. From the plum-bloom blue of the far Magaliesberg, General Clements' heliograph was twinkling and blinking for the remainder of his force and more mounted men. In addition to this Colonel Hicks took out a column. These and other deductions left Krugersdorp with a garrison of 300 men to man a perimeter of some ten or twelve miles, or, roughly speaking, just over fifty yards for each rifle. 'C' company, under Captain Pomeroy, W.I.R. (attached), and Lieutenant Molony, occupied Fort Craig; 'D' company, under Captain Clarke, R.M.L.I. (attached), and Lieutenant Marsh, held Fort Kilmarnock; and 'G' company, under its Captain and Lieutenant Smith, took over Fort Harlech. Major Rutherford took over this fort next day, as the captain of 'G' company had been appointed commander of the town guards and piquets and interior defences. Colonel Hicks had been ordered to Johannesburg to see General French, who informed him that he was to take command of a mixed force * and march to the Losberg, there to dig up a large sum of gold, reputed to amount to nearly 100,000*l.*; after which he was to proceed south to the Vaal, and hold the drifts between Vereeniging and Rensburg.

* 400 Royal Dublin Fusiliers, 200 cavalry, two guns.

BURIED TREASURE

Starting at midnight on the 10th–11th, the column marched till 6 a.m., covering fifteen or sixteen miles. The men then had breakfasts; and, after resting till mid-day, when they had dinners, started again for Orange Grove, the pass in the Gatsrand with which we were by this time so familiar. It was occupied by Boers, estimated at about one hundred in number, who offered considerable resistance, but who were finally shelled out of it, without loss on our side, though charged by a squadron of Carabineers with great dash. Having done about twenty-six miles, the camp was pitched at 6 p.m., outposts being, of course, thrown out on the adjacent hills.

Reveille sounded at 4.30 a.m., and by 5.30 the small column was on the way again. Their destination was plain enough this time, and very grim and formidable it looked in the broad light of day, considering the very small force which was about to attack it. Moreover, on this occasion it held something besides oranges. Advancing from the north in the direction of the spot from which we had advanced to the attack a few days before, Colonel Hicks made a demonstration as though about to attack the eastern peak, then, suddenly opening a heavy shell fire on the nek between the two, he launched his real attack against the other summit. Although the hill was held by a considerable number of the enemy, estimated at 500, these tactics proved eminently successful, for when they discovered the direction of the main attack shrapnel was bursting all over the nek along which they would have had to gallop to meet it, and they gave up the idea and evacuated the position, which fell into Colonel Hicks' hand with a loss of one man, who had the misfortune to be hit in no less than five places. A guide had been sent with the column who knew where the gold was, and a party was told off to dig it up and bring it in. The guide may or may not have known where the gold *was*, but he certainly did not know where it was *then*, and the search proved entirely abortive. He was a murderer under sentence of death, and was to save his life by showing the gold and ten buried guns. The force started at 5 a.m. next morning for Lindeque Drift. There was a certain amount of sniping all the way, principally at the cavalry, who were riding wide on either flank, collecting cattle and burning straw and hay, in addition to guarding the flanks. Lindeque was reached at 5.30 p.m., a camp of our people being in view on the far bank of the river, with whom communication was opened by signal. The drift was very deep, but an orderly managed to get across with a letter. Orders also arrived from General French giving Colonel Hicks thirty miles of river to watch, which seemed a good deal, considering the paucity of the numbers at his disposal.

At 6.30 a.m. a helio message was received calling the column at once back to Krugersdorp, and a start was made for the return journey at 8 a.m. The Boers endeavoured all day to cut off the rearguard, but met with no success, the gunners shelling them whenever they got close enough to be unpleasant.

The 15th proved to be almost a repetition of the day before, the enemy hanging persistently on the flanks and rear of the little column, but showing no signs of any desire to make their closer acquaintance. Indeed, that morning Colonel Hicks had prepared a small surprise for them which fully realised his anticipations. Whenever columns were moving about it was the invariable custom of the enemy to at once occupy the vacated camping-ground in search of any odds-and-ends that might have been left about, but more especially ammunition, which used to drop out of our men's pouches in surprising quantities, in spite of the most stringent orders on the subject. On this occasion the Colonel left a small party in ambush when he moved off, with the result that when half-a-dozen Boers began rummaging about in the camp they were suddenly invited to hold their hands up, a

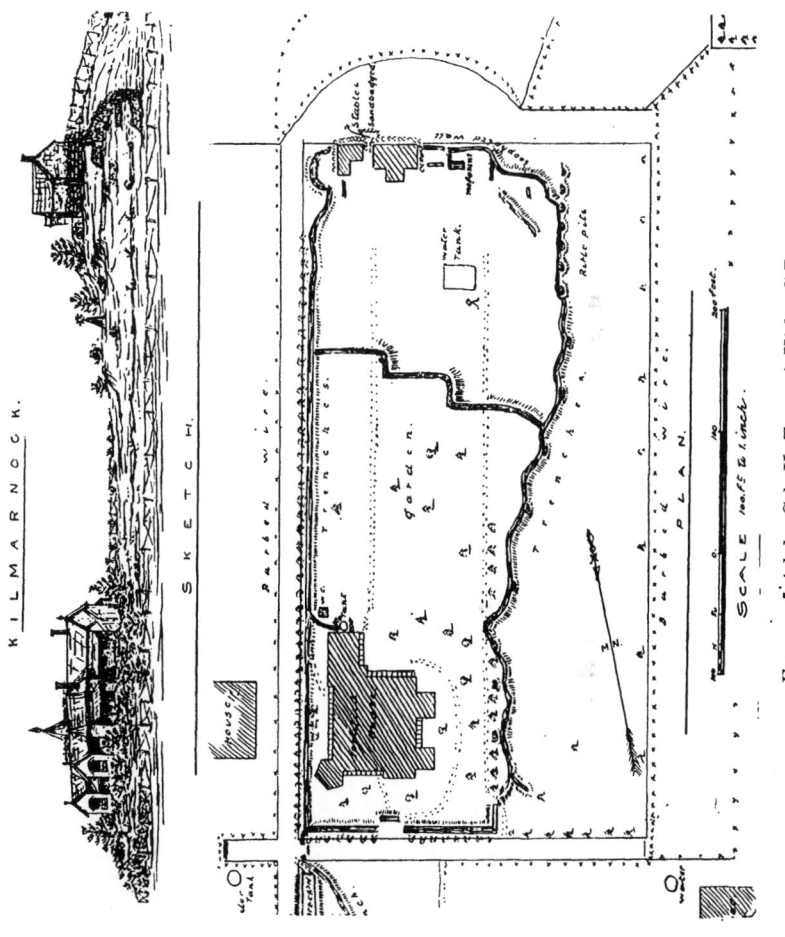

From a sketch by Col. H. Tempest Hicks, C.B.

BURIED TREASURE

request which they had of necessity to comply with, one of them being a Field-Cornet and a man of some local imporance. A halt was made in sight of Randfontein, on the slopes of which a column, under Colonel the Hon. Ulick Roche, could be seen proceeding in the direction of Krugersdorp. Next day was Dingaan's Day, and rumour stated that the Boers under De la Rey, flushed with their victory over Clements, were going to attack Krugersdorp.

The column marched the remaining fifteen miles by 2.30 p.m. next day without seeing any sign of the enemy. During the six days they had been away they had marched 102 miles, skirmished with the enemy nearly every day, taken a strong position by a fine example of tactics, captured a good many prisoners, and brought in a large quantity of cattle, sheep, &c. : a very fine six days' work.

Since May 30th the headquarters of the battalion had marched well over 1200 miles. On three occasions it had exceeded thirty miles in twenty-four hours—the record, of course, being the thirty-eight miles in sixteen hours from Klerkskraal to Pochefstroom in September. But the most wonderful part of its work was the strange immunity it experienced from any of the determined attacks which were so constantly being made on other columns. Whether it was good or bad luck, good or bad scouting, whatever it was, the fact remained that with the exception of the almost daily scrapping and sniping, which constant use had made to appear as part of the day's work, no action of any importance came our way in spite of the countless marches and counter-marches we made to bring one on. With the solitary exception of the afternoon at Frederickstadt, when the Boers dropped a few shells into our camp, and the two following days, when General Liebenburg paid a similar attention to the detachment left behind on the hill, we had not been under shell-fire.

In the meantime, the disaster to General Clements at

2ND BATT. ROYAL DUBLIN FUSILIERS

Nooitgedacht had drawn all eyes to the state of Krugersdorp, which with its small garrison seemed to offer a tempting bait to De la Rey, and column after column arrived to assist in repelling the assault which was threatened for Dingaan's Day. Before the reinforcements arrived the General had taken every sort of precaution ; amongst others, arresting most of the principal inhabitants of the town, and holding them as hostages. The festival, however, passed without incident, and the tide of men and horses, guns and waggons, which had reached a record height in the history of the town, soon began to ebb once more, and then everything settled down to the quiet, peaceful state of affairs which almost always characterised Krugersdorp. The band played in the market square, and concerts were arranged in the town hall, while the General set a fine example to his troops for their guidance in his treatment of those of our late enemies who had observed their oaths of neutrality, as a large number of them most religiously did. Ever foremost in aggressive tactics in the field until the enemy was overcome, the General adopted a policy of conciliation at other times which undoubtedly had far-reaching effects as regarded the conduct of the inhabitants of Krugersdorp.

On December 19th, 400 men of the regiment, under Major Bird, started off to join the force under General French which was going to sweep the Eastern Transvaal, very much on the same lines that the various columns had been sweeping the Western Transvaal. Their special duty was to act as a baggage-guard to the various mounted corps, a duty which they shared with a battalion of Guards. Their lives for the next two or three months were very much the same as they had been for the previous two or three months, though they covered an even greater number of miles, and, owing to the rains and thunderstorms of the South African summer, experienced an even harder time. It is the custom to speak in terms of high praise of the climate of South Africa, but

THE EASTERN TRANSVAAL

if the British Army had been consulted on the subject after some of these treks, it is doubtful if their vocabulary would have been large enough to enable them to thoroughly ventilate their opinions. The fact is that the spring, summer, and autumn are ruined by the desperate storms which are of such common occurrence at those times of year. There are, it is true, four winter months of glorious weather: fine, frosty, starlit nights, and clear days of brilliant sunshine when the the heat is never unpleasant. But of these four months, two are completely ruined by the high winds which sweep the broad veld, and which, in the vicinity of the mines, fill the air with minute particles of gritty dust from the waste-heaps, penetrating eyes and nostrils, throats and lungs.

The first portion of the trek was, however, spent in the country that General Hart had been operating in. The following account of some of their hardships and privations is given by Lieutenant and Quartermaster Burke:—

With General Knox's Brigade in the sweeping movement by General French on the eastern side of the Transvaal. Detail of a few orders as showing the hardships the troops suffered through bad weather and scarcity of food.

Brigade Orders. 'Witcomb, 8.2.01. Owing to the late arrival of the convoy, the force will go on ⅔ biscuits.'

This all the time we were marching daily and fighting.

16.2.01. Our force reached Piet Retief.

Brigade Orders. '20.2.01. The following will be the scale of rations until further orders:—2 ozs. rice, 4 ozs. jam, ½ lb. mealie meal, 1½ lb. meat. No coffee, tea, biscuits, vegetables, or salt.'

Orders received from General French:—'Convoy under General Burn-Murdoch is terribly delayed by swollen rivers and bad roads. The Pongola is fifty yards and the Intombi 300 yards wide. You must use your utmost resources to economise food, and so meet this unfortunate state of affairs,

2ND BATT. ROYAL DUBLIN FUSILIERS

which will assuredly last till the weather improves. No forage for horses and mules. Send parties for food to search out as far as ten miles. Kaffirs to receive 1*l.* in gold for a bag of mealies, or a heifer for five bags.'

21, 22, 23.2.01. 1 oz. jam, ½ lb. mealie meal, 1½ lb. meat, nothing else.

24, 25. Same.

26. No jam, ½ lb. mealie meal, 1½ lb. meat, nothing else. I paid a shopkeeper at Piet Retief 2*s.* 6*d.* for a quarter-handful of salt.

Brigade Orders. 27.2.01. By General French: ' O.C. units will take steps to let the troops know how highly their spirits and bearing under the privations they are suffering from bad weather and short rations are appreciated by the Lieutenant-General Commanding.'

27.2.01. Burnt mealie cobs issued for coffee.

Telegram from Lord Kitchener to General French, Piet Retief, 28.2.01 :—' Explain to the troops under your command my admiration of the excellent work they have performed, and the difficulties they have overcome.'

8.3.01. Full rations, first issue since 14.2.01.

To show that the troops, besides suffering from frightful bad weather (constant rain for a month), had to work hard, the following results are shown.

General Orders. The following results of our operations since 27.1.01, is published for officers and men :—

Boers, killed, wounded, and captured, 393 ; surrendered, 353. Total accounted for, 746.

Cannon taken, excluding a maxim, 4.

Rifles, 606. *Ammunition*, 161,630.

Horses and mules, 6504. *Trek oxen*, 362.

Other cattle, 20,986. *Sheep*, 158,130.

Waggons and carts, 1604.

Mealies and oat hay, over 4,000,000 lbs.

H. BURKE, LT.

THE DEFENCES OF KRUGERSDORP

Colonel Hicks now set every one to work improving the various posts round Krugersdorp, setting a fine example to all by the interest he took in the work, and showing his thoroughness by the attention he devoted to even the most trivial details. He also took infinite pains to make Christmas as pleasant as he could for every one. The regiment was, of course, very much split up in the various forts and fortified houses, but headquarters still remained till the end of the year in our old camping-ground.

On the very last day of the year an escort of forty men returning to Krugersdorp had a near shave of being cut off; they lost four men captured, and would assuredly have lost more but for the prompt action of Major English, who went out from Kilmarnock with twenty men to help them in.

So ended 1900. It had been a hard year for every one, but one and all had done their best, and no sign of failing spirits was visible anywhere. It was difficult to see anything like an end to the campaign, however, for the process of attrition, which now seemed the sole solution, was necessarily a slow one, and considerably interfered with by the various 'regrettable incidents' that occurred from time to time in the huge theatre of the war. These not only assisted our indomitable foes with extra supplies of clothing, arms, ammunition, &c., but also had the effect of keeping up their *morale*.

On January 4th, 1901, the 400 men under Major Bird passed through on their way to Elandsfontein, but nobody knew about the move in time to go up to the station and see them.

Large bodies of the enemy were now known to be in the neighbourhood, and a spy came in saying that it was an open secret among the Boers that Krugersdorp was De la Rey's objective as soon as a favourable opportunity should present itself. In spite of this it was difficult to make the danger of going beyond the outposts appreciated, and this

2ND BATT. ROYAL DUBLIN FUSILIERS

resulted in the death of one of our men, Private Hyland, servant to one of the clergymen. It was supposed that the poor fellow had gone out in a cape-cart with the object of getting some flowers for the church; his body was found on the 8th simply riddled with bullets, as was also that of the Cape-boy who had driven him.

On the 10th, Major Pilson, Royal Dublin Fusiliers, one of the first officers selected to proceed to South Africa on special service before the war, arrived—not, unfortunately, to join the regiment, but the South African Constabulary.

On the 11th the enemy blew up the railway just beyond Roodeport, the first station out of Krugersdorp on the way to Pochefstroom. Lieutenant Marsh and twenty men of the regiment were sent out as escort to guard the Engineers who repaired it.

The storms continued to be very severe. Kilmarnock House was struck by lightning, and the sentry on guard at the Court House in the town sent spinning, fortunately only receiving a severe shaking.

On the 23rd the sad news of the death of Her Majesty Queen Victoria was made known to the troops, by whom it was received in deep and impressive silence.

A salute was fired by the Artillery on the 24th with plugged shell, to celebrate the Accession of King Edward VII.

At the end of the month General Hart left us. The regiment had been continuously under his command since the formation of the Irish Brigade; officers and men alike had learned to entertain a deep respect and admiration for their General, than whom no braver man ever went into action. He on his part loved the regiment, and fully appreciated the *esprit de corps* which permeated it, from the Colonel to the last-joined recruit. His farewell letter to Colonel Hicks, another on the subject of our camping arrangements, and his farewell order to his brigade, may all be found in the Appendix, and afford proof of his

THE DEFENCES OF KRUGERSDORP

regard for his troops and the spirit which he breathed into them.

Colonel Groves took over command of Krugersdorp and its defences, and gave Colonel Hicks a free hand: he also rode round the inner defences with the commander of the town-guards and piquets, and arranged for their being made stronger also.

In spite of the presence of a good many of our columns, the enemy was very active all over the Magaliesberg and the Gatsrand at this time. It will be remembered that on the return from the Klip River trek, a party of the South Wales Borderers had been left to watch the Modderfontein Pass.

This small force was now surrounded and being fiercely attacked, and offering as determined a resistance. A force was hastily organized to proceed to their relief, under command of Colonel the Hon. U. Roche, of the South Wales Borderers. With half or more of the battalion away under Major Bird, we could only supply 180 men, under command of Captain Shewan, for this column.

They marched that night, and the following morning found all the hills for ten miles held by the enemy, Colonel Roche wiring in that the Boers were in too great force for his column to proceed. Indeed, the column had to fight hard enough to maintain its position and to save itself from being surrounded. General Conyngham, hastily gathering together another 500 men and a battery, marched off to reinforce Colonel Roche, but before they could get to the unfortunate post at Modderfontein, it had fallen to superior numbers. The Boers, who were under the command of General Smuts, sent in a flag of truce, giving notice of the capture of the post, stating that there were many British wounded, and suggesting that an ambulance and doctors should be sent out to them. This incident was very hard lines on a most gallant regiment, and in no way reflects adversely on them for one instant. They defended their position splendidly as long as

2ND BATT. ROYAL DUBLIN FUSILIERS

defence was possible, and suffered greatly from want of water as well as from the enemy's fire. Colonel Roche reported that Captain Shewan and his men had done very well, and had held a hill on the left of his position, until he recalled them.

Colonel Hicks never for a moment remitted his exertions in the fortifying of the various posts and houses in the section of the command for which he was responsible, with the result that he very soon had them in a most efficient state. Ammunition, food, and water, in sufficient quantities to withstand a regular siege, were stored in each post, while the wire entanglements would have effectually precluded any attempt on the part of the enemy to rush them. Indeed, no precautions were omitted, and one began to enjoy one's sleep considerably more than had been the case for some months past.

On the 7th, the headquarters of the regiment at last moved into Kilmarnock, a house which had belonged to a Mr. Burger, a brother of Mr. Schalk Burger, the acting President. Here they remained until the regiment left for Aden in January 1902.

THE HAIR-DRESSER'S SHOP.

CHAPTER VII.

THE LAST TWELVE MONTHS.

'In the morning thou shalt say, Would God it were even! and at even thou shalt say, Would God it were morning!'—Deut. xxviii. 67.

WITH the occupation of Kilmarnock by the headquarters of the regiment arrived the third and last phase of the war. It had begun with four months' hard fighting, continued with twelve months' hard marching, and

KILMARNOCK, KRUGERSDORP.

was to end with twelve months of weary escorts to convoys, occupation of blockhouses, and garrison work generally. It was, perhaps, in its way, the most trying period of the three, for in addition to unceasing vigilance there was added the dead monotony of week after week in the same place, surrounded by the same faces, and feeding on the same indifferent food. One was buoyed up by the reports published

2ND BATT. ROYAL DUBLIN FUSILIERS

from time to time of the hauls of prisoners made by the various columns, but there was always some pessimist handy to discount one's hopes, and even though the result proved their dismal croakings more or less correct, they might have had the grace, even if they had not the common sense, to keep their miserable opinions to themselves. Thank goodness there were not many of these gentlemen in the regiment. Throughout the war I only heard one man grumble sulkily, and only heard of one man who paid too great a regard to the use of cover. The high tone with which the war had been entered upon was maintained to the very end, and if the regimental officer came out of it with credit, the N.C.O. and private soldier did every bit as well. Hardship, fatigue, stress of weather—everything was accepted as part of the general day's work, and as such cheerfully met and thoroughly done.

Lieutenants B. Maclear and J. P. B. Robinson joined about this time, the former a brother of Percy Maclear, Adjutant of the 1st Battalion.

In spite of all the work, however, time was yet found for a certain amount of play, the exercise of which was very beneficial. Cricket matches were played against the town, the S.A.C., and amongst ourselves, and later on football matches against the town and other regiments. We proved more successful at the latter game than the former: not to be wondered at, seeing that two of our officers—Lieutenants Maclear and Newton—were later on to become International three-quarter backs, the former playing for Ireland and the latter for England.

Lieutenant Knox joined on March 23rd, having been detained nine months through illness on the way up.

In March, Major-General Mildmay Willson, a Guardsman, took over from Colonel Groves the command, which now became 'the District West of Johannesburg.'

On April 17th, Major English proceeded to Bank in command of a small mixed force (one hundred Royal Dublin

THE LAST TWELVE MONTHS

Fusiliers) to try and catch a Boer force who had been for some time hovering round that station. He returned on the 19th, having seen no Boers.

On the 21st, Captain Watson, formerly in the regiment, came to see us. He was then Adjutant of the Scottish Horse, and was shortly afterwards killed at Moedwil. He had distinguished himself on many occasions, and had received special promotion into the Lancashire Fusiliers.

On the 30th, Major Bird and his half-battalion at last got back. They had done a lot of marching and good work in the Eastern Transvaal with General French's columns, but had not had much fighting. They all seemed glad to be back; it is always satisfactory to have the regiment together, as we have a feeling of dependence on one another that one cannot have when working with other troops, however good they may be.

On May 3rd Captain Kinsman, Royal Dublin Fusiliers, came to see the battalion. He was then in the S.A.C. He had been badly wounded some time ago, having been with the force under General Plumer since the beginning of the war, and present at the relief of Mafeking, and had seen a deal of fighting.

On May 7th Lieutenant Seymour joined the regiment, in which his father had also served.

On May 25th a force* went out to escort the S.A.C. to a fort they were to build. The column was under command of Colonel Hicks, and almost immediately met with opposition, the Scottish Horse, on the left, coming in for a good deal of sniping. Sending out his mounted men well ahead, and occupying a ridge in front with the Worcesters, the Colonel then rode on with Colonel Edwardes, S.A.C., to select a spot for the erection of the work. The only casualties were two men wounded and five horses killed, and the force then bivouacked on the positions they held. Next

* 400 Royal Dublin Fusiliers, 100 Worcestershire Regiment, 200 S.A.C., 220 Scottish Horse, two guns.

2ND BATT. ROYAL DUBLIN FUSILIERS

day building was commenced on a small fort and three blockhouses, the building parties being sniped for some time until a detachment of the regiment under Captain Fetherstonhaugh and Lieutenant Maclear went out and drove the Boers away. By the 27th the fort and posts were nearly completed, the enemy still hovering round the neighbourhood, and next day the column returned to Krugersdorp, meeting and dispersing a few Boers on the way back.

A BLOCKHOUSE.

On June 3rd Colonel Hicks took over command of the Krugersdorp sub-district, as Colonel Groves was down with measles, as was also Lieutenant Bradford—an extraordinary disease for a man of the Colonel's time of life.

On the 15th of June Colonel Groves handed over the Krugersdorp sub-district to Brigadier-General Barker, R.E. Before leaving he said some very nice things about the regiment, and we on our part were sorry to lose him, as he had always had a good opinion of the battalion, and had assisted the Colonel in his endeavours to put Krugersdorp in a thorough state of defence.

THE LAST TWELVE MONTHS

On the 27th Lieutenant Frankland, 2nd Royal Dublin Fusiliers, came to see us. It will be remembered that he was taken prisoner at the very beginning of the war in the armoured-train disaster. Since the capture of Pretoria he had been occupied on the line of communications. He told us that Lieutenant Le Mesurier had probably never got over the exposure to which he was subjected during his escape from Pretoria and on his long march to Delagoa Bay, as he no sooner got over one attack of fever than he was down with another. He also gave us an account of the escape, which was a most gallant affair, and in the light of what has since happened to the only other officers who escaped—Captain Haldane and Mr. Winston Churchill—it seems hard luck that Le Mesurier should have received nothing. He added that Lieutenant Grimshaw had been attached to the Mounted Infantry since the relief, and that Captain Lonsdale had got into the Staff College.

On July 1st two convoys went out, one under Major English and the other under Captain Fetherstonhaugh, not returning until the 6th. The remainder of the month brought forth nothing novel, however, and was spent in strengthening posts and escorting convoys.

August also passed uneventfully, but on September 16th Colonel Hicks was given command of a mixed force some 1000 strong, 170 of whom belonged to the regiment, with orders to move along through the same old Gatsrand country, visit posts, burn farms, collect cattle, &c., &c. He marched accordingly, but met with little opposition until well inside the hilly country, where some sniping took place. After a fortnight's trek he arrived in Pochefstroom, where he found General Willson, who informed him that he was to succeed General Barker in command of the Krugersdorp sub-district. He returned to that place on the 30th, only to find a wire ordering him to go back for the present to his column and to move to a place on the Vaal south of Pochefstroom and

2ND BATT. ROYAL DUBLIN FUSILIERS

turn out a Boer force which was occasioning considerable trouble. Colonel Hicks by a rapid march anticipated the Boers at a pass leading into this valley, their commander, George Hall, afterwards declaring that this step saved us a hundred men, as he had determined to hold the pass till the last.

On October 5th he encountered a force of Boers who were prepared to dispute the ownership of some cattle with him, but he had little difficulty in convincing them that under the circumstances might was undoubtedly right. On the 6th the seven-pounder gun lost by the S.A.C. was recovered, and George Hall, a prominent Boer leader, captured. The Colonel induced him to send a letter out to his commando advising them to give in, which resulted in twenty-two of them surrendering at Pochefstroom a few days later. In addition to this the column captured about fifteen prisoners and brought or sent in very large quantities of stock, mealies, cattle, &c. The Colonel got back to Krugersdorp on the 12th, having returned by train to take over his command.

Lieutenants Frankland and Weldon of ours were present at the fight at Bakenlaagte, when Colonel Benson was killed, and had a hot time of it. Our mounted infantry lost two killed and six wounded. The following description is supplied by Lieutenant Weldon :—

THE ROYAL DUBLIN FUSILIERS MOUNTED INFANTRY AT BAKENLAAGTE.

On the afternoon preceding the move from Zwakfontein, where Colonel Benson's column was camped, I was ordered to escort Lieutenant Biggs, R.E., to a drift some miles away on the road to Bakenlaagte : this we accomplished, bringing back one prisoner, whom we took near the drift. At daybreak on the following morning our outposts were attacked before the column had moved out of camp, and the rearguard action com-

THE LAST TWELVE MONTHS

menced. Our mounted infantry formed the right and left flank guards to the light transport, the right under Lieutenant Grimshaw, and the left under Lieutenants Frankland and Weldon. The enemy did not pay much attention to us at first, but after going a little way I galloped with my section to take possession of a small kopje which commanded the route. The Boers made a simultaneous dash for it, resulting in a spirited race, in which we proved victors, having been expedited on the way by two 'belts' from our own pompom. On gaining the hill we at once poured a heavy fire into our opponents, who withdrew. In the meantime considerable difficulty was experienced in getting the transport over the drift, which gave the Boers time to get round us. Eventually, however, most of it was got across and the march resumed. On nearing camp our mounted infantry closed in a bit, when we were suddenly fired on from a farmhouse flying the Red Cross flag, and sustained five or six casualties. We were detailed to a section of the defence of Bakenlaagte, which was practically surrounded. We lay down on the slopes with our heads downhill, and kept the enemy well away, taking the opportunity to improvise some sort of head-cover whenever their fire slackened. Although we fully expected an attack in the night, or at dawn, none was made, there being no sign of the enemy next day. KENNETH WELDON.

On December 6th Captain Romer took over the appointment of C.S.O., Krugersdorp Sub-District, from our old friend, Captain Hart, who was appointed to General Knox's staff. We were very sorry to lose him, as from first to last he had done his best to oblige all, and during his term of office made friends with everybody.

On the 9th Lieutenant Britton and fifty men of the regiment proceeded to Middelvlei to relieve a party of the Border regiment.

On the 17th Lieutenant Robinson had to perform the

THE LAST TWELVE MONTHS

unpleasant duty of carrying out the sentence of death on a Boer prisoner, who had been tried and condemned for shooting three of our men after having surrendered.

General Cooper arrived on the 19th, to say good-bye to the regiment, as he was on his way home. He brought the very welcome intelligence that we were shortly to be relieved, but of course this was only made known to the Colonel at the time.

Lieutenant Renny, who had been A.D.C. to General Cooper, rejoined on the 27th, and brought further rumours to the effect that the regiment was shortly to leave the country, and as orders had come to get in all our employed men, and men from forts, blockhouses, and stations all over the country, it began to look as if there was some truth in the rumours.

On the very last day of 1901 a severe thunderstorm passed right over headquarters, two of our men being struck by lightning.

1902.

On the first day of the New Year the order for the battalion to leave South Africa arrived at the brigade office, its destination being Gibraltar, the best of the Mediterranean stations; but next day a wire arrived cancelling the move.

On the 5th, however, Lord Kitchener passed through Krugersdorp, when the Colonel saw him and ascertained that the regiment was to go to Aden.

At 8.30 p.m. on the 11th, part of the 1st Battalion Royal Dublin Fusiliers, under Majors Shadforth and Gordon, Captains Swift and Maclear, and Lieutenant Le Mesurier, with some other officers, arrived to take over the defences from the 2nd Battalion.

On the 14th, 300 of the 1st Battalion, under Major Gordon, proceeded down the Pochefstroom line to take over the posts at present held by us.

KRUGERSDORP from
Kilmarnock House.
shewing The Gold mines,
Monument, Camps &c.

From a sketch by Col. H. Tempest Hicks, C.B.

2ND BATT. ROYAL DUBLIN FUSILIERS

On the 20th, Captains Kinsman and Rowlands (now serving in the S.A.C.) arrived to say good-bye, and on the 23rd, Colonel Mills and Major Bromilow, 1st Battalion, arrived.

On January 26th the regiment fell in for the last time at Kilmarnock, and marched through Krugersdorp to the station. They had made many friends during their stay, and the entire town, Boers as well as Britons, turned out

THE 'BLUE CAPS' RELIEVING THE 'OLD TOUGHS.'

and enthusiastically cheered the corps as it marched out of the town it had first marched into on June 19th, 1900. The night was spent at the railway station, and a start made at 4 a.m. on the 27th. A good view of Talana, from a distance of about five miles, was obtained on the morning of the 28th, and it may easily be imagined with what mixed feelings our thoughts flew back to that grey morning of October 20th, 1899, and our well-loved comrades who had given their lives to gain that gallant victory. Ladysmith was reached about 1 p.m., and Maritzburg in the small hours of the 29th, which was unfortunate, as the regiment had so many friends

THE LAST TWELVE MONTHS

there. In spite of the hour, however, a large number of the inhabitants were on the platform with various small presents of cigarettes, &c., for the men. Durban was reached a few hours later, when an illuminated address was presented to the regiment, as well as refreshments to officers and men, after which the battalion embarked on board the s.s. *Sicilian* for conveyance to Aden.

PART III.

CHAPTER I.

THE ADEN HINTERLAND.

'For this relief much thanks.'
Hamlet.

THE voyage from Durban to Aden was a welcome change, but quite uneventful, with the exception of one sad event, the death of Sergeant Pearson, who had embarked in a state of collapse, with little or no prospect of recovery. He was a most promising N.C.O., and his father had served in the regiment before him. Aden was reached on February 11th, 1902, and the battalion disembarked that afternoon.

The year passed without any incident calling for remark, and on October 1st the following notice appeared in battalion orders:—' It is notified for general information that the battalion will leave Aden for home in H.M.T. *Syria*, on or about the 11th of February, arriving home on 24th February, 1903.' 'There is many a slip 'twixt the cup and the lip,' however, and the old adage was once more to be exemplified.

For some time past rumours of approaching trouble with regard to the delimitation of the Turkish frontier in the Hinterland had been rife. A force of Turkish troops was encamped near Dthala, about one hundred and ten miles from Aden, and the Sultan of Dthala finally appealed to the British for support. The result was that instead of going home, a column was organized under the command of Brevet-Lieutenant-Colonel F. P. English, 2nd Royal Dublin Fusiliers, to watch the frontier.

The following is an extract from the Aden District Orders:—

2ND BATT. ROYAL DUBLIN FUSILIERS

DISTRICT ORDERS BY LIEUTENANT-COLONEL H. T. HICKS, C.B., 2ND ROYAL DUBLIN FUSILIERS, COMMANDING ADEN DISTRICT.

No. 450.   *Aden, Friday, December 12th, 1902.*

In supersession of previous instructions, a column composed as under will be held in readiness to proceed, on field-service scale, from Aden into the interior of Arabia:—

In Command: Lieutenant-Colonel F. P. English, 2nd Royal Dublin Fusiliers.

Staff Officer: Major S. M. Edwards, D.S.O., 2nd Bombay Grenadiers.

Supply and Transport Officer: Captain W. C. W. Harrison, Supply and Transport Corps.

Staff Medical Officer: Captain I. A. O. MacCarthy, Royal Army Medical Corps.

2nd Royal Dublin Fusiliers (including section of maxim gun and twelve signallers) ... ... 225 N.C.O.'s and men.

No. 45 company, Royal Garrison Artillery (with two seven-pounder mountain guns and four nine-pounders)... ... ... 80 ,,

Aden Troop ... ... { 25 horsemen. 12 camelmen.

2nd Bombay Grenadiers ... ... A double company.

Section A. No. 16 British Field Hospital.

,,   ,, 68 Native ,,   ,,

If the column is required to move out, they will be joined *en route* (if necessary) by a detachment of No. 3 company Bombay Sappers and Miners.

(By Order)   C. H. U. PRICE, *Major*, *D.A.A.G. Aden District.*

THE ADEN HINTERLAND

The following officers of the regiment accompanied the column:—Lieutenant Haskard, Lieutenant Wheeler, Lieutenant Smith, Second Lieutenant Tredennick, Second Lieutenant W. F. Higginson.

The following standing orders are quoted in full, as they give a good idea of the scope of the operations, the difficulties likely to be met with, and the precautions taken to overcome those difficulties:—

COLUMN STANDING ORDERS BY LIEUTENANT-COLONEL F. P. ENGLISH, COMMANDING ADEN COLUMN.

December 24th, 1902.

1. *Water.*—It is anticipated that in all probability it will be difficult to obtain good drinking water in sufficient quantities on some of the marches into the interior. All ranks are therefore cautioned to husband their drinking water as much as possible. Troops and followers should be forbidden to draw water from the camel tanks without permission from the officer in charge, and be cautioned against drinking water from any but authorised sources, as some of the water on the route is brackish and liable to bring on diarrhœa.

Each unit will detail an officer or selected N.C. officer to be in charge of the water camels, who will see that their supply is only drawn on by order of the officer commanding, and that great care is taken to prevent wastage. Whenever possible, water tanks and bottles should be replenished; halts will be made for this purpose. Water-bottles will be filled overnight. On arrival in camp, the sources of water supply will be pointed out by the staff officer, and sentries posted to see that the right people draw from the right source.

2. *Country and Inhabitants.*—It should be remembered that the country through which the column will march

to Dthala is in the British Protectorate, and that the inhabitants and their property must not be interfered with. All supplies must be paid for, and foraging is strictly forbidden.

3. *Camps.*—On arrival at the camping-places, the staff officer will point out the sites for the camps of the different units to N.C.O.'s detailed for that purpose. Officers commanding units will see that their respective camping-grounds are cleared up before departure.

4. *Transport.*—On arrival in camp the transport in charge of each unit will be picketed near its camp.

5. *Order of March and Baggage.*—Each unit will be complete in itself, being followed by first line transport, viz :—

1. Signalling equipment. 2. First reserve ammunition. 3. Entrenching tools. 4. Water camels. 5. Stretchers. 6. Great-coat camels.

All followers not required with the above are to accompany the baggage of their corps. The transport officer will act as baggage-master, and all baggage-followers and baggage-guards will be under his orders. He will see that the baggage moves off the ground in the following order, viz :— Field hospital with its baggage in rear of fighting portion of column; ammunition second reserve and ordnance park; staff baggage, including supplies; regimental baggage with supplies in regimental charge in order of march of unit; supply go-down; spare animals in transport charge; rearguard.

(By order)   S. M. EDWARDS, *Major*,
S.O. Aden Column.

January 2nd, 1903, *Sheikh Othman.*—On January 2nd, 1903, the column assembled at its rendezvous, Sheikh Othman, some ten miles from Aden.

January 3rd, Bir Sayed Ali Wells (2½ *miles north of Firush.*)—An early start was made, though as it was the first day's march as a column it was not intended to go very far.

THE ADEN HINTERLAND

The going, moreover, was bad. It takes time to accustom oneself to marching through deep sand, just as it takes time to acquire the 'heather-step' in August. However, every one did well, the water was good and fairly plentiful, though somewhat scattered, and the spirits of the little force rose high at the possibilities of the prospect before them.

January 4th, Bir Salim.—The water at this camp was good, but insufficient in quantity, necessitating the watering of the animals some mile away.

January 5th, Shaika.—Another good march, the only incident of which was the breaking down of the treasure-camel, an important item of the force.

January 6th.—Owing to the necessity of making very early starts, long before daybreak, Lieut.-Colonel English gave orders for bonfires to be built overnight. These proved a great success, and enabled the packing-up in the morning to be accomplished with facility and dispatch.

January 7th, Alhaja.—This place was reached after a long and trying march, but the water proved bad in quality and small in quantity. Captain Harrison, however, luckily joined the force here with a good supply from Aden, so all was well.

January 8th, Hadaba.—Another tiring march, but a spring in the river-bed provided a plentiful supply of good water. As there were 1300 human beings and animals to provide for, it can easily be understood that the problem of the water-supply was a never-ceasing care to the staff. Its solution would have been still more difficult had not the O.C. column arranged that the Bombay Grenadiers and native hospital should march a day behind the rest of the force.

January 9th, Arrado.—A short march, and more water than was expected.

January 10th, Dthala.—There was a difficult pass to ascend before the column reached its objective; three camels were in consequence lost *en route*, one falling over a precipice

2ND BATT. ROYAL DUBLIN FUSILIERS

and two dying from exhaustion. By 1 p.m., however, all difficulties had been overcome, and the camping-ground was reached without opposition.

January 11th.—The remainder of the column arrived safely.

The rest of the month was occupied in putting the camp

DTHALA CAMP.

in a state of defence, and the usual camp life. A force of 400 Turkish troops, with four guns and twenty-five mounted men, was encamped only two miles off at Jelala, and, as the condition of affairs, according to the political officer, Colonel Wahab, was very acute, it was necessary to observe the strictest precautions at all times. On January 30th the detachment of the Royal Dublin Fusiliers was relieved by one from the Hampshire Regiment, and marched off on their way back to Aden, under command of Lieutenant Haskard. Colonel

THE ADEN HINTERLAND

English did not return, having received orders from Lord Kitchener to remain in command of the field force, whose total strength now consisted of 818 officers and men, and 735 animals.

February 1st.—The situation now, however, became more serious. Colonel English received a wire at 2.30 p.m. directing him to stop Haskard's return march at Nobat-Dakim, and another at 6 p.m. informing him that the whole of the Dublin

DTHALA VILLAGE FROM CAMP.

Fusiliers were coming up, and also half the 23rd Bombay Rifles. On February 10th instructions were received to recall Haskard, who marched on the 12th, arriving at Dthala on the 14th. On the 18th, headquarters and the remainder of the Dublin Fusiliers left Aden, reaching Dthala on the 26th, when Colonel Hicks took over command of the column, Lieut.-Colonel English assuming command of the battalion.

On March 22nd the Turks, however, evacuated Jelala, retiring behind Kataba. Jelala was at once occupied by two companies of the Bombay Rifles. Captain Rooth, Brevet-

2ND BATT. ROYAL DUBLIN FUSILIERS

Major Carington Smith, Captains Garvice, Grimshaw, and Taylor arrived on the same day.

On April 27th a detachment, consisting of 100 Royal Dublin Fusiliers, two guns 6th Mountain Battery, and 100 Bombay Rifles, with supply and transport, the whole under the command of Lieutenant-Colonel English, occupied Sanah, where they remained until July 11th, when they returned to Dthala.

On May 18th a detachment of 100 men of the Royal Dublin Fusiliers, under Brevet-Major Smith, joined a column under command of Colonel Scallon, C.I.E., D.S.O., 23rd Bombay Rifles, which proceeded on a punitive expedition to Hardaba. They met with some slight opposition, in which No. 7274 Private Martin, Royal Dublin Fusiliers, was slightly wounded. The column returned to Dthala on May 25th, after suffering considerably from heat.

On August 31st a small flying column, under Major Delamain, left for the Bunna River. Lieutenant Wheeler, Royal Dublin Fusiliers, acted as Staff Officer to this force. On September 4th, Lieutenant Haskard, Royal Dublin Fusiliers, with thirty-five men, went out to Delamain with a convoy, returning on September 6th.

Considerable trouble had for some time been caused by the depredations of the Arab tribes, who had been killing camel-men, and generally making themselves obnoxious on the line of communications. Information was now received that these Arabs were beginning to get very excited, and that they contemplated an attack on a post under Captain Shewell, at Awabil. A force was immediately got together, and placed under the command of Colonel English. He marched on September 13th, only to find, however, on arrival that Shewell had beaten off the attack by himself, with a loss of one man killed and five wounded. Colonel English then returned to Dthala, which place he reached on September 19th.

THE ADEN HINTERLAND

On October 5th the same officer took command of another column, to punish the Dthanbari tribe and destroy their chief town, Naklain. The column consisted of Royal Dublin Fusiliers, 4 companies; 6th Mountain Battery, Royal Artillery, 1 section; Camel Battery, 2 guns; Aden Troop, 17 sowars; Bombay Grenadiers, 1 double company; 23rd Bombay Rifles, 23 men.

A FRONTIER TOWER. ABDALI COUNTRY.

Colonel English arrived before Naklain at 8.25 a.m. on October 7th, after pushing back the enemy, who disputed the passage of a difficult gorge for some time. He then proceeded to destroy the place, and at 11.15 a.m. started on his return march. The enemy clung to his flanks, and kept up a long-range fire until 2.30 p.m., when he repassed the gorge mentioned above. His casualties consisted of one killed (No. 5710 Private Andrew Keegan), and six wounded,

2ND BATT. ROYAL DUBLIN FUSILIERS

while there were in addition six cases of sunstroke. The column did not return to Dthala, but marched straight to Aden, where it arrived on October 14th.

The remainder of the battalion left Dthala on October 10th, reaching Aden on the 16th, where, on October 24th, it embarked on the transport *Soudan* for home.

For his services in the Aden Hinterland, Lieutenant-Colonel English was awarded the D.S.O. It was never better earned. But no medal was issued to the regiment, in spite of the fact that for ten months they had been living under active service conditions, which necessitated unceasing vigilance by day and night. It is true they had not suffered many casualties, or seen much fighting, but as this was undoubtedly due to the excellent manner in which the operations were conducted, and to the precautions taken, it seemed a little hard that the coveted distinction of a medal should be withheld, although the little campaign is ranked in war services as active service.

However, the experience and the knowledge of the country gained will doubtless prove beneficial to all concerned, who still look back upon Dthala with affection, and speak of it with regret. On the night after Colonel English had dealt with the Dthanbari tribe, Major Carington Smith, who was in command of a small detachment, after posting his outposts was just thinking of retiring when he heard the sentries challenge; this was immediately followed by a rush of horsemen, headed by a most gorgeously dressed officer. Reining up almost at Smith's feet he informed him that his master, a neighbouring potentate, friendly to the English, had sent him and his men to assist in the repulse of the bloodthirsty Dthanbari tribe, who might be expected to attempt to rush the camp that night. Although not anticipating anything of the kind, Major Smith was far too polite to say so, and after thanking his allies, suggested that they should take up a line of cossack posts in front of his out-

THE ADEN HINTERLAND

post line. To this they consented, but before leaving declared their earnest conviction that an assault would be delivered. Shortly after midnight Smith was awakened by a fiendish din. Grasping his sword with one hand and his pistol with the other, he rushed out to meet the crisis. From every direction his allies came galloping in as fast as their horses could lay legs to the ground, while the detachment sprang to arms in a second, fully expecting to be attacked by every Arab in the Hinterland. Reining up his horse as before, the leader of the cavalry once more saluted Smith, and made the following report: 'Sah, I have honour to salute you, and inform your Honour that Dthanbari tribe have not yet arrived.'

The following description of the action at Naklain appeared in the home press:—

'An Arab Drive.

'Hot Fighting in the Aden Hinterland.

'The expedition, under Brevet-Lieutenant-Colonel English, was sent out to destroy the chief village and crops of the tribe Naklain, as punishment for the shooting of Government camels and the looting of his Majesty's mails. The tribe is very warlike, and their country had never hitherto been penetrated.

'After leaving As Suk camp, the British column began to wind among the mountains, which rise very abruptly from the plain, and, as they met with no opposition for a considerable time, they began to think there would be no resistance. Suddenly, without warning of any sort, a ragged volley was opened on the advance-guard, apparently from some very broken ground, fifty to a hundred yards in front.

'This seemed to be a prearranged signal, for from the hills on both flanks the firing was taken up, the enemy constantly changing their positions after firing. The guns

2ND BATT. ROYAL DUBLIN FUSILIERS

were brought into action almost at once, and the infantry, extending at the double, soon covered a wide front and swept along the hills parallel to the advance.

'Moving Forward.

'After the surrounding hills had been shelled, the whole column moved forward, the infantry pushing the enemy back step by step until the village of Naklain was reached. While parties of men were told off to keep down the enemy's fire from points of vantage, others proceeded to blow up the houses with gun-cotton, and the more inaccessible houses were shelled.

'The crops were then destroyed by the men with their bayonets and swords. There was a fierce fire while this was proceeding, the enemy evidently not having expected such a reprisal. The work having been completed, the arduous retirement commenced, the enemy following the force up step by step the whole way back, at one time coming to comparatively close quarters and necessitating a most careful management of the rearguard.

'As Suk was reached after a trying march of twenty miles, the troops being under fire most of the time, with scarcely any water and exposed to a burning sun. The British casualties were seven men of the Dublin Fusiliers wounded (one since dead) and one native and one gunner slightly wounded.'

2nd Lieut. H. St. G. S. Scott; 2nd Lieut. B. Maclear; 2nd Lieut. E. St. G. Smith; 2nd Lieut. J. P. Tredennick.

Bt.-Major E. Fetherstonhaugh; Lieut. A. H. D. Britton; Lieut. and Qr.-mr. Burke; Major S. G. Bird, D.S.O.; Lieut. Haskard; Lieut. Wheeler; and Lieut. R. F. B. Knox; 2nd Lieut. J. P. B. Robinson; 2nd Lieut. A. W. Newton.

Lieut. C. Garvice, D.S.O.; Capt. G. N. Cory, D.S.O.; Capt. M. Lowndes; Lieut.-Col. H. T. Hicks, C.B.; Lieut. L. F. Renny; Capt. H. W. Higginson; 2nd Lieut. E. F. E. Seymour; Lieut. A. de B. W. W. Bradford (absent).

OFFICERS OF THE 2ND BATTALION ROYAL DUBLIN FUSILIERS WHO EMBARKED FOR ADEN.

CHAPTER II.

THE RETURN HOME AND RECEPTION.

> 'I must to England.
> I pray you give me leave.'
> *Hamlet.*

EARLY in October, 1903, the 2nd Battalion at length heard the good news that the date of their departure from Aden had been definitely fixed, and on the 23rd of the month it sailed in the s.s. *Soudan*, arriving at Queenstown late in the evening of November 9th. The tour of foreign service had lasted for twenty years all but two months, and only one man in the whole battalion had seen it through from start to finish without coming home, the present quartermaster, Lieutenant J. Burke.

The 2nd Battalion Royal Dublin Fusiliers left England for Gibraltar on January 9th, 1884, and in February, 1885, proceeded to Egypt, where it was quartered first at Ramleh, and later on at Cairo. Early in 1886 the battalion went to India, headquarters being stationed successively at Poona, Nasirabad, Karachi, Quetta, and Bombay.

In May, 1897, it was suddenly ordered to South Africa, and quartered at Maritzburg, as already stated in the opening chapter.

The details were at Buttevant, County Cork, and thither the battalion proceeded on their arrival in Ireland.

Just two days prior to the arrival home of the 2nd Battalion the regiment had been honoured by having appointed as its Colonel-in-Chief Field-Marshal H.R.H. A. W. S. A. Duke of Connaught and Strathearn, K.G., K.P., K.T., G.C.B., G.C.M.G., G.C.I.E., G.C.V.O.

On November 13th, 1903, the battalion proceed to Dublin

2ND BATT. ROYAL DUBLIN FUSILIERS

to attend a public reception and also to receive their medals at the hands of H.R.H. the Duke of Connaught. The following is the account of the proceedings as published in the *Irish Times* of November 14th, 1903, to whom the thanks of the regiment are due for their kindness in permitting its reproduction :—

(*Extract from* ' *Irish Times*,' *Saturday, November* 14*th*, 1903.)

HOME-COMING OF THE ROYAL DUBLIN FUSILIERS.

The officers, non-commissioned officers, and men of the 2nd Battalion of the Royal Dublin Fusiliers may well feel proud of the reception accorded them on their return to their native land and city after a long and arduous service under the British flag in foreign lands. There was quite a contest for places on the gallery in the great Central Hall of the Royal Dublin Society's buildings at Ballsbridge to see the heroes of a regiment which had gained undying laurels in Burmah, India, and South Africa. Exceptional arrangements had been made for the entertainment of the battalion at Ballsbridge, and the reception committee, which had for its chairman the Earl of Meath, must be congratulated on the manner in which they carried out the entertainment and provided for the enjoyment of such a large number of guests. The arrangement of the hall was admirable in every respect. At the further end a slightly-raised daïs was placed and profusely decorated with palms and evergreens, and immediately behind the chair subsequently occupied by H.R.H. the Duke of Connaught was the regimental emblem introducing the figures of an elephant and a tiger; the former bringing to mind the doughty deeds of the Dublin Fusiliers in Burmah and the latter their equally splendid record on the historic field of Plassey. At the back was the regimental motto, *Spectamur Agendo*, and the roof and gallery railings were handsomely draped with red, green, and blue muslin, while

THE RETURN HOME AND RECEPTION

the names of the various engagements in which the men took part were prominently displayed. On the right-hand side of the hall four long rows of tables were placed, handsomely prepared for the dinner, while the centre of the building facing the daïs was kept clear for the men to be drawn up in proper formation to receive H.R.H. the Duke of Connaught.

HOMEWARD BOUND AT LAST AFTER TWENTY YEARS' FOREIGN SERVICE.

The spacious galleries reserved for ticket-holders were crowded long before the hour fixed for the ceremony, 12.30 o'clock. Shortly before 10 o'clock a large number of reservists of the battalion, about 250, and some reservists from other battalions of the regiment assembled at the Marshalsea Barracks, and under the command of Captain Perreau, Royal Dublin Fusiliers, Adjutant 5th Battalion, and Major Baker, D.S.O., marched viâ Thomas Street, Cork Hill, Dame Street, Nassau Street, Merrion Square North, Lower Mount Street, and

2ND BATT. ROYAL DUBLIN FUSILIERS

Northumberland Road to Ballsbridge. The men were dressed in civilian clothes, but wore their medals and other decorations, and many showed by their appearance that they, too, had played no insignificant part in the recent campaign. They were accompanied by the massed bands of the 3rd, 4th, and 5th Battalions Royal Dublin Fusiliers. The 2nd Battalion of the regiment arrived from Buttevant by train at the Ballsbridge siding at 11.30 a.m., and marched across the roadway into the Royal Dublin Society's premises. A great crowd of people watched the men detraining, and several hearty rounds of cheering greeted their appearance. The men looked in splendid form as they defiled into the main hall and took up the positions allotted to them. It was at first stated that the strength comprised 25 officers, 2 warrant officers, 8 staff sergeants, 54 sergeants, and 528 rank and file; but the figures given yesterday were 18 officers and 523 rank and file. Be the numbers as they may, the appearance of the men thoroughly maintained the regimental nickname of 'The Old Toughs.' Hardy, wiry warriors they looked—thoroughly capable of accomplishing the daring and courageous deeds which have covered the Dublin Fusiliers with special glory. It is worthy of note that the majority of the non-commissioned officers served through the South African campaign from the Battle of Dundee, and that Lieutenant and Quartermaster Burke is the only remaining one who left England with the battalion nineteen years ago. The officers and men of the battalion were dressed in general service (khaki) uniform, and carried their rifles and bayonets. They also wore Indian helmets with puggarees, while the mounted company were attired in the clothing suited to this particular branch of the Service. They were under the command of Colonel Tempest Hicks, C.B., Colonel English, and Major Fetherstonhaugh, and when they marched into the hall and took up position on either side, in line of half-battalions, they were greeted with loud cheering, and when the order

THE RETURN HOME AND RECEPTION

'stand at ease' was made a number of reservists and other friends rushed forward to exchange greetings with former acquaintances. There was nearly a half-hour's wait for the arrival of the Duke of Connaught, and in the interval the bands of the Fusiliers and Warwickshire Regiment played some selections. At a quarter-past twelve precisely, H.R.H. the Commander of the Forces in Ireland arrived in an open carriage, accompanied by H.R.H. the Duchess of Connaught and Princesses Margaret and Patricia of Connaught, and attended by the following staff: Major-General Sir William Knox, Major-General Sir John Maxwell, Colonel Hammersley, Colonel Davidson, Colonel Dickinson, Colonel Congreve, V.C., and Major Murray, A.D.C.

The Duke, who wore the uniform of a Field-Marshal, was received by the following members of the reception committee: Major Domville, D.L. (vice-chairman), Mr. Justice Ross, Sir Wm. Thompson, Sir Charles Cameron, C.B., Major Davidson Houston, Colonel Finlay, Colonel Davidson, Major-General Sir Gerald Morton, K.C.B., Colonel Paterson, Colonel G. T. Plunkett, C.B., Captain Lewis Riall, D.L., Colonel Vernon, D.L., and Alderman Harris.

Major-General Vetch, commanding the Dublin District, was accompanied by Major Lowndes, A.D.C., Major Gilles (Brigade-Major), and Captain Fox Strangways (Garrison Adjutant). A guard of honour of the Royal Irish Rifles was drawn up outside the Show Buildings, and the band of the regiment played the National Anthem when the Duke and Duchess of Connaught drove up.

Their Royal Highnesses having taken seats on the daïs, the Duke of Connaught, who spoke in a tone which was easily heard in all parts of the building, said, 'Colonel Hicks, officers and non-commissioned officers, and men of the 2nd Battalion Royal Dublin Fusiliers, allow me to welcome you most warmly home again to old Ireland after your very arduous four years' service. I am sure I am only

2ND BATT. ROYAL DUBLIN FUSILIERS

the mouthpiece, not only of the General Officer Commanding this Army Corps, but also of every loyal Irishman, when I assure you how warm and how hearty is the greeting that is given you on your return to your native country, and especially in this capital of Ireland. You are an old and distinguished regiment; raised originally for service in India as the Royal Madras and Royal Bombay Fusiliers. During the time that you bore this name and the numbers 102 and 103, you took a very honourable part in all those great battles that assured us the conquest of India. Now, since the year 1881, you have become closely associated not only with Ireland, but with its capital. Your first service since you became the Royal Dublin Fusiliers was in South Africa, and through the arduous services in that country you, men, whom I have now the honour of addressing, nobly maintained the traditions of those fine soldiers who went before you. When you were sent from India amongst the first reinforcements of the troops in South Africa in 1897—soon afterwards the war broke out—you took a leading part in the Battle of Talana. You then went back to Ladysmith, and after falling back across the Tugela, you were attached to the army of Sir Redvers Buller, in the Irish Brigade under General Hart. During all those weary months on the Tugela, you took a leading part in every action that took place, and you distinguished yourselves so much at Pieter's Hill that when the relief force of Ladysmith marched in, the general officer commanding gave you the post of honour, and you led the troops that marched into Ladysmith. (Cheers.) Men of the Royal Dublin Fusiliers, this occasion is one of especial pleasure and satisfaction to myself, as His Majesty has done me the great honour of appointing me your Colonel-in-Chief—(cheers)—and I hope that in this you will recognise not only His Majesty's high appreciation of the distinguished services you have rendered to his throne and his empire, but also that you will see in it his wish that

THE RETURN HOME AND RECEPTION

you will have some special mark of distinction when he has made me, his only brother, Colonel-in-Chief of the regiment. I hope I shall long have the honour to be your Colonel-in-Chief, and to have a connection with a regiment of which every Irishman feels so proud.' (Cheers.)

Colonel G. T. Plunkett, C.B., read the following letter, received from the Earl of Meath, H.M.L. for the County and City of Dublin:—

'*Ottershaw, Chertsey.*

'MY DEAR PLUNKETT,—Owing to absence from Ireland, I shall be unable to be present in person with you on the 13th, when you and the Reception Committee entertain the 2nd Battalion Royal Dublin Fusiliers on their return home from foreign service, but I shall be with you in spirit, and I hope you will let the officers and men know how sorry I am that I cannot personally welcome them on their return to Ireland, and to Dublin, after so many years spent abroad in the service of their Sovereign.

'The fame which the regiment has acquired by daring deeds of valour performed during the late war has travelled far beyond the shores of Ireland. Military men the world over, and all who have studied the South African War, have heard of the famous deeds of the Dublin Fusiliers. The citizens of the Metropolitan county and City are proud of the men who, mindful of their origin, have known how to make the name of Dublin to be honoured in all lands. Both officers and men have done their duty to King and country, and we, their Irish brothers, accord them a hearty welcome on their return to the dear land of their birth.

'Believe me, yours sincerely,
'MEATH,
'*H.M.L. for County and City of Dublin.*'

The Duke of Connaught then said: 'I have been particularly requested by His Excellency the Lord Lieutenant

2ND BATT. ROYAL DUBLIN FUSILIERS

of Ireland to assure you of his warm welcome. He is away in England at present, but he has sent his military secretary and senior A.D.C. to represent him, and to give you his warmest wishes.' (Applause.)

His Royal Highness then distributed the medals and other distinctions to the officers and rank-and-file of the battalion who were entitled to them. The following officers were decorated, the Duke cordially shaking hands with each recipient:—Colonel Hicks, C.B., Colonel English, Major Fetherstonhaugh, Major Carington Smith, Captain H. W. Higginson, Captain Cory, D.S.O., Captain Garvice, D.S.O., Lieutenants Grimshaw, D.S.O., Haskard, Britton, Wheeler, St. George Smith, Knox, Tredennick, Seymour, Robinson, and Maclear, and Lieutenant and Quartermaster J. Burke and Sergeant-Major Sheridan. His Royal Highness pinned distinguished-conduct medals on the breasts of Lieutenant and Quartermaster J. Burke, Corporal Connell, and Privates C. N. Wallace, M. Farrelly, and M. Kavanagh, each recipient being loudly cheered.

The following officers who had served with the battalion during the war, but who had previously come home through wounds or sickness, availed themselves of the opportunity to have their medals presented to them by the Duke:—Captain Downing, Captain Dibley, Lieutenants Renny, Supple, Newton, Weldon, Molony, Armstrong, and Cooper. The distribution of the medals occupied over half an hour.

When this important portion of the programme had been completed, the order to 'stack arms' was given, and the men filed into their seats at the four long rows of tables which had been admirably prepared for the dinner by the caterers, Messrs. Mills & Co., of Merrion Row. Messrs. Mills & Co. had a picked staff of forty-two persons to carve the various dishes and wait at table. Dinner consisted of several courses, with selected fruit; while in addition to liberal supplies of ale, stout, and mineral waters, 300 bottles

THE RETURN HOME AND RECEPTION

of champagne were placed before the honoured guests. This last-mentioned luxury was the generous gift of Messrs. Perrier-Jouet & Co., of Epernay, the famous wine shippers, who kindly and thoughtfully presented this supply of their extra-quality wine through their Irish representatives, Messrs. James McCullagh, Son, & Co., 34 Lower Abbey Street. When the guests were seated, H.R.H. the Duke of Connaught, the Duchess of Connaught, and the Princesses Margaret and Patricia of Connaught, with the Reception Committee, a number of ladies, and a resplendent military *entourage*, walked slowly down between the rows of tables, stopping to speak a few gracious words to the non-commissioned officers and men who had made themselves conspicuous even amongst their comrades for valorous deeds and unflinching devotion to duty. Many of the reservists who sat beside former 'chums' at table, and on whose less warlike garb, the ordinary civilian clothes, medals and clasps shone out in high relief, also received kindly congratulations from the Commander-in-Chief in Ireland. Meanwhile the string band of the 21st Lancers, who occupied a good position on the gallery, played a beautiful selection of airs, principally Irish, not the least being 'The Wearin' of the Green.' The Royal party on walking down the centre of the hall was enthusiastically cheered, and the Duchess and her daughters left the building at about half-past one.

The Duke remained for lunch with his staff and the officers of the battalion. The health of His Majesty the King was drunk amidst much enthusiasm. After dinner, cigars and cigarettes and tobacco were liberally distributed, officers of the regiment performing most of this agreeable duty, and each man was presented with a nice briar pipe before leaving, the gift of Messrs. Lalor & Co., of Nassau Street.

In the interval between dinner and leaving the premises

2ND BATT. ROYAL DUBLIN FUSILIERS

at Ballsbridge, many friends and relatives of the members of the battalion were afforded an opportunity for a pleasant chat, and most of these accompanied the men in their subsequent march through the city. One figure attracted much attention during the afternoon—a sturdy soldier who formerly belonged to the Royal Dublins, and who appeared in the quaint, and, in this country, unusual uniform of a West African regiment. It would be certainly less than unwarranted to refer to the general appearance and behaviour of the men. Clean, smart, soldierly fellows, they all appeared to be impressed with the one idea—that they belonged to a crack corps with unrivalled traditions to maintain.

The departure from Ballsbridge occasioned unbounded enthusiasm on the part of thousands of eager spectators, who, unaware of the exact time at which the entertainment would finish, had patiently waited for a couple of hours to catch a glimpse of the 'Old Toughs.' The main thoroughfare from the Show-grounds to Pembroke Road was lined by detachments of the Warwickshire, East Lancashire (with band), and Middlesex Regiments, while a guard of honour of the Royal Irish Rifles (with their band) was stationed opposite the main entrance. About 3.15 o'clock H.R.H. the Duke of Connaught, preceded by two mounted policemen and an escort of the 21st Lancers, drove out, and passed over the route to be traversed immediately afterwards by the Fusiliers. The Field-Marshal was loudly cheered as he proceeded to the Royal Hospital, and repeatedly returned the cordial salutations of the large crowds who were assembled at different points. The appearance of the fêted warriors was the signal for an astonishing ovation at Ballsbridge.

The scene was a striking one. A splendid body of the 21st Lancers, numbering fifty, occupied first place in the procession, and these were followed by four or five bands

THE RETURN HOME AND RECEPTION

and the heroes of the day. Another detachment of fifty Lancers brought up the rear, and a number of men of the same dashing cavalry regiment marched on either side of the advancing column. Many relatives and friends of the Fusiliers had now an opportunity to exchange greetings, and strict army discipline was at an end. There was nothing reprehensible, however, and the progress to Kingsbridge was of the most orderly and praiseworthy description.

The route followed was the main road from Ballsbridge—Pembroke Road, Upper Baggot Street, Lower Baggot Street, Merrion Row, Stephen's Green, North Grafton Street, College Green, Dame Street, Parliament Street, and the south lines of quays to Kingsbridge. At different points, like Baggot Street Bridge, Stephen's Green, and Grafton Street, the reception was of a most cordial nature, while an immense crowd in College Green raised deafening cheers as the sturdy warriors marched past. Enthusiasm reached its height when the tattered colours of the battalion, borne by two stalwart young ensigns, came into view. The officers and men appeared delighted with the cordial reception extended to them on all sides. At Grattan Bridge the band of the Seaforth Highlanders, which had already delighted a large concourse of people with some choice selections, struck up a lively air as Dublin's guests moved past, while a splendid send-off characterised the entrainment of the battalion at Kingsbridge for Buttevant, co. Cork.

The Railway Company made excellent arrangements for the men, who, considering their long day and its happy experiences, went through the ordeal in first-class style. After all, one could scarcely expect less from soldiers who carry six or seven, or even nine clasps, on their medal ribbons.

It is right to mention that a number of members of the Army Veterans Association, decorated with their medals and other distinctions, visited Ballsbridge, and cordially

2ND BATT. ROYAL DUBLIN FUSILIERS

congratulated the Fusiliers on their return from foreign service.

On reaching Buttevant, the men will be supplied with new clothing and granted a general furlough.

Shortly after the reception the battalion was once again supplied with their home service full-dress head-gear—the busby, and it was with much gratification that the men wore their new busby hackle for the first time. This distinction was granted in 1902, when by Army Order 57 it was directed that the Royal Dublin Fusiliers should wear a blue and green hackle in their busbies: that for the officers to be blue and green, eight inches long, and that for the non-commissioned officers and men a similar but shorter one, in recognition of their services during the war in South Africa. In explanation of the colours of the hackle it may be stated that blue is the distinguishing colour of the 1st Battalion ('Blue Caps'), and green that of the 2nd Battalion ('Old Toughs').

On November 27th, 1903, the regiment was honoured by having appointed as its Colonel Major-General W. F. Vetch, C.V.O., commanding Dublin Garrison, *vice* Lieut.-General Sir John Blick Spurgin, K.C.B., G.C.S.I., deceased.

General Vetch joined the 102nd Foot on March 8th, 1864, was promoted Lieutenant, July 1st, 1869; Captain, May 22nd, 1875; Major, June 18th, 1881; Lieut.-Colonel, June 7th, 1884; Colonel, June 7th, 1888; and Major-General, April 1st, 1900.

After a quiet and uneventful stay at Buttevant for nearly three years the battalion proceeded to Fermoy on September 14th, 1906, and took up quarters in the New Barracks at that station.

CHAPTER III.

THE MEMORIAL ARCH.

'Even so great men great losses should endure.'
Julius Cæsar.

ON August 19th, 1907, the memorial arch to the officers and men who fell in South Africa was opened by H.R.H. the Duke of Connaught, Colonel-in-Chief the Royal Dublin Fusiliers. The 2nd Battalion was marching from Kilworth Camp to Ballyvonaire Camp on that day, but the authorities very kindly did everything in their power to make the ceremony a success, and Colonel English, Major Bromilow, and every one of any importance who had taken part in the war proceeded to Dublin by special train on the morning of the 19th, while the Depôt and Militia officers also assembled in good force.

The officers and men of the regiment were very sensible of the honour shown to them by H.R.H. the Duke of Connaught in personally opening the arch, and so identifying himself with it and them, while every Dublin Fusilier present felt an added pride in himself and his uniform as he saw it worn by His Royal Highness the brother of His Majesty the King.

The following account of the ceremony is taken from the Dublin *Daily Express*, to whose proprietors our thanks are due for permission to reproduce it:—

'ROYAL DUBLIN FUSILIERS' MEMORIAL IN STEPHEN'S GREEN INAUGURATED BY THE DUKE OF CONNAUGHT.
LUNCHEON AT SHELBOURNE HOTEL.

'To-day the Royal Dublin Fusiliers' Memorial to the officers and men of the regiment who fell in South Africa was

2ND BATT. ROYAL DUBLIN FUSILIERS

formally inaugurated by the Duke of Connaught, Inspector-General of the British Army. His Royal Highness arrived at Amiens Street terminus by the early morning train from Belfast, and was received by the Viceroy's Military Secretary. The Duke of Connaught at once drove to the Shelbourne Hotel, where he was received by the following members of the Memorial Committee :—The Earl of Meath, President ; the Earl of Drogheda, Mr. Justice Ross, Colonel Vernon, Sir Frederick Shaw, Bart., D.S.O., Sir Maurice Dockrell, Mr. Richard Dowse, Colonel Gore-Lindsay, Colonel Finlay, Sir Thomas Drew, R.H.A., Sir Charles Cameron, C.B., &c.

'Lunch was served immediately afterwards, and was presided over by the Earl of Meath, K.P., who was supported on his right by H.R.H. the Duke of Connaught, K.P., the Earl of Drogheda, Major-General Vetch, C.V.O., and Mr. Justice Ross, P.C. ; and on his left by Lord Grenfell, G.C.B., Commander-in-Chief of the Forces in Ireland ; Viscount Iveagh, K.P. ; Major-General Sir Herbert Plumer, K.C.B. ; Lieut.-Colonel Sir F. Shaw, D.S.O., 5th Royal Dublin Fusiliers. There were also present :—

'Sir G. Holmes, K.C.V.O. ; Col. Vernon, D.L. ; Brig.-Gen. Hammersley, Col. Lindsay, D.L. ; Brig.-Gen. Monro, C.B. ; Col. R. St. L. Moore, C.B. ; Lieut.-Col. Hackett, 4th R.D.F. ; Sir Daniel Hegarty, Captain Seymour, A.D.C. ; Sir T. Myles, Major D. C. Courtney, Alderman Cotton, D.L. ; Mr. Gerald M'Guinness, Col. Doyly Battley, Capt. Cameron, Dr. Wheeler, Mr. G. S. Dockrell, Capt. Halahan, Col. Chapman, 1st R.D.F. ; Sir Horace Plunkett, P.C. ; Col. Finlay, Sir John Arnott, Brig.-Gen. Cooper, C.B. ; Mr. G. A. Stevenson, M.O. ; Col. Hutcheson Poe, D.L. ; Mr. P. Hanson, Sir John Moore, Major Carington Smith, Major Domville, D.L. ; Col. Lyster Smythe, D.L., A.D.C. ; Major Skeet, Capt. Garvice, Capt. Thompson, Mr. H. M. Dockrell, Mr. Wm. Graham, Mr. John Laverty, Col. F. P. English, D.S.O., 2nd R.D.F. ; Mr. R. Dowse, B.L. ; Major-Gen. Sir John Maxwell,

THE MEMORIAL ARCH

K.C.B. ; T. A. O'Farrell, J.P. ; Surg.-Gen. Edge, C.B. ; Col. the Hon. E. Lawless, Col. O'Neill, 3rd R.D.F. ; Sir W. Watson, D.L. ; Col. Colville Frankland, Major Lowndes, Mr. James F. Darcy, D.L. ; Mr. J. H. Pentland, R.H.A. ; Mr. Key, A.D.C. ; Mr. J. A. Pigott, Mr. Robert Mitchell, Mr. R. H. A. M'Comas, Mr. Major Gorman, Mr. George Healy, Mr. R. Tyson, Mr. R. A. Falconer, Major-Gen. Bunbury, C.B. ; Sir Maurice Dockrell, Brig.-Gen. Mills, C.B. ; Sir John Ross of Bladensburg, K.C.B. ; Sir T. Drew, R.H.A.; Sir G. Moyers, D.L. ; the Hon. M. Ponsonby, A.D.C. ; Sir William Thomson, Sir C. Cameron, C.B. ; Sir L. Ormsby, Col. D. Browne, Mr. R. H. Jephson, Major Knight, Mr. A. E. Kennedy, Mr. W. A. Shea, Mr. Milward Jones, Mr. F. J. Usher, Mr. J. H. Reid, Mr. Henry L. Barnardo, Mr. R. P. Jephson.

'After lunch, which was admirably served,

'The Earl of Meath arose, amidst applause, and said :—
"The toast list to-day is short, and contains but one toast, that of The King (applause). His Majesty King Edward occupies a position amongst rulers which is absolutely unique. He not only rules over twelve million square miles, one-sixth of the earth's surface, and governs four hundred millions of subjects of all races, colours, creeds, and conditions of civilisation, from the most advanced to the most backward, but he is a Monarch whose personal qualities are of so distinguished an order that he has come to be regarded as a statesman of the first rank (applause). The world watches His Majesty's movements with breathless interest. Under his masterful touch international difficulties which seem insuperable are solved, political sores are healed. His presence seems to breathe the spirit of peace and of goodwill, so that when he undertakes a journey it needs no strong imagination to picture to oneself the Angel of Peace hovering over his footsteps with healing in her wings (applause). King Edward is no stranger to Ireland ; certainly not to Dublin

2ND BATT. ROYAL DUBLIN FUSILIERS

(renewed applause). We knew him and loved him as Prince of Wales, and our affection for him has only increased since he became King, and since we recognised that Ireland and the Irish are as dear to him as he is to us (applause). We are an open-hearted race, and on each occasion that he has visited these shores, his kindly, sympathetic, and genial nature has captivated our hearts. He is just such a monarch as we love (applause). May he be long spared to reign over us and may he often grace this island with his genial and captivating presence." (Loud applause.)

'The toast was duly honoured, and the festive proceedings terminated.

'INAUGURATION CEREMONY BY THE DUKE OF CONNAUGHT. BRILLIANT FUNCTION.

'Brilliant and strikingly picturesque was the ceremony of unveiling the Royal Dublin Fusiliers' war memorial in St. Stephen's Green, which took place at four o'clock this afternoon. The weather was, fortunately, bright, although inclined to be showery, and no heavy rain fell at any stage to mar the success of the interesting proceedings, which were attended by a very large and distinguished gathering. Long before the ceremony commenced, a great crowd had assembled in the Green and its vicinity.

'The military arrangements were of a most elaborate nature, and thoroughly in keeping with the occasion. The troops of the Dublin Garrison and representative detachments of the Line and Militia battalions of the Royal Dublin Fusiliers were drawn up in the vicinity of the Memorial Arch, and presented a very imposing appearance. There was also a representative gathering of ex-soldiers who had served in the Royal Dublin Fusiliers during the South African war and of members of the Veterans' Club, who were accommodated in special places reserved for them on the outside of the arch. After the troops had been drawn up, the massed bands of the

THE MEMORIAL ARCH, DUBLIN.

ERECTED TO THE MEMORY OF THE OFFICERS, N.C.O.'S, AND MEN OF THE ROYAL DUBLIN FUSILIERS. OPENED BY H.R.H. THE DUKE OF CONNAUGHT, K.G., ETC., COLONEL-IN-CHIEF THE ROYAL DUBLIN FUSILIERS, AUGUST 19TH, 1907.

THE MEMORIAL ARCH

13th Infantry Brigade played a number of pleasing selections whilst awaiting the arrival of H.R.H. the Duke of Connaught.

'The magnificent monument, which takes the form of a triumphal arch spanning the north-west corner of St. Stephen's Green, was greatly admired by the crowd. The noble archway is undoubtedly a most beautiful and artistic ornament to the city. Twelve feet in width, it springs from rusticated piers, each intersected by a pedestal and a pair of pilasters supporting a Doric entablature. The frieze bears on its four elevations the names in gold of the principal actions in the South African War in which the regiment took part. The entablature is surmounted by an Attic storey broken over the pilasters, and bearing two inscription panels. The front keystone supports a bronze cartouche, flanked by branches of bay bearing the arms of the regiment. Within the arch appear the names of the gallant 212 who perished in the war.

' Loud cheers were raised when, at a quarter to four o'clock, Field-Marshal H.R.H. the Duke of Connaught arrived on the scene and was received with a Royal salute. He was accompanied by the Right Hon. the Earl of Meath, President of the Memorial Committee; General the Lord Grenfell, K.C.B.; Sir George Holmes, K.C.V.O.; the members of the committee, and others who had attended the luncheon at the Shelbourne Hotel. More cheers rose from the expectant gathering when, a few minutes later, their Excellencies the Lord Lieutenant and the Countess of Aberdeen arrived, and were received with a Royal salute. The flag on the Memorial Arch was then half-masted, and the order was given for the troops to "reverse arms" and "rest on their arms reversed." The massed bands of the 13th Infantry Brigade played the "Dead March in Saul," after which "Oft in the Stilly Night" was played by the band of the 2nd Battalion Royal Dublin Fusiliers. The massed bugles of the 13th Infantry Brigade

2nd BATT. ROYAL DUBLIN FUSILIERS

then sounded "The Last Post," and the flag on the Memorial Arch was mast-headed.

'His Excellency the Lord Lieutenant extended a hearty welcome to the Duke of Connaught, and congratulated the Memorial Committee, and every one connected with the undertaking, upon the successful manner in which it had been carried out.

'The Earl of Meath, in requesting his Royal Highness the Duke of Connaught to open the gates of the archway, said:—"Your Royal Highness, we meet to-day for the purpose of honouring the memory of the gallant men belonging to the Royal Dublin Fusiliers who sacrificed their lives for King and country in the late South African war. By the aid of subscriptions raised throughout the city and county of Dublin and its neighbourhood, a large sum of money has been collected, and I trust that your Royal Highness will agree with the general opinion that a very handsome and satisfactory memorial has been raised, worthy of the heroes whose fame it is destined to perpetuate. As the only surviving brother of the gracious and mighty Sovereign whose uniform these heroes wore when they died in the defence of their country's interests, and as Colonel of the regiment in which they so faithfully served, it is fit and proper that you, Sir, should have been invited to perform the ceremony of opening the gates of the arch erected to their memory. We who have been actively concerned with the erection of the memorial most sincerely and gratefully thank your Royal Highness for the honour you have done the regiment by thus personally identifying yourself with the effort to keep fresh in the minds of their fellow-countrymen the gallant deeds performed by those heroes whom to-day we delight to honour. Irish gallantry and Irish fidelity to King and country are well known. Wherever British arms have penetrated, there the record of Irish valour need not be sought in brass or stone, but in the soil itself, which has been made

THE MEMORIAL ARCH

sacred to Erin's sons by the knowledge that it holds the mortal remains of hearts which have been faithful to duty and to high ideals of Irish valour even to the gates of death. But, sir, it may safely be said that not in the Peninsula, nor in India—where this regiment under its old title, in a hundred fights never knew the meaning of the word defeat—did Irish soldiers ever cover themselves with greater glory than did the Dublin Fusiliers in the battles of South Africa —Talana, Colenso, Tugela Heights, Hart's Hill, Ladysmith, and Laing's Nek. These glorious contests are commemorated on the memorial arch which your Royal Highness will shortly declare open. Situated in the centre of the Irish capital this memorial, recording the gallant deeds of brave men, will be an ever-present reminder to coming generations of the citizens of Dublin of the obligations of loyalty, of faithfulness to duty and to honour which Ireland demands of all her sons. I have the honour, sir, on behalf of the Dublin Fusilier Memorial Committee, to ask your Royal Highness to declare the gates of the archway to be open."

'As his Royal Highness formally opened the gate, the massed bands played the National Anthem.

'Headed by H.R.H. the Duke of Connaught, the troops then marched through the arch with bayonets fixed, the Royal Dublin Fusiliers leading, and the other battalions following in regimental seniority, headed by their bands. Loud cheers were raised as the soldiers passed out into Grafton Street, and proceeded down that thoroughfare, which was thickly lined on either side with spectators. At College Green the troops separated, and marched off to their respective quarters.

'The memorial which was inaugurated to-day forms a handsome addition to the ornamental architecture of the city. It stands in one of the most prominent and most beautiful parts of the city, and is a striking adornment to the main entrance to Stephen's Green Park. The luxuriant

2ND BATT. ROYAL DUBLIN FUSILIERS

trees and foliage of the park form a capital background to the fine imposing arch, the design for which was suggested by Sir Thomas Drew, composed entirely of Irish granite; the height of the memorial is thirty-two feet six inches, and the breadth twenty-seven feet three inches. The ornamental iron gates leading into the principal carriage-drive of the park are cast out of metal taken from guns captured by the British Army from enemies in the past, and suspended over the keystone there will be an interesting trophy consisting of the Crest and Arms of the regiment. In front a large millstone will bear the inscription :—

FORTISSIMIS SUIS MILITIBUS
HOC MONUMENTUM
EBLANA DEDICAVIT. MCMVI.*

'In big letters in the frieze appear the names of the important battles in which the battalions of the regiment took part, and on the back of the arch the inscription :— "In memory of the officers, non-commissioned officers, and men of the Royal Dublin Fusiliers who died in the service of the country during the South African War, 1899–1902."

'The Earl of Meath, H.M.L., President of the Memorial Committee, and his colleagues, including the Earl of Drogheda, Sir Maurice Dockrell, Sir Thomas Drew, Colonel Gore Lindsay, and Colonel Vernon, are to be congratulated upon the successful result of their indefatigable efforts. When the project was first mooted, it met with enthusiastic support, and the necessary sum of 1800*l.* was quickly raised to cover the cost of erection.

'The plans were designed by Mr. Howard Pentland, of the Board of Works, in consultation with Sir Thomas Drew, and Messrs. Laverty & Son, Belfast, carried out the contract.

* 'To her brave soldiers Dublin has dedicated this Monument. 1906.'

THE MEMORIAL ARCH

'The losses of the 1st and 2nd Battalions of this famous regiment in the Boer war totalled 31 officers and 655 non-commissioned officers and men. The glorious and inspiring deeds performed by these two battalions during the terrible engagements which led to the relief of Ladysmith are still fresh in the memory of their proud countrymen. Throughout the whole of the arduous campaign, indeed, the regiment nobly upheld the finest tradition of the Irish soldier, and gained the admiration and respect of friend and foe alike. The 5th Battalion lost, in several minor engagements, two officers and ten men killed, and eight wounded.'

2ND BATT. ROYAL DUBLIN FUSILIERS

EPILOGUE.

WITH the opening of the Memorial the curtain drops on the last scene of the drama of the South African war, and the regiment's share in it. To the large majority of those present the ceremony was probably merely a spectacular entertainment, but its real significance was borne fully home to us, even without the sight of more than one poor woman, silently weeping from the re-opening of the never-healed wound in her heart. For there is nothing truer than that a victory is only less terrible than a defeat, and as the sad strains of the wailing music fell on our ears, our thoughts flew back through the many happy years of good-comradeship we had spent with the gallant friends whom we have never ceased to mourn, and whose names will be treasured memories as long as the regiment endures.

But with the opening of the gates by our Colonel-in-Chief a fresh chapter in the history of the regiment commenced, and all that remains for us who share in the triumph of the present is to emulate in the future the noble deeds of those who gave their lives in willing, cheerful sacrifice for their sovereign, their country, and their regiment.

THE END.

THE SOUTH AFRICAN MEMORIAL, NATAL.

APPENDIX.

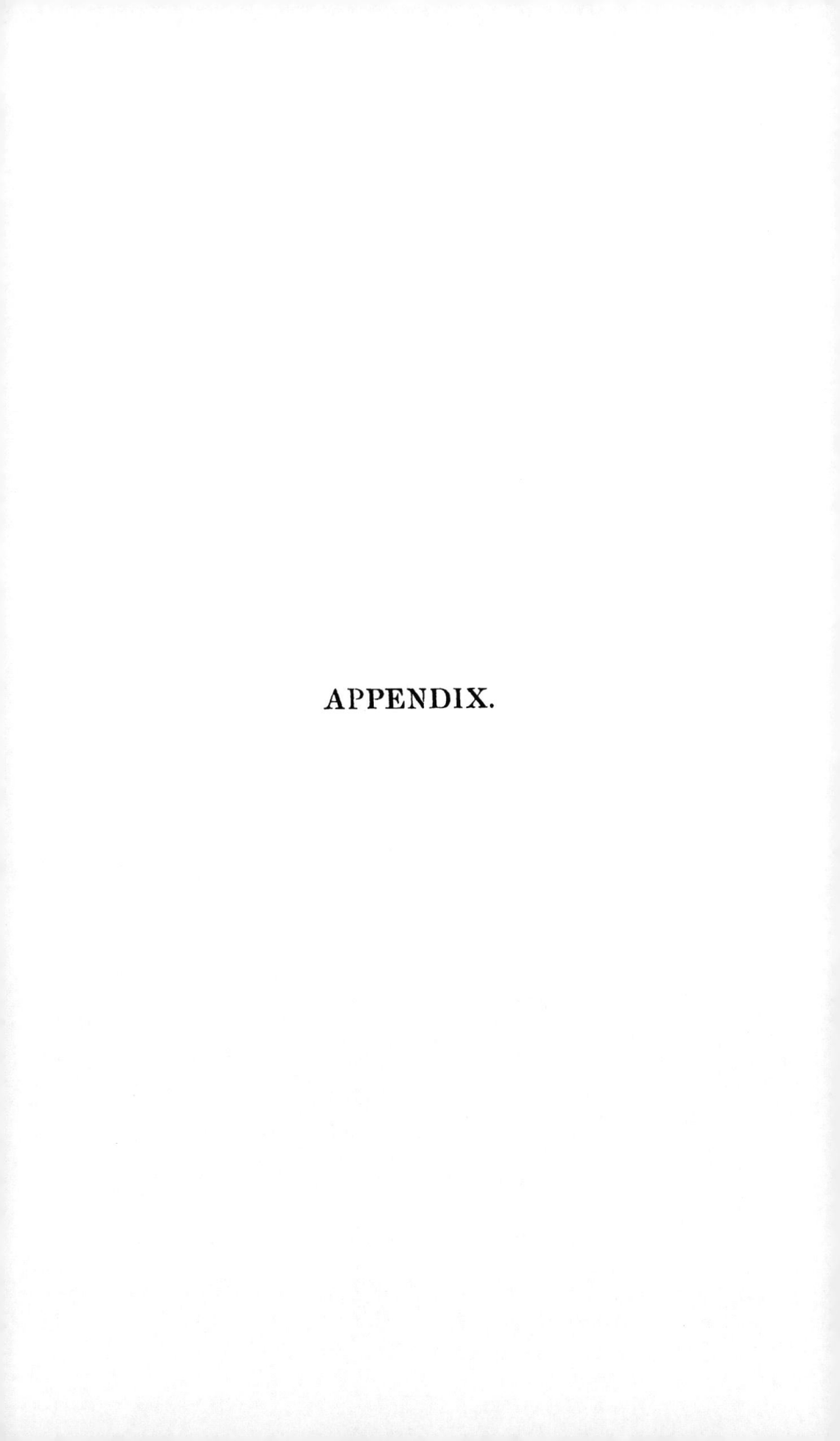

APPENDIX

I.

ROLL OF DEATH CASUALTIES.

KILLED IN ACTION.

No.	Rank and Name.	Place of Death.	Cause.	Date.	Remarks.
	Capt. Weldon	Talana Hill	Killed in action	20/10/99	
5103	Pte. Cahill	,,	,,	,,	
5794	,, Merrill	,,	,,	,,	
5933	,, Crotty	,,	,,	,,	
5918	,, Callaghan	,,	,,	,,	
5795	,, Balfe	Chieveley	,,	15/11/99	Armoured train
5031	,, Birney	,,	,,	,,	,,
5546	,, O'Shea	Colenso	,,	1/11/99	While on patrol,
	Lieut. Henry	,,	,,	15/12/99	[M.I.
3441	Sgt. Hayes	,,	,,	,,	
4488	Pte. Smith	,,	,,	,,	
5930	,, Sinnott	,,	,,	,,	
5123	,, Broderick	,,	,,	,,	
5319	L.-Cpl. Coyne	,,	,,	,,	
5833	Pte. Dillon	,,	,,	,,	
4795	,, Murphy	,,	,,	,,	
4380	,, Doolan	,,	,,	,,	
4299	,, McAlpine	,,	,,	,,	
5044	,, Moore	,,	,,	,,	
4560	,, Clifford	,,	,,	,,	
4838	,, Flood	,,	,,	,,	
6287	L.-Cpl. Gibson	,,	,,	,,	
6134	Pte. Pearse	,,	,,	,,	
6044	L.Cpl. Cathcart	,,	,,	,,	
4462	Pte. Murphy	,,	,,	,,	
6165	,, Bennett	,,	,,	,,	
6297	,, Campion	,,	,,	,,	
4679	,, Bowen	Potgieter's Drift	,,	8/2/00	
	Capt. Hensley	Venter's Spruit	,,	20/1/00	
5668	L.-Sgt. Taylor	,,	,,	,,	
	Lt.-Col. Sitwell	Hart's Hill	,,	24/2/00	
	Capt. Maitland	,,	,,	,,	
4261	Cpl. Seymour	,,	,,	,,	
4871	Pte. White	,,	,,	,,	
5359	,, Galbraith	,,	,,	,,	
6296	,, Allen	Pieter's Hill	,,	27/2/00	
3303	,, Timmins	Hart's Hill	,,	24/2/00	Militia 4th R.D.F.
4012	,, Armstrong	,,	,,	,,	Militia 5th R.D.F.
2037	,, Whelan	,,	,,	,,	,,
2872	,, Wade	,,	,,	,,	,,
5073	,, Kinsella	Pieter's Hill	,,	27/2/00	
5618	,, Purcell	,,	,,	,,	
1769	Sgt. Brennan	,,	,,	,,	Section 'D'
1717	Pte. Shirwin	,,	,,	,,	Militia 5th R.D.F.
2327	,, Grimes	,,	,,	,,	,,
5573	,, Tyrrell	Near Talana	,,	20/10/99	

2ND BATT. ROYAL DUBLIN FUSILIERS

KILLED IN ACTION (continued).

No.	Rank and Name.	Place of Death.	Cause.	Date.	Remarks.
5987	Pte. Mahoney	Near Talana	Killed in action	20/10/99	
4864	,, Byrne	,,	,,	,,	
5861	,, McGuire	Chieveley	,,	15/11/99	Armoured train
2112	,, Kelly	Hart's Hill	,,	23/2/00	Section 'D'
6171	,, Kavanagh	Colenso	,,	15/12/99	
6011	Cpl. Sinnot	Steelkoolspruit	,, [Boers	25/10/01	[bullets
4621	Pte. Hyland	Nr. Krugersdorp	Murdered by	6/1/01	Found riddled with

II.
DIED OF WOUNDS.

No.	Rank and Name.	Place of Death.	Cause.	Date.	Remarks.
1166	2nd-Lt. Genge	Talana Hill	Of wounds	21/10/99	
5263	C.Sgt. Anderson	,,	,,	,,	
3467	Pte. Johnston	Maritzburg	,,	27/11/99	Arm. train disaster
6293	Clr.-Sgt. Gage	,,	,,	20/12/99	Battle of Colenso
1823	Pte. Crosbie	Spearman's Cmp.	,,	26/1/00	,, Venter's Spruit
219	,, Finnegan	Hart's Hill	,,	25/2/00	Section 'D'
3648	,, Oldham	Chieveley	,,	3/3/00	Battle of Hart's Hill
5745	,, Norton	Maritzburg	,,	2/3/00	,, ,,
6299	,, Brady	Colenso	,,	,,	,, Pieter's Hill
5349	,, Kelly	Maritzburg	,,	8/3/00	,, ,,
3094	,, Bracken	,,	,,	16/3/00	,, Hart's Hill
2753	Sgt. Broughton	Dundee	,,	22/10/99	,, Talana
4029	Pte. Frahill	,,	,,	28/11/99	,, ,,
5706	,, Quirke	Colenso	,,	1/3/00	,, Colenso
6347	,, McEvoy	Johannesburg	,,	11/11/01	
5710	,, Nugent	Bakenlaagte	,,	31/10/01	
	,, Keegan	Dthala	,,	8/10/03	

III.
DEATHS BY DISEASE.

No.	Rank and Name.	Place of Death.	Cause.	Date.	Remarks.
5102	Pte. Phelan	Frere	Enteric	24/12/99	
642	Q.M.S. Hynes	Maritzburg	Pneumonia	7/1/00	
2865	Sgt. Linehan	Pretoria	Dysentery	16/12/99	
5519	Pte. Brennan	Maritzburg	Abscess liver	7/1/00	
3498	,, Dunphy	,,	Dysentery	19/1/00	
6129	,, Homan	Mooi River	Enteric	22/2/00	
4593	,, Keating	,,	,,	15/2/00	
5368	,, Walsh	Cape Town	Tumour brain	26/11/99	
2775	,, Ward	Ladysmith	Enteric	7/2/00	
5317	,, Maher	Estcourt	,,	8/3/00	
6510	,, Tobin	Ladysmith	Dysentery	22/3/00	
5909	,, Dixon	,,	,,	25/3/00	
5801	,, Martin	Chieveley	,,	24/4/00	

APPENDIX

DEATHS BY DISEASE (continued).

No.	Rank and Name	Place of Death	Cause	Date	Remarks
5790	Pte. Greene ...	Mooi River	Enteric	15/4/00	
	2nd Lt. Dennis	Aliwal North	,, ...	2/5/00	
1600	Pte. O'Brien ...	,,	,, ...	,,	3rd R.D. Fus.
4791	,, O'Connor	Mooi River	,, ...	3/5/00	
5200	,, Hart ...	,,	Fractured thigh	1/5/00	
3380	,, Cummings	Aliwal North	Enteric pneumonia	5/5/00	3rd R.D. Fus.
3760	,, Keogh ...	Chieveley ...	Enteric	,,	
4012	,, Mack ...	Aliwal North	,, ...	12/5/00	
5847	,, O'Carroll	,,	Enteric phthisis	15/5/00	
4566	,, Gray ...	Kimberley ...	Enteric	17/5/00	
5622	,, Corr ...	Maritzburg	Ague	28/2/00	
4131	Cpl. Looney ...	Woolwich ...	Dysentery	24/3/00	
	Lieut. Ely ...	At sea	Enteric	15/4/00	
6049	Pte. Neill ...	Kimberley ...	,, ...	23/5/00	
6309	L.Cpl. McGinley	,, ...	,, ...	8/6/00	
6608	Pte. Behan ...	,, ...	,, ...	19/6/00	
4686	,, Ears ...	Wynberg ...	,, ...	25/6/00	
7049	,, Roach ..	Heidelberg	Pneumonia ...	14/7/00	
5881	,, Pooley ...	,,	Enteric	18/7/00	
4499	O.R.S. Hanrahan	Maritzburg	g.s. skull	2/7/00	Suicide
5873	Pte. Hunt ...	At sea ...	Enteric	26/4/00	
3998	,, Kenny ...	Krugersdorp	Pneumonia ...	12/9/00	
1741	,, Burke ...	Johannesburg	,, ...	11/9/00	Section 'D'
4737	Cpl. Wilson ...	Maritzburg	,, ...	27/10/00	
5741	Pte. Dwyer ...	Germiston ...	Enteric	31/10/00	
5697	,, Davis ...	Pretoria ...	.. ...	29/11/00	Died in hospital, [prisoner of [war
5181	,, Clark ...	Kaalfontein	Lightning	24/11/00	
6800	,, Connor ...	Johannesburg	Enteric	25/11/00	
5967	,, Sutton ...	Krugersdorp	Jaundice	18/1/00	
2961	,, Ambrose	Johannesburg	Enteric	3/2/01	
6770	,, Cassidy...	Bloemfontein	,, ...	22/3/01	
1346	,, Hanlon ...	Maritzburg	,, ...	5/4/00	
6109	,, Buckley	Cork ...	Insane	...	
3910	L.Cpl. Stewart	Gaskraal ...	,, ...	28/8/01	
6491	Pte. O'Connor	,, ...	.. ..	,,	
5532	,, Peel ...	Krugersdorp	Enteric	14/8/01	
4657	,, Mooney	,,	,, ...	22/12/01	
5397	,, Melia ...	Kroonstad ...	,, ...	27/12/01	
5540	,, Quinn ...	Krugersdorp	Drowned	14/1/02	
6028	Sgt. Pearson ...	At sea	Enteric	7/2/02	
5303	Pte. Furlong ...	Aden	Heat apoplexy ...	29/5/02	
4938	,, Moore ...	,, ...	Heart disease ...	9/8/02	
4921	Sgt. Smith ...	,, ...	Syncope	13/9/02	
4565	Pte. Dunne ...	,, ...	Multiple neuritis	10/10/02	
5686	,, Gray ...		Diseased liver ...	11/10/02	
3661	,, Mooney	Krugersdorp	Enteric	6/7/01	4th R.D. Fus.
6332	,, Merrigan	Aden	,, ...	8/11/02	
7547	Boy Roberts	Dthala ...	Pneumonia ...	8/3/03	
7182	Pte. Dempsey	,, ...	Enteric	13/10/03	
5944	,, Wynne ...	Aden	Consumption ...	2/3/04	

2ND BATT. ROYAL DUBLIN FUSILIERS

IV.

LIST OF WOUNDED.

Reg. No.	Rank and Name.	Date.	Place.	Nature of Wound.	Remarks.
	Capt. M. Lowndes	20/10/99	Talana	g.s. leg	
	,, Dibley	,,	,,	g.s. head	
	Lieut. Perreau	,,	,,	g.s. shoulder	
5686	Pte. Gray	,,	,,	...	...
2753	,, Frahill	,,	,,	...	...
5310	,, Black	,,	,,	...	...
4815	,, Doyle	,,	,,	...	...
4700	,, Leonard	,,	,,	...	...
4894	Sgt. Grace	,,	,,	...	...
5430	Pte. Babester	,,	,,	...	...
5317	,, Maher	,,	,,	...	...
4790	,, O'Brien	,,	,,	...	...
5047	,, Greer	,,	,,	...	...
4359	,, Smith	,,	,,	...	...
4699	,, Callaghan	,,	,,	...	...
4931	,, Righton	,,	,,	...	...
5947	,, Dwyer	,,	,,	...	...
43	Sgt.-Maj. Burke	,,	,,	...	...
3770	Col.-Sgt. McNeice	,,	,,	...	...
5426	Sgt. Walton	,,	,,	...	...
3139	,, McKenna	,,	,,	...	...
6264	Pte. Carroll	,,	,,	...	...
6125	,, Dempsey	,,	,,	...	...
5038	,, Richardson	,,	,,	...	...
5523	,, Ryan	,,	,,	...	...
4620	,, Summerville	,,	,,	...	...
5635	,, Tracey	,,	,,	...	...
6084	,, Brady	,,	,,	...	...
4910	Dmr. Brudnell	,,	,,	...	...
5078	Pte. Gorman	,,	,,	...	...
5643	,, Cullen	,,	,,	...	...
5011	,, Brennan	,,	,,	...	...
4382	,, Jordan	,,	,,	...	...
4766	,, Murphy	,,	,,	...	...
4592	,, Cullen	,,	,,	...	...
6096	,, Gilhooley	,,	,,	...	...
3704	,, Kearns	,,	,,	...	...
4857	,, Butler	,,	,,	...	...
4767	,, Byrne	,,	,,	...	...
6022	,, Cassin	,,	,,	...	...
5156	,, Fitzpatrick	,,	,,	...	...
5118	,, Magee	,,	,,	...	...
5142	,, Murray	,,	,,	...	...
5063	,, Kelly	,,	,,	...	...
5595	,, Reynolds	,,	,,	...	...
4948	,, Wilby	,,	,,	...	...
2156	Cpl. Hogan	,,	,,	...	...

APPENDIX

LIST OF WOUNDED (continued).

Reg. No.	Rank and Name	Date	Place	Nature of Wound	Remarks
5634	L.-Cpl. Keenan	20/10/99	Talana	...	
4593	Pte. Flood	,,	,,	...	
5137	,, McGrath	,,	,,	...	
4785	,, Hopkins	,,	,,	...	
5531	,, Hatt	,,	,,	...	
4444	,, Creegan	,,	,,	...	
4347	,, Lahey	,,	,,	...	
5914	,, Coyle	15/11/99	Armr. Train	shell, arm	
	Capt. Shewan	15/12/99	Colenso	g.s. thigh	
4341	Sgt. Doherty	,,	,,	g.s. shoulders	
4986	L.-Sgt. Gibbons	,,	,,	g.s. arm	
5668	,, Taylor	,,	,,	g.s. shoulder	
3150	Sgt. Towey	,,	,,	g.s. hand and foot	
501	,, Hamilton	,,	,,	g.s. foot	
5108	,, Bodkin	,,	,,	g.s. leg	
5628	L.-Sgt. Church	,,	,,	g.s. leg	
5374	Cpl. Loughran	,,	,,	g.s. thigh	
6684	Pte. O'Brien	,,	,,	g.s. hand	
5117	,, Lillis	,,	,,	g.s. foot	
4589	,, Whelan	,,	,,	g.s. hand	
5637	,, Taylor	,,	,,	g.s. thigh	
4898	,, Walker	,,	,,	g.s. head	
5687	,, Enright	,,	,,	g.s. hand	
5869	,, Mackey	,,	,,	g.s. knee	
5584	,, Carr	,,	,,	g.s. hip	
6145	,, Byrne	,,	,,	g.s. elbow	
6103	,, Cooney	,,	,,	g.s. foot	
4997	,, Ludlow	,,	,,	g.s. arm	
4201	Dmr. Webb	,,	,,	g.s. thigh	
5970	L.-Cpl. Cooper	,,	,,	g.s. leg	
6094	,, Hanley	,,	,,	g.s. leg	
5760	Pte. Brown	,,	,,	g.s. leg	
5765	,, Welsh	,,	,,	g.s. foot	
4545	,, Flood	,,	,,	g.s. thigh	
4959	,, Smith	,,	,,	g.s. hand	
5672	,, Sanders	,,	,,	g.s. leg	
5661	,, Murphy	,,	,,	g.s. foot	
4582	,, McCarthy	,,	,,	g.s. head	
4395	,, Ellis	,,	,,	g.s. arm	
4290	Sgt. Hunt	,,	,,	g.s. wrist and thigh	
4987	Pte. Reilly	,,	,,	...	
4552	,, Kelly	,,	,,	g.s. thigh	
3362	Dmr. Murphy	,,	,,	...	
4411	Pte. Murray	,,	,,	...	
5716	,, Lahey	,,	,,	...	
6038	,, Kelly	,,	,,	...	
3013	Sgt. Healey	,,	,,	...	
4726	Pte. O'Brien	,,	,,	...	
5848	,, Townsend	,,	,,	...	

2ND BATT. ROYAL DUBLIN FUSILIERS

List of Wounded (continued).

Reg. No.	Rank and Name.	Date.	Place.	Nature of Wound.	Remarks.
5834	Pte. McBride	15/12/99	Colenso	g.s. hip	
5520	,, Hackett	,,	,,	...	
4441	L.-Sgt. Merry	,,	,,	g.s. thigh	
5023	L.-Cpl. Hayes	,,	,,	g.s. feet	
4543	Pte. Keating	,,	,,	g.s. foot	
6123	,, Kelly	,,	,,	...	
4800	,, Walsh	,,	,,	...	
4226	,, Reilly	,,	,,	g.s. hand	
6137	,, O'Brien	,,	,,	g.s. thigh	
2442	,, Leary	,,	,,	...	
5151	,, Clark	,,	,,	...	
	Maj. English	20/1/00	Vent. Spruit	g.s. leg	
6105	L.-Cpl. Kidd	,,	,,	g.s. neck	
6796	Pte. Burke	,,	,,	g.s. foot	
6285	,, Healey	,,	,,	g.s. back	
3141	,, Rooney	,,	,,	g.s. arm	
4644	,, Burke	,,	,,	g.s. hip, thigh	
5997	,, Davis	,,	,,	g.s. thigh, leg	
5458	,, Burke	,,	,,	g.s. neck	
5873	,, Hunt	,,	,,	g.s. head	
5659	,, Walsh	,,	,,	g.s. leg	
5069	,, Lee	,,	,,	g.s. hand	
6121	,, Brien	,,	,,	g.s. thigh	
2892	L.-Sgt. Ryan	21/1/00	,,	g.s. foot	
3548	Sgt. Cragg	,,	,,	g.s. hand	
6047	Pte. Cole	,,	,,	g.s. arm	
6391	,, Richardson	,,	,,	g.s. foot	
4898	L.-Cpl. Walker	,,	,,	...	
6366	Pte. Molloy	,,	,,	g.s. right leg	
6310	,, Gibney	,,	,,	g.s. leg	
5883	,, Marshall	,,	,,	g.s. hand	
5283	,, Shaughnessey	,,	,,	g.s. left leg	
5904	,, Edwards	,,	,,	g.s. right hand	
4636	Cpl. Reynolds	,,	,,	g.s. chin	
4368	Pte. Githens	,,	,,	g.s. arm	
5056	,, Lordan	22/1/00	,,	g.s. thigh	
4794	,, Murray	23/1/00	,,	g.s. right forearm	
4689	L.-Sgt. O'Higgins	,,	,,	g.s. chest	
4384	Pte. Ring	,,	,,	g.s. head, shoulder	
5888	,, Kenny	,,	,,	g.s. head, shoulder	
6484	,, Duffy	,,	,,	g.s. hip	
5882	Sgt.-Dmr. Smith	25/1/00	,,	...	
5900	Pte. Mason	,,	,,	g.s. hand	
6569	,, Conroy	,,	,,	g.s. foot	
	2nd Lieut. Lane	23/2/00	Hart's Hill	g.s. head	
	,, Dennis	,,	,,	g.s. left leg	
2872	Pte. Wade	,,	,,	...	5th R.D. Fus.
4012	,, Armstrong	,,	,,	...	,,
3303	,, Timmins	,,	,,	...	,,

246

APPENDIX

List of Wounded (continued).

Reg. No.	Rank and Name.	Date.	Place.	Nature of Wound.	Remarks.
5167	Pte. McDonnell	23/2/00	Hart's Hill	...	...
5928	,, Pender	,,	,,	g.s. right hand	...
4791	,, Connor	,,	,,	g.s. chest	...
4817	,, Iliffe	,,	,,	...	...
4559	,, McCabe	,,	,,	...	...
2426	,, O'Beirne	,,	,,	...	...
6522	,, Ryan	,,	,,	g.s. right hip	1st Battalion
5461	L.-Cpl. Dennehy	,,	,,	...	...
5387	Pte. Brannagan	,,	,,	g.s. chest	...
4771	,, Johnston	,,	,,	g.s. left thigh	...
5765	,, Ward	,,	,,	g.s. arm and knee	
4557	,, McCarthy	,,	,,	g.s. back	...
5811	,, Ryan	,,	,,	g.s. arm	...
2921	,, Thompson	,,	,,	...	...
6355	,, Fagan	,,	,,	...	...
148	,, Metcalf	,,	,,	g.s. right arm	5th R.D. Fus.
2096	,, Farrell	,,	,,	...	...
1557	,, Kinsella	,,	,,	...	...
4530	,, Brown	,,	,,	g.s. groin	...
5684	,, Hetherston	,,	,,	g.s. chest	...
6333	,, Newsome	,,	,,	g.s. left arm	...
3631	,, McDonald	,,	,,	g.s. left shoulder	...
1997	,, Brady	,,	,,	...	5th R.D. Fus.
6110	,, Kelly	,,	,,	...	...
2387	,, Strain	,,	,,	g.s. buttock	...
3068	,, Adams	,,	,,	...	...
5069	,, Lee	,,	,,	...	...
4424	,, Mulvaney	,,	,,	...	...
4621	,, Hyland	,,	,,	g.s. left thigh	...
5836	,, Cullen	,,	,,	g.s. right wrist	...
3313	,, Concannon	,,	,,	g.s. right shoulder	
6498	,, Flannagan	,,	,,	g.s. chest	...
1741	,, Burke	,,	,,	g.s. left arm	...
2422	,, Morgan	,,	,,	...	...
2787	,, Brien	,,	,,	g.s. left knee	...
4325	,, Curran	,,	,,	g.s. left leg	...
6108	,, Bernes	,,	,,	...	...
5908	,, McDonald	,,	,,	...	...
1881	,, Reynolds	,,	,,	...	4th R.D. Fus.
4015	,, Lynch	,,	,,	...	...
2348	,, Maddox	,,	,,	g.s. left shoulder	...
4029	,, Quirk	,,	,,	...	...
6217	,, Valentine	,,	,,	...	...
3881	,, Talbot	,,	,,	...	...
6314	,, Early	,,	,,	...	...
5224	,, McNeill	,,	,,	...	...
4277	,, Mack	,,	,,	...	...
4994	,, Knoctor	,,	,,	g.s. right leg	...
3441	,, O'Grady	,,	,,	g.s. left hand	4th R.D. Fus.

2ND BATT. ROYAL DUBLIN FUSILIERS

List of Wounded (continued).

Reg. No.	Rank and Name.	Date.	Place.	Nature of Wound.	Remarks.
5982	Pte. Tighe	23/2/00	Hart's Hill	g.s. head	
347	,, Doyle	,,	,,	g.s. left hand	
6130	,, Mason	,,	,,	...	3rd R.D. Fus.
5141	,, Kirwan	,,	,,	g.s. right foot	
4569	,, Gorman	27/2/00	Pieter's Hill	g.s. shoulder	
5399	,, Connor	,,	,,	...	
5828	,, Kegney	,,	,,	...	
847	,, Mangan	,,	,,	...	3rd R.D. Fus.
1716	,, Quinn	,,	,,	...	,,
5716	,, Leahy	,,	,,	...	
5981	,, Broad	,,	,,	...	
5698	,, Toomey	,,	,,	...	
350	,, Murphy	,,	,,	...	3rd R.D. Fus.
1846	,, Kealey	,,	,,	...	,,
4741	,, Moore	,,	,,	...	
4903	Cpl. Marshall	,,	,,	...	
5379	Pte. Pryor	,,	,,	...	
2368	,, Byrne	,,	,,	...	
4878	,, Clark	,,	,,	...	
6524	,, Quaid	,,	,,	...	
1554	,, Brennan	,,	,,	...	5th R.D. Fus.
5757	,, Kelly	,,	,,	...	
5284	,, Farrell	,,	,,	...	5th R.D. Fus.
3361	,, Brady	,,	,,	...	,,
1765	,, Fagan	,,	,,	...	
6429	,, Fox	,,	,,	...	
4777	,, Mullane	,,	,,	...	
3253	,, Mellington	,,	,,	...	5th R.D. Fus.
5280	,, Daly	,,	,,	...	
639	,, Whelan	,,	,,	...	5th R.D. Fus.
6139	,, Dignam	,,	,,	...	
2917	,, Ferris	,,	,,	...	5th R.D. Fus.
3242	,, McHale	,,	,,	...	,,
3266	,, Evans	,,	,,	...	
1377	,, Farrell	,,	,,	...	
4474	,, McLoughlin	,,	,,	...	
6113	,, McCormack	,,	,,	...	
1651	,, Kinsella	,,	,,	...	5th R.D. Fus.
3639	,, Brien	,,	,,	...	,,
3282	,, O'Brien	,,	,,	g.s. hand	
1846	,, Gradwell	,,	,,	...	5th R.D. Fus.
174	,, Lawless	,,	,,	g.s. foot, right hand	,,
1284	,, Molloy	,,	,,	...	,,
1508	,, Donnelly	,,	,,	...	
5704	,, Kennedy	,,	,,	...	
2236	,, Tuite	,,	,,	g.s. right heel	5th R.D. Fus.
4317	,, Carpenter	,,	,,	...	
3231	,, Mallon	21/7/00	Zuikerbosch	g.s. right thigh	4th R.D. Fus.
2853	,, O'Brien	,,	,,	g.s. left thigh	,,

APPENDIX

List of Wounded (*continued*).

Reg. No.	Rank and Name.	Date.	Place.	Nature of Wound.	Remarks.
1143	Pte. Stanton	21/7/00	Zuikerbosch	... ...	4th R.D. Fus.
2961	Col.-Sgt. Cossey	,,	,,	... [eye	
	Maj. English	,,	,,	slight shell splinter,	[duty
6786	Pte. Reilly	15/9/00	Nr. Frdkstdt.	... ...	On convoy
2392	Sgt. James	21/9/00	,,	very slight g.s. leg	
6070	Pte. Angleton	2/10/00	Near Irene	g.s. foot	With M.I.
	Lieut. Haskard	27/2/00	Pieter's Hill	right elbow	
	2nd Lieut. Bradford	,,	,, [dorp	shoulder	
2692	Pte. Doyle	31/12/00	Nr. Krugers-	g.s. buttock	
5767	,, Lang	,,	Nooitgedacht	... [slight	
2052	,, Armstrong	2/2/01	Gatsrand ...	g.s. left arm, very	
6265	,, Roach	,,	,,	g.s. right leg, slight	
4981	,, Sheehan	,,	Nr. Carolina	g.s. neck	
5718	,, Kavanagh	,,	,,	g.s. left knee	
4365	,, Moran	,,	,,	g.s. left shoulder ...	
4680	,, Fitzgerald	,,	,,	g.s. left arm	
6057	,, Goff	,,	,,	g.s. chest	
5433	,, Holmes	28/8/01	Gaskraal ...	... ...	
4840	,, Nolan	,,	,, [fontein	... ...	
4858	,, Butler	27/7/01	Nr. Wonder-	... ...	
4680	,, Fitzgerald	25/10/01	Swartzfontein	g.s. hand, severe ...	
5706	,, McEvoy	,,	,,	g.s. buttock, groin	
3761	Sgt. Carroll	30/10/01	Bakenlaagte	g.s. leg, very slight	
4473	Pte. Hand	,,	,,	g.s. knee, severe ...	
4448	,, Murphy	,,	,,	g.s. foot, slight ...	
4513	,, Connor	,,	,,	g.s. hip, severe ...	
5706	,, Moran	,,	,,	g.s. hand, severe ...	
6347	,, Nugent	,,	,,	g.s. abdomen ...	
4686	Cpl. Curtis	15/12/99	Colenso ...	g.s. hand	
5548	Pte. Metcalf	,,	,,	g.s. left leg	
4453	,, White	,,	,,	g.s. both legs ...	
6330	L.-Cpl. Matthews	21/1/00	Vent. Spruit	g.s. leg	
5330	Pte. Holohan	27/2/00	Pieter's Hill	... ...	
5973	Cpl. Gaffney	7/10/03	Aden Hntlnd.	g.s. severe, foot ...	
6367	Pte. Daly	,,	,,	g.s. very slight ...	
5584	,, Carr	,,	,,	g.s. severe, chest ...	

2ND BATT. ROYAL DUBLIN FUSILIERS

V.

BATTLE OF TALANA.

Reported Missing since October 21st, 1899.

Reg. No.	Rank and Name.	Reg. No.	Rank and Name.
2615	Clr.-Sgt. Gage	5489	Pte. Geoghegan
2078	Sgt. Martin	6019	,, Curran
4388	,, Guilfoyle	5918	,, Callaghan
3761	,, Carroll	4411	,, Cooney
5328	L.-Sgt. Payne	5706	,, McEvoy
5178	,, Crean	5600	,, Gleeson
5094	Cpl. Corrigan	5000	,, Nulty
5544	,, Richards	4974	,, Costello
6028	,, Pearson	5889	,, Keogh
5004	,, Kiernan	5501	,, Mannix
5601	L.-Cpl. Lee	5127	,, Battersby
5143	,, Flynn	5352	,, White
5304	,, Whelan	4864	,, Byrne
4812	,, Lyons	5390	,, Doyle
4868	,, Green	5126	,, Farrell
5033	,, Byrne	5714	,, Finnigan
4947	,, Harper	5055	,, Reidy
4638	Pte. Mahon	5345	,, Dunne
4966	,, Murphy	5789	,, Flood
4359	,, Hall	4964	,, Gibney
4655	,, Cullen	5987	,, Mahoney
5175	,, Reddy	5030	,, Callaghan
5143	,, Flynn	5126	,, Delaney
5759	,, Dowling	4692	,, McGuinness
5070	,, Angleton	6018	,, McDonagh
5402	,, Rourke	5693	,, Keating
5209	,, Dunne	4532	,, Kirwan
5793	,, Murphy	6866	,, Molloy
4513	,, Connor	5427	,, Carr
5055	,, Reidy	4142	,, Lyons
5609	,, Connor	6120	,, Cullen
5162	,, Macken	4927	,, Kane
5929	,, Carroll	5545	,, Reilly
5956	,, Rourke	5702	,, Byrne
4498	,, Watts	5724	,, Dempsey
4884	,, Kenny	5218	,, Reilly
5876	,, Molloy	5880	,, Carroll
5647	,, Harrison	5144	,, Williams
6087	,, Tyrrell	5027	,, Doody
4788	,, Toomey	4473	,, Hand
4366	,, Doyle	4566	,, Glynn
5931	,, Bracken	5184	,, Dowler
3752	,, Travers	5551	,, Finn
5733	,, Kavanagh	5912	,, Kavanagh
6055	,, Gough	5182	,, Cavanagh
5266	,, Bigley	5350	,, Farrell
5479	,, Brien	4692	,, McGann

APPENDIX

VI.
REPORTED MISSING SINCE OCTOBER 22ND, 1899.

Reg. No.	Rank and Name.	Reg. No.	Rank and Name.
5022	Pte. Rourke	4327	Pte. Neill
4998	,, Hawthorn	5321	,, Moran
5246	,, McGuinness		

VII.
REPORTED MISSING SINCE OCTOBER 30TH, 1899.

Reg. No.	Rank and Name.	Reg. No.	Rank and Name.
5524	Pte. Wall	5503	Pte. Hennessey

VIII.
REPORTED MISSING SINCE NOVEMBER 15TH, 1899 (ARMOURED TRAIN DISASTER).

Reg. No.	Rank and Name.	Reg. No.	Rank and Name.
3672	Sgt. Hassett	3715	Sgt. Osborne
5114	Cpl. Hallahan	5795	Pte. Balfe
5800	Pte. Buckley	5316	,, Daly
6293	,, Kempster	5516	,, Scully
5499	,, Byrne	4443	,, Hoey
4497	,, Barry	5031	,, Bierney
5755	,, Collins	5697	,, Davis
6140	,, Dunphy	5297	,, Drew
5741	,, Dwyer	5841	,, Hoy
5256	,, Kavanagh	5287	,, Lynch
5691	,, O'Rourke	5908	,, Murphy
5626	,, Buckley	6308	,, Connell
5968	,, Glynn	6116	,, Harty
5057	,, Kirwan	6228	,, Meehan
5017	,, Pakenham	5297	,, Doogan
5239	,, Herbert	6319	,, Burke
6283	,, Cragg	4676	,, Driscoll
5790	,, Murray	4865	,, Reynolds
5210	,, Rice	6354	,, Sheridan
5329	,, Stanton	5861	,, McGuire
4680	,, Fitzgerald	4542	,, Flannagan
5548	,, Metcalf		

2ND BATT. ROYAL DUBLIN FUSILIERS

IX.

List of Officers in Natal Campaign.

Rank and Name.	Remarks.
Col. Cooper	Commanding 2nd Royal Dublin Fusiliers.
Maj. Bird	2nd in command.
,, English, A Company	Wounded at Venter's Spruit and Zuikerbosch.
Capt. Hensley, G Company	Killed at Venter's Spruit.
,, Weldon, E Company	Killed at Talana.
,, Fetherstonhaugh, D Coy.	Acted as Adjutant after Capt. Lowndes was wounded.
,, Dibley, B Company	Wounded at Talana, and sent into Intombi Hospital.
,, Lonsdale, M. I. Company	Captured at Talana.
Lieut. Shewan, H Company	Wounded at Colenso.
,, Perreau	Wounded at Talana, and sent into Intombi Hospital.
,, Le Mesurier	Captured at Talana. Escaped from Pretoria.
,, Grimshaw	Captured at Talana.
,, Cory	Was sent with M.I. Section to Dundonald's Brigade.
,, Renny	Transport Officer. Left in Ladysmith.
2nd Lieut. Haskard	Wounded at Pieter's Hill.
,, Henry	Killed at Colenso.
,, Frankland	Captured in Armoured Train.
,, Genge	Killed at Talana.
Capt. Lowndes (Adjutant)	Wounded at Talana, and sent into Intombi Hospital.
Lieut. and Qtmr. Rowland	Went to S A.C.
Lieut. Garvice	Joined battalion at Dundee ; captured at Talana.
2nd Lieut. Ely	Joined battalion at Dundee, and died of enteric, 1900.
Lieut. H. W. Higginson	Joined on posting, and shared in siege of Ladysmith.
Capt. Romer	Joined from Staff College on Oct. 30th.
Capt. Haldane and Lieut. Maitland (of Gordon Highlanders)	The former was captured in the Armoured Train, and escaped from Pretoria with Lieut. Le Mesurier ; the latter killed at Hart's Hill.
2nd Lieut. Britton	Joined on November 5th. After Colenso he acted as Transport Officer.
Brevet-Lieut.-Col. Sitwell	Joined on November 8th, and commanded C Company. He was killed at Hart's Hill.
2nd Lieut. Lane	Joined on December 6th. He was wounded at Hart's Hill.

APPENDIX

X.

The following Officers of the 1st Battalion and other corps joined on December 7th and subsequent dates:—

Rank and Name.	Remarks.
Maj. Hicks	Returned to 1st Battalion after Colenso. Succeeded Col. Cooper in command of 2nd Battalion, March 1900.
,, Gordon	Wounded at Colenso.
Capt. Bacon	Killed at Colenso.
2nd Lieut. De Salis	Promoted into another regiment.
,, Brodhurst Hill ...	Wounded at Hart's Hill.
,, Halahan	
,, Macleod	Wounded at Colenso.
,, Winnington	(Worcestershire Regiment). Attached.
,, Wheeler	Joined December 23rd.
,, Dennis	Joined December 27th, and died of enteric at Aliwal North.
Capt. Venour	Joined on January 30th.
Lieut. Hill	Joined on January 30th. Wounded at Hart's Hill.
2nd Lieut. Bradford	Joined on January 30th. Wounded at Pieter's Hill.
Capt. Sir Frederick Frankland, Bart.	(3rd Bedford Regiment). Joined on March 2nd.
Lieut. G. S. Higginson	Joined on March 11th.
Lieut. Nelson, R.M.L.I.	Joined on March 29th.
Capt. Clark, ,, ...	Joined on April 1st.

Col. C. D. Cooper took over a brigade, with Lieut. Renny as his A.D.C., early in 1900. It will thus be seen that Capt. Fetherstonhaugh was the only officer who was with the regiment from start to finish who was not hit.

2ND BATT. ROYAL DUBLIN FUSILIERS

XI.

TOTAL CASUALTIES OF OFFICERS OF THE
1ST AND 2ND BATTALIONS ROYAL DUBLIN FUSILIERS.

Name.	Nature of Casualty.	Place.
Capt. Weldon	Killed	Talana.
Lieut. Genge	,,	,,
Capt. Bacon	,,	Colenso.
Lieut. Henry	,,	,,
Capt. Hensley	,,	Venter's Spruit.
Lt.-Col. Sitwell	,,	Hart's Hill.
Capt. Maitland (Gordon Highlanders, attached)	,,	,,
Capt. Macbean	,,	Nooitgedacht.
,, Watson	,,	Western Transvaal.
Lieut. Ely	Died of disease	
,, Dennis	,,	
Capt. Dibley	Wounded	Talana.
,, Lowndes	,,	,,
Lieut. Perreau	,,	,,
Maj. Gordon	,,	Colenso.
Capt. Shewan	,,	,,
Lieut. Macleod	,,	,,
Maj. English	,,	Venter's Spruit and Zuikerbosch.
Capt. Hill	,,	Pieter's Hill.
Lieut. Brodhurst Hill	,,	,,
,, Lane	,,	Hart's Hill.
,, Dennis	,,	,,
,, Bradford	,,	Pieter's Hill.
,, Haskard	,,	,,
Capt. Carington Smith	,,	Sanna's Post and Heidelberg.
Lt.-Col. Mills	,,	Alleman's Nek.
Lieut. Seppings	,,	,,
,, Taylor	,,	Parys.
Capt. Kinsman	,,	Near Mafeking.
,, Chapman	,,	Itala.
Lieut. Lefroy	,,	,,

APPENDIX

XII.

HONOURS AND REWARDS OF OFFICERS OF THE 2ND ROYAL DUBLIN FUSILIERS.

C.B.
Colonel C. D. Cooper.
„ G. A. Mills.
„ H. T. Hicks.

D.S.O.
Major S. G. Bird.
„ W. H. O. Neill.
Brevet-Major A. F. Pilson.
„ W. J. Venour.
Captain H. M. Shewan.
„ G. N. Cory.
Lieutenant E. A. A. De Salis.
„ C. Garvice.
„ Lefroy.
„ W. F. Stirling.
„ C. T. W. Grimshaw.
„ A. Moore.
Captain-Quartermaster R. Baker.

BREVETS.
Major F. P. English.
Brevet-Major Godley.
Captain McBean.
Major A. W. Gordon.
Captain E. Fetherstonhaugh.
„ C. F. Romer.
„ P. Maclear.
„ H. Carington Smith.
Major A. J. Chapman.
Captain M. Lowndes.

SPECIAL PROMOTIONS.
Lieutenant Watson.
„ E. A. A. De Salis.
„ Lefroy.

XIII.

N.C.O.'S AND MEN OF 2ND ROYAL DUBLIN FUSILIERS AWARDED DISTINGUISHED CONDUCT MEDAL.

Reg. No.	Rank and Name.		Reg. No.	Rank and Name.	
3423	Sgt. M. Connor			L.-Cpl. Melia	
4290	„ Hunt			Pte. W. Connell	
1664	„ Sheridan	A.O. 163 of 1901		„ W. Cullen	A.O. 15 of 1902
	L.-Cpl. J. Kelly			„ A. Dowling	
	Pte. W. Holmes			„ M. Farrelly	
	„ P. Kelly			„ M. Kavanagh	
	„ E. Reid			„ J. McCormack	
	Sgt.-Mj. F. A. Whalen 5th R.D. Fus.		6642	„ C. N. Wallace	
	Qmr.-Sgt. B.T. Bruen 5th R.D. Fus.	A.O. 15 of 1902	43	Sgt.-Maj. J. Burke	A.O. 10 of 1903
	Col.-Sgt. F. Gage		4637	Col.-Sgt. J. Ambrose	
	Arm.-Sgt. T. H. Ford, attached R.D. Fus.		5178	„ T. Crean	
	Sgt. W. Brown			„ M. Dunne	
2892	„ J. Ryan			Cpl. P. Flannery	
	Cpl. G. F. Frost, 1st Batt. R.D. Fus.			Pte. P. Furlong	
				Col.-Sgt. J. H. Robinson, 1st Batt. R.D. Fus.	A.O. 172 of 1903

2ND BATT. ROYAL DUBLIN FUSILIERS

XIV.

AN ADDRESS PRESENTED BY THE NATAL UNITED IRISH ASSOCIATION.

The Officers, Non-commissioned Officers, and Men of the 2nd Battalion Royal Dublin Fusiliers.

THE recent war, from which we welcome you back, marks another epoch of glory in the annals of your distinguished battalion. It was our privilege on several occasions to be favoured at social functions with the presence of officers and men of the DUBLIN FUSILIERS, and we felt assured that the goodness of character and disposition which shed their radiance at those gatherings, would shine with added lustre when in the face of danger and death. The popularity of your regiment in Natal has only been exceeded by your distinguished gallantry in the field, and as we followed your fortunes with feelings of deepest interest throughout the campaign, our hearts thrilled with pride as we read of your gallant and heroic deeds. As you held the position of honour at the march to Lucknow, so were you by the unanimous consent of the army awarded a similar position in the entry to Ladysmith. The marvellous bravery displayed by your regiment in the terrible fighting between Talana Hill and Tugela, forms a fitting sequel to your magnificent record in the Indian Peninsula; and we as Irishmen can take a legitimate pride in the fact that your muster-roll of glory is replete with familiar names which abound throughout the hills and valleys of our far-off motherland. The name and fame of your regiment are world-wide; and whether on frozen shores or in tropical climes, a light-heartedness, an uncomplaining endurance of hardship and fatigue, and a ready adaptability to circumstances, afford abundant proof that the best traditions of our race have been maintained by the DUBLIN FUSILIERS. In the vast territories of Hindostan as in South Africa, you have shown the world the material of which an Irish soldier is made. In the many engagements in which you have taken part, you have seen your enemies fall thick around you, and seen, too, the crimson tide ebb from the heart of many a brave comrade, whose last good-bye will

APPENDIX

remain for ever hallowed in your memory. You have returned triumphant from this WAR, and though, alas! your numbers are fewer, your hearts are as stout and your spirits as intrepid as ever. The land which claims you as her sons has in proportion to her capabilities given more hostages to glory than any land beneath the sun, and well and nobly have you upheld that national renown. You have won a name and *éclat* that will go down through the ages, and with the hope that countless honours are yet in store to further illumine the aureole of your prestige,

We are yours faithfully,

CHAS. DONNELLY, *President*.
JAMES P. DONNELLY, *Hon. Treasurer*.
E. G. O'FLAHERTY, *Hon. Secretary*.

Vice-Presidents:

CRAWFORD LINDSAY.   THOS. KELLY.
A. TRIMBLE.   J. F. E. BARNES.

Committee:

W. P. BOWEN.   C. W. KAY EVANS.
W. J. LYONS.   R. S. W. BARNES.
P. O'NEILL.   J. J. O'NEILL.
E. BUTLER.   D. LANE.
N. F. BLACK.

XV.

ADDRESS FROM THE EUROPEAN INHABITANTS OF ADEN TO THE MEMBERS OF THE SERGEANTS' MESS, 2ND ROYAL DUBLIN FUSILIERS.

To the Members of the Sergeants' Mess, 2nd Battalion Royal Dublin Fusiliers.

WE, the undersigned, take advantage of this occasion, the eve of your departure from among us, to place on record our very high esteem of the many sociable qualities displayed by you since your battalion arrived in this station from South Africa in February, 1902.

Coming to Aden at a time when, after the brilliant services you had rendered to your Sovereign and country in that uncertain field of the reputation of battalions as

2ND BATT. ROYAL DUBLIN FUSILIERS

well as individuals—South Africa, you had every reason to expect a far better station, a union with those near and dear to you, and therefore every reason to be despondent. Instead, you threw yourselves into the social life of this place in such a way that, before you were here many weeks, it was felt that you, who had displayed the brilliant qualities so characteristic of your race on many a hard-fought field in South Africa, were not lacking in those social qualities which tend to enhance the popularity of His Majesty's forces, and make life a little less irksome in what all must admit is not a pleasant spot.

Words fail to express what we all feel at being compelled to say good-bye to you, who have been more than friends to so many of us, and in leaving Aden for return to your homeland, we assure you that you carry with you the sincerest good wishes of all.

We shall always have a kindly feeling for you, and watch your future with great interest, and, above all, we trust that you will find those from whom you have so long been separated in the best of health, and that a long life and prosperity is before you.

W. SMITH.
C. ELLIOTT.
W. WILLOWS.
E. B. BATCHELOR.
T. GRAVES.
R. GRIFFITHS.
A. HANDY.
C. A. HOLLAND.
C. J. HOCKING.
J. M. GILTINAN.
F. C. BREWIN.
F. WELLS.
E. HALL.
F. J. CLAY.
G. R. CHAMARETT.
P. C. KELLY.

F. WISEMAN.
G. C. KENNEDY.
R. THORLIN.
H. M. HANLEY.
E. B. OWEN.
J. A. RUPERT JONES.
J. R. DEANE.
T. W. TWADDLE.
C. O. CRAVEN.
J. MALLIA.
J. INGLOTT.
G. NOEL.
J. F. FIELD.
E. HESSLETON.
F. PENHA.

APPENDIX

XVI.

EXTRACT FROM BATTALION ORDERS ISSUED AT LADYSMITH, 27/10/99.

Para. 2. Strength.—The following officers and men, killed in action on the 20th inst. at the Battle of Talana, are struck off the strength :—

Capt. G. A. Weldon.
No. 5103 Pte. P. Cahill, A Coy. | No. 5931 Pte. P. Crotty, E. Coy.
„ 5794 „ A. Merrill, E Coy. | „ 5918 „ P. Callaghan, H Coy.

Died of wounds received in action on 21st :—

2nd Lieut. C. J. Genge.
No. 1166 Col.-Sgt. F. Anderson, F Coy.

The Commanding Officer, while expressing his deep regret at these casualties, can fully testify to the gallant manner in which each and all met their death, fighting for their Queen and upholding the regimental honour.

XVII.

EXTRACT FROM BATTALION ORDERS, DATED FRERE, 18/12/99.

Para. 3. Strength.—The following officers, N.C.O.'s, and men, having been killed in action at Colenso on the 15th inst., are struck off the strength of the battalion from that date :—

2ND BATTALION.
Lieut. Robert Clive Bolton Henry.

Reg. No.	Rank and Name.	Reg. No.	Rank and Name.	Reg. No.	Rank and Name.
3441	Sgt. Hayes.	5833	Pte. Dillon.	6134	Pte. Pearse.
6287	L.-Cpl. Gibson.	4795	„ Murphy.	4560	„ Clifford.
6044	„ Cathcart.	4380	„ Doolan.	4838	„ Flood.
5123	Pte. Broderick.	4299	„ McAlpine.	5319	L.-Cpl. Coyne.
4488	„ Smith.	5044	„ Moore.	6165	Pte. Bennett.
5930	„ Sinnott.	4462	„ Murphy.		

1ST BATTALION.
Capt. Arthur Henry Bacon.

Reg. No.	Rank and Name.	Reg. No.	Rank and Name.	Reg. No.	Rank and Name.
3993	Col.-Sgt. Magee.	6472	Pte. Hayes.	4095	Pte. Usher.
3514	Sgt. Flynn.	4192	„ Neill.	3108	„ Connell.
4869	„ Callan.	3906	„ Walsh.	6002	„ Wisdom.
5505	Pte. Cole.	4273	„ Nolan.	4387	„ Toole.
4301	„ Carroway.	3273	„ Costello.	4242	„ Joyce.
2943	„ O'Keefe.	2504	„ Bissett.	4672	„ Maddox.
?	„ O'Keefe.	4193	„ Deevey.		

2ND BATT. ROYAL DUBLIN FUSILIERS

The Commanding Officer, whilst deeply regretting, in common with all ranks, the severe loss the regiment has sustained in the deaths of Captain Bacon and Lieutenant Henry and the N.C.O.'s and men killed in action at Colenso on Friday last, desires to place on record his high appreciation of the admirable spirit displayed by all ranks in unflinching pressing forward under a very heavy fire to the attack of a practically impregnable position.

The names of the officers, N.C.O.'s, and men who fell will, he feels sure, be honoured in the annals of the regiment, as having set a noble example of fearless courage and devotion to duty.

XVIII. *Colenso*, 18/12/99 (5).
TELEGRAM RE DECEASE SERGEANT LINEHAN.
'*From Censor to G.O.C. L. of Comn.*'

'No. 5514 Cable from Lorenzo Marquez says that Sergeant Linehan, Fusiliers, died Racecourse, Pretoria, of Dysentery, Friday last. Buried Catholic Cemetery.'

XIX. *Frere*, 25/12/99 (3).
THE QUEEN'S MESSAGE, CHRISTMAS, 1899.

'I wish you and all my brave soldiers a happy Christmas. God protect and bless you all.—V.R.I.'

XX.
Spearman's Camp, 29/1/00 (6).
CAPTAIN C. A. HENSLEY DIED OF WOUNDS 21/1/00; STRUCK OFF STRENGTH; ORDER REGRETTING HIS LOSS.

The following Officer and N.C.O. having been killed in action and died of wounds on the dates opposite their names, are struck off the strength of battalion accordingly:—

Captain C. A. Hensley, died of wounds 21/1/00.
No. 5668 Lance-Sergeant Taylor, D company, killed in action 20/1/00.

Whilst in common with all ranks deeply deploring the severe loss the battalion has sustained by the death of Captain Hensley, the Commanding Officer desires to place on record

APPENDIX

his great appreciation of the services rendered on all occasions by the late Captáin Hensley, whose zeal, devotion to duty, and gallantry in action was ever conspicuous since the present war began. He feels sure he is but expressing the sentiments of all ranks in saying that his name will always be handed down in honour to future generations of the regiment as one of those who have nobly striven to shed additional lustre on the regiment's reputation.

XXI.

Spearman's Camp, 31/1/00 (3)

PRESENT OF TOBACCO FROM PAST OFFICERS, AND LETTER, &c.

The following letter, accompanying a present of 400 pounds of tobacco sent to the N.C.O.'s and men of the battalion by some former officers of the battalion, has been received to-day:—

'From the old Officers of the 2nd Battalion Royal Dublin Fusiliers to the N.C.O.'s, rank and file of the 2nd Royal Dublin Fusiliers, in token of their high appreciation of the conspicuous gallantry displayed by the battalion during the campaign, now in progress in South Africa, in which they have so brilliantly maintained the ancient traditions of the "Old Toughs."'

The following names are appended to the above:— Colonel R. Taylor, Colonel Colville Frankland, Colonel C. E. Glasse, Colonel W. Holmes, Colonel F. Taylor, Colonel W. C. Riddell, Lieut.-Colonel Reeves, Lieut.-Colonel F. W. Graham, Lieut.-Colonel A. A. Godwin, Lieut.-Colonel R. H. Mansel, Lieut.-Colonel M. J. Hickley, Lieut.-Colonel J. R. Povah, Major the Hon. H. M. Hobart Hampden, Major R. L. Shaw, Major S. J. Wynne, Major E. Pearse, Captain A. M. Horrocks, Captain R. D. Vincent, Captain H. J. Guyon, Lieutenant W. S. Burmester.

REPLY.

'Colonel Cooper, the Officers, N.C.O.'s and men of the 2nd Battalion the Royal Dublin Fusiliers desire to return their very heartfelt thanks to Colonel Frankland and the old Officers of the battalion for their kind thoughtfulness in providing the men with tobacco.

2ND BATT. ROYAL DUBLIN FUSILIERS

'They beg to assure the old Officers that their gift is most thoroughly appreciated, as also the expression of goodwill and admiration of the battalion's services in the present campaign which accompanies it.

'To know that the old Officers still continue to follow with interest and admiration the fortunes and doings of the "Old Toughs" will ever be an incentive to all ranks to do all that lies in their power to maintain the reputation which the old Officers helped to win for the corps in days gone by.'

XXII.

Spearman's Camp, 1/2/00 (5).

LANCE-SERGEANT MERRY PROMOTED FOR GALLANTRY.

The Commanding Officer has been pleased to specially promote the undermentioned N.C.O. to the rank of Sergeant from January 12th for meritorious service in the field:—

No. 4441 Lance-Sergeant J. Merry, H company.

XXIII.

Ladysmith, 5/3/00 (2).

LOSSES IN ACTION, INCLUDING COLONEL SITWELL AND CAPTAIN MAITLAND, NOTED AND DEPLORED.

The following Officers, N.C.O.'s and men having been killed in action on the dates opposite their names, are struck off the strength of the battalion, or cease to be attached to it as the case may be, from those dates accordingly:—

Major and Brevet-Lieut.-Colonel C. H. G. Sitwell, D.S.O., 24/2/00.
Captain S. C. Maitland, 2nd Gordon Highlanders (attached), 24/2/00.

No. 4871 Pte. J. White.	No. 4743 Pte. T. Reid (attached).
,, 4262 Cpl. J. Seymour.	,, 5073 ,, Kinsella. [24.2.00
,, 5359 Pte. Galbraith.	,, 6296 ,, Allen.
,, 2872 ,, Wade.	,, 5618 ,, T. Purcell.
,, 4012 ,, J. Armstrong.	,, 1717 ,, Sherwin.
,, 2037 ,, Whelan.	,, 2327 ,, Grimes.
,, 3303 ,, Timmins.	,, 1749 Sgt. T. Brennan.

Died of wounds 2/3/00:—

No. 5745 Pte. Brady.

Whilst in common with the rest of the battalion deeply deploring the loss of so many brave Officers, N.C.O.'s and

APPENDIX

men, and sympathising with those who have been wounded, the Commanding Officer wishes to place on record his high appreciation of the services rendered to the battalion on all occasions by the late Major and Brevet-Lieut.-Colonel Sitwell, whose distinguished career hitherto tended to the honour and reputation of the regiment. All ranks of the battalion join with him, he is sure, in lamenting the loss of such a distinguished soldier and comrade, and a brilliant career thus suddenly though gloriously cut short.

To the late Captain Maitland's stirling qualities as an officer and comrade he would also wish to bear testimony. His services to the battalion during a very trying and critical time were most valuable. On behalf of the battalion he offers the late Captain Maitland's relatives and brother-officers his deepest sympathy.

XXIV. 5/3/00 (4).
The Queen's Message re Relief of Ladysmith.

The following telegram, received by the Commander-in-Chief on the relief of Ladysmith from Her Most Gracious Majesty the Queen, is published for information of all ranks:—

'Thank God for news you have telegraphed to me. Congratulate you with all my heart.—V.R.I.'

XXV. Ladysmith, 5/3/00 (3).
The Queen's Message—'My Brave Irish.'

The Commanding Officer has much pleasure in publishing for the information of all ranks, the following message from Her Majesty the Queen, to the 5th Brigade, which was recently received by the G.O.C. in Chief in Natal.

'*To General Buller, Natal.*

'I have heard with the deepest concern of the heavy losses sustained by my brave Irish soldiers. I desire to express my admiration of the splendid fighting qualities which they have exhibited throughout these trying operations.—V.R.I.'

2ND BATT. ROYAL DUBLIN FUSILIERS

THE FOLLOWING REPLY WAS SENT BY SIR REDVERS BULLER :—

'Sir Redvers Buller has, on the part of the Irish Brigade, to thank the Queen for her gracious telegram of sympathy and encouragement.'

XXVI. 5/3/00 (5)
LETTER TO GORDON HIGHLANDERS, RE CAPTAIN MAITLAND.

The Commanding Officer has, on behalf of the battalion, forwarded the following letter to the Officer Commanding the 2nd Gordon Highlanders.

'*Ladysmith, 5/3/00.*
'DEAR MAJOR SCOTT,—

'On behalf of myself and the officers of the battalion, I write to offer you all our very deeepest sympathy in the severe loss your battalion has sustained by the death of Captain Maitland.

'I find it hard to adequately express to you how very deeply the whole of my battalion laments his loss, and I know I am only expressing the sentiments of all ranks when I assure you that his memory will ever be cherished in the battalion.

'A better or more conscientious officer I have never had under my command. We would all esteem it a very great favour if you could send us a photograph of our late dear comrade, and might I also so far trespass on your kindness, as to ask for one for his company (G) as well, which I need hardly say will be highly prized by them.

'Yours, &c.   (Signed)   C. D. COOPER.'

XXVII. *Ladysmith,* 14/3/00 (3).
NATAL ARMY ORDERS. THE WEARING OF SHAMROCK ON ST. PATRICK'S DAY.

The following extracts from Natal Army Orders are published for information :—

'(1) The General Commanding has to communicate to the troops the following telegram he has received from the C. in C. viz.

'Her Majesty the Queen is pleased to order that in

APPENDIX

future on St. Patrick's Day all ranks in Her Majesty's Irish regiments shall wear as a distinction a sprig of shamrock in their head-dress to commemorate the gallantry of Her Irish soldiers during the recent battles in South Africa.

'WOLSELEY.'

XXVIII. *Ladysmith, 18/3/00.*
MR. WINSTON CHURCHILL'S TELEGRAM TO REGIMENT.

The following telegrams received yesterday, and replies thereto, are published for information :—

'*To Colonel, Dublin Fusiliers, Ladysmith.*

'My earnest congratulations on the honour the Dublin Fusiliers more than any other regiment have won for the land of their birth. We are all wearing the shamrock here.
'(Signed) WINSTON CHURCHILL.'

REPLY.

'*To Winston Churchill, Lord Dundonald's Brigade.*

'Many thanks for your kind message received yesterday, all ranks appreciate your kind expressions.
'(Signed) COLONEL, DUBLIN FUSILIERS.'

XXIX. 18/3/00 (1).
COLENSO RAILWAYMEN'S TELEGRAM TO REGIMENT.

'*To Brigadier-General Cooper, Commanding Irish Brigade, Ladysmith.*

'On St. Patrick's Day the railway men of Colenso respectfully wish to convey to the officers and men of Her Majesty's Dublin Fusiliers their best wishes for a speedy termination of the present war, in which the Dublins have borne so glorious a part. The whole of South Africa rings with praise of the gallant Irish Brigade. We mourn with you the loss of so many gallant men of your command. They have fallen in their defence of a united South Africa, over which, please God, Her Most Gracious Majesty's flag will fly from Cape Town to the Zambesi.
'(Signed) INSPECTOR CAMPBELL.'

2ND BATT. ROYAL DUBLIN FUSILIERS

Reply. 18/3/00 (1).
' *To Inspector Campbell, Colenso.*

' On behalf of the officers and men under my command, please accept our heartfelt thanks for your kind message and expressions of sympathy.   (Signed)   Colonel Cooper.'

XXX.

5th Brigade Orders, 18/3/00 (1).
Cape Town Irishmen send Telegram.

The following telegram has been received by General Sir Redvers Buller :—
' Cape Town Irishmen wish the gallant Irish officers and men under your command many returns of St. Patrick's Day, and would express their heartfelt admiration for the way in which they have maintained unsullied the splendid military traditions of Ireland and the Empire under your gallant leadership.'

XXXI.
Ladysmith, 20/3/00 (2).
The Queen sends Telegram of Thanks.

The following reply to telegram sent by Colonel Cooper on behalf of the battalion to Her Majesty the Queen on Shamrock Day was received yesterday :—
' The Queen thanks her Dublin Fusiliers for loyal message. Windsor Castle, 18th.'

XXXII.
Elandslaagte, 3/4/00 (7).
Colonel Saunderson's Letter.

The following letter was received to-day by the Commanding Officer from Colonel Saunderson, M.P. :—

' Dear Sir,   ' *Castle Saunderson, Belturbet*, 1/3/00.
' I cannot help writing to you to express on my part, and on the part of every loyal Irishman, the pride and sympathy we take in the heroic deeds of the Dublin Fusiliers in South Africa. Your gallant regiment has shed a lustre on the army to which they belong and on the country from which they come.

APPENDIX

'No words of mine can express the admiration we feel for their loyalty, their courage, and their indomitable determination. I hope they realise how our hearts are with them.'

A reply thanking Colonel Saunderson has been sent by the Commanding Officer.

XXXIII.

Fourteen Streams, 12/5 (3).

DEATH OF SECOND LIEUTENANT J. T. DENNIS AT ALIWAL NORTH, MAY 2ND. ENTERIC.

The Commanding Officer deeply regrets to announce the death of Second Lieutenant J. T. Dennis, which occurred at Aliwal North on May 2nd of enteric.

XXXIV. 17/5/00 (4).

GENERAL HART CONGRATULATES 1ST BORDERS AND 2ND ROYAL DUBLIN FUSILIERS ON THEIR MARCHING.

Major-General Hart congratulates the 1st Border Regiment and 2nd Royal Dublin Fusiliers upon the recent instance of their marching powers. For military reasons it was needful after the march forward yesterday to march back at once to Fourteen Streams. As far as he can arrive at a tolerably accurate estimate of the ground gone over, these two battalions in the course of yesterday and last night marched twenty-six miles in the space of nineteen hours. And the strong point is that they arrived at the end of it in compact formation, still going a good pace, and without any straggling or falling out. The Major-General accordingly puts this event on record.

XXXV. *Heidelberg*, 2/7/00 (5).

COLONEL COOPER'S FAREWELL ORDER.

The following farewell order by Major-General C. D. Cooper is published for information. The Commanding Officer regrets that its publication has been unavoidably postponed till now:—

'In bidding farewell to the battalion in which I have

2ND BATT. ROYAL DUBLIN FUSILIERS

served for so many years, I wish to thank all ranks from the bottom of my heart for the kind and efficient support accorded to me during the period of my command—close on five years. It was always my ambition to command the battalion, and on active service, and I feel very thankful that my wish was granted. We have fought together and worked hard for our noble Queen and country, and all ranks have shown that good spirit and bravery that has made the battalion what it is. You may rest assured that I will always take the greatest interest in the doings of the battalion, and I shall never forget the happy days spent amongst you. I much regret that I was unable to wish you Godspeed in person, but I sincerely hope I shall soon see you all again. My very sincere sympathy and regret at our very heavy losses. May God bless you all.

'(Signed)   C. D. COOPER, *Major-General Commanding 4th Brigade.*'

XXXVI.
Heidelberg, 24/7/00 (6).

GENERAL BULLER'S TELEGRAM RE ZUIKERBOSCH.

The following telegram received by the G.O.C. is published for information:—

' *From Sir Redvers Buller.*

' So glad to hear of your fight. Good old Dublins, and tell them so from me, and well done you.'

XXXVII.
Krugersdorp, 4/10/00 (8).

A PATROL UNDER LIEUTENANT GARVICE, &c.

A patrol under Lieutenant Garvice, Commanding Virginia Railway Station, came in contact with some Boers on the 1st. We had one man wounded, Boers three, whom they had to leave on the ground. The casualties in the 2nd Coldstream Guards near Pan were caused by the enemy's fire, the majority of the wounds were caused by explosive bullets: the men behaved very well, and everybody kept their heads, otherwise the loss would have been greater, as the Boers opened fire at sixty yards range.

APPENDIX

XXXVIII.
Krugersdorp, 4/10/00 (8).

COLONEL ROCHFORD'S ATTACK.

Colonel Rochford attacked a small Boer laager between Pretoria and Johannesburg before dawn yesterday, with Royal Dublin Fusiliers and M.I. Fusiliers. He rushed the position with the bayonet. Nine prisoners were captured, most of them men of importance, who have been troubling the district for some time. A small party of Boers made their way to Dewetsdorp and Wepener. General Kelly Kenny has sent troops to occupy both these places.

XXXIX.
Krugersdorp, 16/12/00 (8).

COMMANDING OFFICER'S REMARKS ON TREK.

The Commanding Officer is very well pleased with the way the men marched in this trip, doing 102 miles in six days, an average of seventeen miles a day ; also with their excellent conduct and the cheerful way in which all difficulties were met. The results of the trip were over 1000 head of sheep and cattle and seven waggons captured, thirty barns of forage burnt, and innumerable stocks of oat hay, some of which concealed ammunition.

XL.

LETTER FROM GENERAL HART.
Lieut.-Colonel Hicks, Commanding 2nd Battalion Royal Dublin Fusiliers.

The manner in which the encampment of your battalion is arranged deserves my special commendation. On very bad camping-ground, beset with rocks and bush, and afflicted with dust between, I find your companies excellently established by ingenious and industrious adaptation to circumstances. The regularity and tidiness are conspicuous, and have been noted by me with great satisfaction. I need not say how much neatness of arrangements must conduce to quickness and good quality of soldier work. (Signed) A. FITZROY HART,
Major-General Commanding Irish Brigade.
Fourteen Streams, May 20th, 1900.

2ND BATT. ROYAL DUBLIN FUSILIERS

XLI.
Krugersdorp, 25/1/01 (4).

GENERAL HART'S FAREWELL.

The following Farewell Order by Major-General A. Fitzroy Hart, C.B., is published for information :—

'In leaving to take another command, I wish you, my brother soldiers of my force, farewell.

'It is an article of my faith, that you would go anywhere and do anything required in battle.

'I leave you with deep regret, and of course I must feel this particularly for the last of my old Irish brigade with which I began the war.

'In departing, I give you this scrap of advice: Be individually, whenever opportunity offers personally, not only kind but generous to the inhabitants of this country which we have taken from them, and among whom so many of our countrymen and countrywomen will have to dwell. It will not diminish your soldierly strength, and it will hasten a welcome for the pleasant government of peace.'

XLII.
Fort Kilmarnock, 25/9/01 (6).

LETTER FROM CAPTAIN ANLEY.

The following extracts from a letter received from Brevet-Major Anley, Commanding 3rd M.I., are published for information :—

'The behaviour of your M.I. company continues to be very good. Lieutenant Garvice and thirty men of the company did excellent service the other day, when acting as rearguard to a convoy which was leaving Carolina. It was reported that it was due to the steadiness of the men of the Royal Dublin Fusiliers, and the able manner they were handled by Lieutenant Garvice, that the convoy got in without loss.

'The Inspector-General M.I. wrote and asked me to congratulate Lieutenant Garvice on the behaviour of his men. No. 4701, Private Kelly, R.D.F., was recommended for gallantry on this occasion.

'(Signed)   F. GORE ANLEY,
Brevet-Major Commanding 3rd Battalion M.I.'

APPENDIX

XLIII.

CONSPICUOUS GALLANTRY AT GASKRAAL ON AUGUST 28TH, &c.

The following extract from Army Order No. 418, dated Pretoria, September 28th, 1901, is published for information:—

'No. 1. The following have been brought to notice of the General Officer Commanding-in-Chief, for gallantry and good service:

2nd Royal Dublin Fusiliers: No. 6491, Lce.-Cpl. T. O'Connor (killed). For great and conspicuous gallantry when very closely engaged with enemy at Gaskraal on 28th Aug. 1901.'

XLIV.

LORD KITCHENER'S WIRE.

'I know I am speaking for the whole army in South Africa, when I wish the Dublin Fusiliers Godspeed, and congratulate them on the fine record they have established during their services in the country.'

ANSWER.

'I beg to thank your Lordship in the name of the regiment for your very kind and congratulatory telegram, which is much appreciated by all ranks.'

XLV.

ROLL OF OFFICERS, 2ND ROYAL DUBLIN FUSILIERS, WHO EMBARKED AT DURBAN ON S.S. 'SICILIA,' ON THE 29/1/02, EN ROUTE FOR ADEN.

Rank and Name.
Col. H. T. Hicks, C.B.
Maj. S. G. Bird, D.S.O.
Capt. and Bt.-Maj. E. Fetherstonhaugh.
Capt. and Bt.-Maj. M. Lowndes.
Capt. H. W. Higginson.
 ,, G. N. Cory, D.S.O.
Lieut. C. Garvice, D.S.O.
 ,, L. F. Renny.
 ,, J. McD. Haskard.
 ,, A. H. D. Britton.

Rank and Name.
Lieut. A. de B. W. W. Bradford.
 ,, S. G. De C. Wheeler.
2nd Lieut. A. W. Newton.
 ,, E. St. G. Smith.
 ,, R. F. B. Knox.
 ,, J. P. Tredennick.
 ,, B. Maclear.
 ,, J. P. B. Robinson.
 ,, E. F. E. Seymour.
 ,, H. St. G. M. S. Scott.
Lieut. J. Burke (Quartermaster).

*Printed by Strangeways & Sons, Tower Street,
Cambridge Circus, London, W.C.*